YOU <u>CAN</u>
LEARN TO WRITE

REVISED EDITION

JACK KATES
Writing Teachers In-Service Program

SEAL PRESS
Seal Beach, California

First Printing, May 1976
Second Printing, August 1976-Revised
Third Printing, November 1976
Fourth Printing, July 1977-Revised Edition

Published by:

Seal Press
P.O.Box 3027
Seal Beach, California 90740

Printed by:

Orange County Lithograph
1251 West Katella Avenue
Orange, California 92667

Logo by: .

Jenny Richards

ISBN: 0-930364-01-5

Printed in the United States of America

ACKNOWLEDGMENTS

First of all, I am extremely grateful to Mr. Allan D. Sklove of Hogan High School in Vallejo for his invaluable suggestions on the style and thrust of this book, and to Professor Lorraine Levine of Compton College for her invaluable editorial advice on the entire book. Secondly, I would like to thank Mrs. Nan Wolfe and my wife, Marilyn, for their assistance with Writing Teachers In-Service Program. In addition, I would like to express my gratitude to Professor Ben Ponnech of Compton College, Professor Shirley Blanchard of El Camino College, and my wife for their comments on several chapters. Finally—and with deepest gratitude—I would like to acknowledge the contributions of my students, particularly those whose essays I have selected for reproduction. I have listed the titles of their essays below, along with the students' names and the colleges where they attended my classes and wrote the essays that are published in this book.

Process Analysis

"The Life and Death of a Steak," Virgina Mitchell, Compton College.
"How to Become a Wild Rice Harvester," Granville King, Compton College.
"Lure Fishing," Barbara Fraley, Compton College.
"The Sights and Sounds of Knee-Board Surfing," James Leiby, Compton College.

"The Operation and Flight of the Boeing 737," Michael Nardone, El Camino College.

Persuasion by Thesis-and-Supporting Evidence

"Clear Expression," Eleanor K. Bryant, Los Angeles Southwest College.
"Effects of the Working Woman's Absence from Home," Jeanette Lake, El Camino College.
"Obscenity Laws," Paul Stearns, El Camino College.
"Capital Punishment," John M. Swensek, El Camino College.
"Capital Punishment: A Moralistic and Practical View," Lynn Schreihofer, El Camino College.

Classification

"Progress in Transportation," Ron Miller, Cerritos College.
"Classification of an Orchestra," Barbara J. Wheat, Cerritos College.
"Pollution," Roy Dahleen, El Camino College.
"Music in the Romantic Era," Diane Bell, Cerritos College.

Comparison and Contrast

"My New Job and the Old One," Pat Bryant, El Camino College.
"A Large Office and a Small One," Pam Kerr, El Camino College.
"Married and Single Life for the Man," Robert Guell, El Camino College.
"Life in Los Angeles and Topeka," James Schmidt, El Camino College.
"Advantages of Country Life," Cheryl Peterson, El Camino College.

Definition

"Superstition," Pat Bryant, El Camino College.
"Honor," William Hoban, El Camino College.
"Social Darwinism," Anthony Reed, El Camino College.

TABLE OF CONTENTS

PART I

Why this Book was Written

PART II

How to Write Effective Sentences

PART III

Handbook of Grammar and Usage

CHAPTER SIX: HANDBOOK OF GRAMMAR AND USAGE.   47

PART IV

How to Write Themes: Paragraphs and Essays

PART ONE

WHY THIS BOOK WAS WRITTEN

CHAPTER ONE

PURPOSE OF THIS BOOK

There seems to be some terrible mystery about writing. Whenever somebody asks me what I do for a living and I mention that I'm a writing teacher, I invariably get the kind of stare one gets by walking into the wrong restroom. Sometimes I get an apology, accompanied by an explanation. "I can't write too well. We had a lousy English teacher and she never taught me anything. All we did was grammar. Diagramming sentences. I hated that. I guess that's why I can't write."

"Did you do much writing in class?" I usually ask.

"Writing! Heck no! All we did was busywork. It was boring. I'm lucky I passed. You must be smart to be teaching writing."

"No, not at all. Writing is fun. It's not that hard."

"Are you kidding? I don't think I could ever learn to write."

"Sure you could if you had the right teacher."

Suddenly my listener's face lights up. "Do you mean that?"

"Certainly! Anybody can learn to write."

Then, in a confidential tone, my listener asks, "Say, where do you teach?"

Since I have not described a mere, isolated case but rather one that seems to be all too prevalent today, this book may very well be meant for you. If you are a student in high school or even in college and you need help in learning how to write effectively, this book will help you. It will help you because it is a special book, written especially for you. Most of the textbooks in current use are hard to understand, especially for the average student. The reason they are hard to understand is that they have been written to impress teachers or professors, not students. Even the above average student has a difficult time understanding them. Believe me, I know. By contrast, this book was designed for you—the student. It's written in simple

1

language, with words you can understand, on a level that is easy to grasp for quick comprehension.

This book will illustrate how to write different kinds of sentences *without requiring you to learn a lot of difficult terms.* The examples of sentences used are those that best illustrate how to communicate most effectively with a minimum of effort. The book uses sentences written by students, and some written by me—for you. You will learn how to get your point across quickly and concisely. You will learn how to write so that you can say exactly what you want to say, so that somebody else who reads your writing understands exactly what you mean. Isn't that what good writing is all about? And once you become a good writer, you will be a different person. You will speak differently, you will act differently, and you will think differently. You will have more confidence in yourself, for you will have "something special" that nobody can ever take away.

Another reason this book can help you better than other English handbooks can is that the paragraphs and essays I chose for models are those that were written by my own students, not by professional writers. And where necessary, to illustrate a particular point, I even wrote some paragraphs and essays myself—again for you. Professional writing may be very fine, perhaps excellent. But let's face it. Do you really want to become a professional writer? Or do you just want to learn how to write—properly? If you want to become a professional writer, I've got news for you. You and your children and grandchildren will probably all starve to death before you become recognized, or even before you sell anything. If you want to become a professional writer, this book won't harm you, but it won't necessarily help you. That's not the purpose of this book, because I realize that most people cannot even aspire toward becoming professional writers. However, most people can aspire toward becoming good writers, and I am sure that they would sincerely like to become good writers, for a number of reasons: completing high school or college, improving their status, and gaining self-satisfaction. If you are one of these people, then, this book is for you.

SPECIAL NOTE TO THE TEACHER

This book, however, is not written for students alone. It is written for the conscientious writing teacher who would like to have some additional tips on the teaching of writing skills. In all probability, you have already attended my seminar, "How to Teach English Composition Effectively," and are now using some of the material in this book, material which I provided in your handouts. The book, therefore, will supplement the handouts, by giving you a detailed, sequential, step-by-step approach to the teaching of sentences, paragraphs, and larger themes.

I must emphasize that this "class-tested" book on individualized instruction is *not* designed to replace you in the classroom, nor is it designed to make it easier for administrators to increase your classload. The supposed "threat" of this book—(a term that I must consider as flattery, since it was used in this connection by some publishers who were afraid of alienating teachers by publishing the semi-programmed book),—the supposed threat, I repeat, is toward *excellence,* not toward increased average daily attendance. Therefore, if you would like the challenge of being the best, of requesting and receiving excellence from your students, you will supplement the instruction in this book with your own personal touch. You will provide your students with individual conferences on their written assignments, a specialized technique now in wide use by thousands of writing teachers who have already attended my seminars. While you are conferring with one student, the rest of the class will be engaged in writing or writing-related activities. This book will help you immensely because it will provide a springboard with which to begin your instruction, and it will provide your students with a self-directed series of lessons that will enable them to work individually—at their own rate.

This book is an outgrowth of ten years of teaching experience at all levels—secondary, post secondary, and post graduate—during which time I have taught thousands of students, of all colors and creeds and mental capacities and from all walks of life, how to write. In addition to my classroom teaching and conducting seminars for writing teachers and language arts specialists, I have conducted massive, scientific research on individualized instruction, population profiles, and pre-post essay tests. *The Report on the Kates Survey of College Freshman Composition Writing Skills: Sixteen First-Semester English Composition Classes from Eleven Community Colleges and Universities,* ERIC ED 077 498 (June, 1973), was the first study of its type to reveal a shocking illiteracy rate in writing among college students. Copies of the study were requested by and delivered to both the Assembly and Senate of California. Following publication of the study, numerous other studies throughout the United States have surfaced, all with findings similar to those revealed earlier by the *Kates Survey.* Among the more important findings of the *Survey* were the unreliability of objective placement tests and college workbooks. Those students who outguessed the objective placement tests or who did enough workbook exercises in the college remedial courses to qualify for the transfer credit course were still unable to write a proper essay within a given time limit. The placement tests did not determine the student's ability to write, and the remedial courses utilizing workbooks as the main source of instruction did not correct the student's deficiencies in writing. Far from it! Altogether too many students were simply "processed" through high school and college without learning how to write adequately.

This handbook, I believe, will help to remedy the entire problem of Johnny's inability to write, by *teaching* him the *basics* of *essay writing*. If he sincerely wants to learn, if he studies the book carefully, and if he does each assignment conscientiously and thoroughly, *he will learn how to write*. If he also makes use of a dictionary, a speller, and a thesaurus, his writing will improve immensely. Finally, and perhaps most importantly, if he consults with a good writing teacher, one who provides him with meaningful feedback as well as encouragement on his written work, he will eventually become a good writer.

Suggestions for the Teacher

Because this book has been published as a personal handbook, not only for students at all grade levels but also for writing teachers regardless of their assignments, I would like to offer you, the teacher, these suggestions, which will help you to individualize your instruction, so that each student can progress at his own rate.

1. Assume nothing. Begin your course with an essay pre-test that actually determines the student's writing ability. Forewarned is forearmed.

2. Use the "building block" approach by teaching—in their proper *sequence*—sentences, paragraphs, and larger themes. Part II deals with sentences. Make sure that each student masters each chapter in that section before he proceeds to the next.

3. After the student has mastered Part II, he is ready to *apply* what he has learned, by writing paragraphs and larger themes, as detailed in Part IV. Do not hold him back. He does not have to learn all the rules of grammar and usage before proceeding to the actual writing of themes. But again—and this is most important—use building blocks in their proper sequence. This means Chapter IX before Chapter X, and so on.

4. Allow your students to work at their own rate, but provide each with an individual conference on his written work, so that he does receive meaningful feedback (and encouragement). During the conference, focus on two or three glaring weaknesses, such as agreement, vague pronoun references, omissions, or whatever you feel

detracts from his intent—to communicate. In short, teach grammar and usage as it applies to his particular need.

5. In addition, arrange for some large group lecture time, during which you can teach the whole class the various aspects of grammar and usage that are outlined in Part III. Please remember, though, it is not necessary to learn the parts of the car before one learns how to drive. Part III is intended as a "reference tool," both for you and for your student. It is not intended to be used as a substitute for the writing experience.

6. At the end of the course, use an essay post-test (identical to the pre) to determine the achievement of your class. And do not be too disappointed if some of your students haven't met with your expectations. Good writing takes time to produce. One does not learn the skill overnight, or even in a semester.

7. If your colleague teaches a composition course at a "higher" grade level, it might be to his advantage to use this same text. He might then take the student from where he is and truly challenge him. For example, the same medical textbook is often used in a more advanced course. The subject matter doesn't change just because a person is a year older.

SUMMARY: STUDENT AND TEACHER

In summary, this book is designed for you—the student, who would like to improve your writing skills,—and for you—the teacher, who would like to help your student become a good writer. The book is based on the premise: there is only one way to learn a skill—by practicing it. There is no other way. All the grammar and usage exercises in the world will not help you to learn how to write *unless you write.* In order to write, you must first think of something to say. Then you must organize your thoughts. Finally, you must put them down on paper so that your reader understands what you are trying to say. This book will help you in every way possible. It will give you ideas on what to write about. It will require you to write. And it will illustrate through step-by-step models the organizational pattern for sentences, for paragraphs, and for essays. If you study these models carefully, and if you imitate them as required in the assignments, you will learn how to write. I can promise you that. This method has worked for thousands of my own students and for hundreds of thousands (or perhaps even millions) of other students. It can work for you too.

There is one final point I must make: You must have confidence in yourself. If you want to improve, you must get rid of any mental blocks you have. I don't care how many times you've failed English or how many times you've failed—period. I don't care how many times somebody has told you or implied that you can't write properly or that your work is no good or that you "don't have it." In fact, I don't care to hear anything like that because *I don't believe in* the word *failure*. Starting now—right now—I want you to believe one thing: you're going to make it. You're going to be able to write. Say to yourself: "I am going to write. I am going to write well." Think about what you have just said. Keep on thinking about it. Memorize it. Now write it down, exactly as it is written, and sign your name. You have already made a commitment. Now you must live up to it. You must be positive. If you believe that you can succeed, you will.

PART TWO

HOW TO WRITE EFFECTIVE SENTENCES

CHAPTER TWO

THE SIMPLE SENTENCE

I. OVERVIEW.

In this chapter you will learn what a simple sentence is, and even more importantly, you will be required to write simple sentences. Most importantly, though, you will write several kinds of simple sentences correctly.

II. DEFINITION OF A SENTENCE.

A sentence is a group of words that makes sense as written. Obviously, the words must be arranged in a certain order or pattern—a meaningful sequence—so that they make sense. When you learn what this sequence is, and when you learn what components must be included, you will have no trouble in writing a *simple sentence*. A simple sentence expresses a simple idea, without explaining why. A simple sentence is very easy to read and very easy to write. This particular sentence is a simple sentence.

III. DETERMINING THE SEQUENCE.

The groups of words listed below are meaningless because the words are mixed up—out of sequence. Can you arrange them in their proper sequence so that they make sense?

1. often cry babies.
2. writing enjoys he.
3. the threw pitcher ball the young.
4. on working this simple I am exercise.
5. to very man bank the a the long old tired slowly wrote letter.

IV. SOLUTION.

Since a sentence usually *begins* with the *something* or *someone that does something* or *is in a particular condition* being described, the *first* thing a writer must do is to determine *what* the *something is,* or *who* the *someone* is that he wants to write about. It's that simple. *This SOMETHING* that performs the action, or is somewhere, or is in a particular condition is called the *SUBJECT* of the sentence. It is called the subject because that is what the sentence is all about.

A. Subjects.

Let us now consider the first example: *often cry babies.* **Question:** What is the something or somebody that is doing something? Is it *cry?* Is *cry* doing something? Of course not. Is it *often?* Is *often* doing something? No. Obviously, then, it must be *babies.* Are *babies* doing something? Yes. The *SUBJECT* of the sentence, therefore, is *babies,* because that is what the sentence is all about. *Babies* are doing something. Let us begin rewriting the sentence, then, as follows:

    a) Babies

B. Verbs.

Now we must determine what is happening. The something (subject)—in this example *babies*—must be doing something, or must be somewhere, or must be described in a particular condition. This *ACTION WORD* that tells the reader what the *babies* are doing—what is happening—is called a *VERB.* Let us, therefore, figure out the *ACTION WORD*—the *VERB*—that tells us what the babies are doing.

POSSIBLE ANSWERS:

a) Babies often . . . **Babies often what?** We still don't know what babies do. Complete the sentence.

b) Babies *cry* . . . Correct. Now we know what babies do. They cry. Now complete the sentence.

SOLUTION: a) Babies cry often.
              b) Babies often cry.

Both sentences a) and b) are correct.

C. Modifiers.

What function is served by the word *often?* What does the word *often* do? Why is it necessary? The answer to all of these

8

questions is very simple. The word *often* modifies *(EXPLAINS)* the action. It tells us in what manner babies cry; it tells us when they cry. Such a word is called a *MODIFIER*. It describes.

NOTE: A *MODIFIER* may also be composed of a group of words. (He ran *very quickly.* He ran *as fast as he could.)*

A modifier may also *DESCRIBE* a subject. (The *young* pitcher threw the ball. The book *on the table* is mine.)

A modifier may also *DESCRIBE* objects. (I wrote a *very long* letter. I wrote a *very long* and *interesting* letter.)

A modifier may also modify additional parts of speech, and although you need not know the specific "grammatical" names or labels often used for these parts of speech, you should know how they function and you should be able to use them correctly. The most important thing to remember about modifiers is this: *place them as close as you possibly can to what they are supposed to modify.* Otherwise, the reader may not understand what you are trying to say, or he may misinterpret your sentence altogether. This point will be discussed in later chapters, particularly Chapter Five.

D. Completers.

A *COMPLETER* is a word or group of words that *completes the meaning* of the sentence and, therefore, is placed at the *end.* Completers may consist of any or all of the following: objects, complements, or modifiers.

1. OBJECTS. a) An object may receive direct action from a verb, in which case it is known as a direct object. (Examples: I threw the *ball.* We saw *Jerry.* We heard *him.)*

b) An object may also receive indirect action as a result of an intervening word, called a "preposition." In such a case, the object is often referred to as an indirect object. (Examples: I threw the ball to *him.* I wrote a letter to *my wife.* I heard about the *incident.* NOTE: It is not vitally important that you be able to label a word "direct object" or "indirect object," so long as you know what an object is (a word that receives action) and where it is placed (at the end).

2. COMPLEMENTS. A complement is a word or group of words that does any one of the following:

a) renames the subject (I am *he.* John is *his name.* John is *president.);*

b) follows any form of the verb *to be* (This is *he*. He was *president.*);
c) follows any form of a linking verb (He might have been *president*. He seemed *polite*. He became *president.*);
d) describes any of the five senses—look, taste, smell, sound, feel (You look *prosperous*. The roses smell *sweet*. I feel *well*. The music sounded *loud.*).

In short, a complement, by *following* a linking verb or a verb describing our sensations, renames the subject or describes it in terms of the senses. Thus, *a complement completes the meaning of the sentence.*

3. MODIFIERS. As already mentioned, a modifier is a word that explains or describes something. Modifiers may take any position in the sentence, but very often they follow the subject (The book *on the table* is mine.), or they follow the verb (He swam very quickly *with all of his might*. He swam very quickly, with all of his might, *toward shore*. He swam very quickly, with all of his might, toward shore, *late that afternoon.*) To summarize, completers are words that complete the meaning of the sentence and, therefore, are placed at the end.

E. Sentence Pattern or Sequence.

This is the sequence:
1) *Subject, verb.* or 2) *Subject, verb, completers.*

EXERCISE 1.
Figure out the sequence of the groups of mixed-up words on page 7 (III. Determining the Sequence) and rewrite them as sentences.

F. Summary: Sentence Definition.

A sentence is a group of words that makes sense as written. A sentence *always* begins with a capital letter, and a sentence always ends with a period (if the sentence is a statement), or it ends with a question mark (if the sentence is a question), or it ends with an exclamation mark (if the sentence is a strong command or exclamation). A sentence usually contains a subject explicitly expressed, or it may contain one that is merely implied. A sentence always contains a verb. And a sentence may also contain other components such as modifiers and completers in order to complete an idea. Above all, *a sentence makes sense.*

V. SIMPLE SENTENCES AS STATEMENTS.

1. A simple sentence may make a simple statement. (*I am here.*)

2. The sentence must begin with a capital letter and end with a period. Remember, we are talking about statements.

3. The subject usually comes first, followed by a verb, and completers if necessary.

4. The simple sentence usually contains only one subject.

5. Sometimes a simple sentence contains two or more subjects acting as one; these are called compound subjects. (*John and Mary love their son.*)

6. A simple sentence usually contains only one verb. (*I enjoy swimming.*)

7. Sometimes, however, a simple sentence contains more than one verb. (*I swim and surf every summer. I went to the store and returned.*)

8. Usually a simple sentence expresses one idea—very simply—without qualifying or explaining it. In short, A SIMPLE SENTENCE COMES RIGHT TO THE POINT—WITHOUT EXPLAINING WHY. (This book is easy to understand.) Why is this book easy to understand? The simple sentence does not explain why. It merely makes a statement.

VI. SIMPLE SENTENCES AS QUESTIONS.

A simple sentence may also take the form of a question, in which case all of the rules you have just learned, in section F above, apply with these exceptions:

1. The verb or part of the verb usually comes before the subject. (*Are you here? Have you been here? Did you see the movie?*)

2. The sentence ends with a question mark. (*Does John love her?*)

VII. SIMPLE SENTENCES AS COMMANDS.

A simple sentence may also take the form of a command, in which case the subject is usually implied instead of being expressed, and the terminal (end) punctuation is an exclamation mark.
(*Get out of here! Pay attention!*)NOTE: The subject *you* is implied. However, the subject may also be expressed in a command. (*John, get out of here! Get out of here, John!*)

ASSIGNMENTS: EXPLANATION.

You have now learned the definition of a sentence, and more specifically, you have learned one particular type of sentence—the simple sentence. Now, in order to apply what you have learned, you must complete the following assignments. Even though you think the assignment is simple—and indeed it is—you must do it to reinforce what you have learned. Remember, I promised to teach you how to write by taking you through this course one step at a time. This is the first step, and you must take it. Of all the skills we use, writing lends itself least to short cuts. COMPLETE THIS ASSIGNMENT AND EVERY ONE THAT FOLLOWS! Take out a piece of paper, get a pencil or pen, clear the table or desk, and do the assignment now!

NOTE: This assignment contains four sections, each one requiring you to write simple sentences using a particular component (subject, verb, completer) that is supplied for each sentence. Write the complete sentence on a separate piece of paper; don't just complete the exercise in the book. And remember: begin each sentence with a capital letter, and end each sentence with the proper punctuation! Use a period for statements. Use a question mark for questions. And use an exclamation mark for commands.

I. Writing Simple Statements from a Given Subject.

Use each of the following subjects to begin a sentence, and complete the sentence as a statement. The statement must be a simple sentence. It must make sense.

EXAMPLES: I have been here.
          John loves his wife.
          Nevada contains the largest gambling casinos in the nation.

1. I. . . . .
2. You. . . . .
3. He . . . .

4. She...

5. We..

6. You three people..

7. They..

8. Harry...

9. Sue...

10. Bill and Fred...

11. This exercise...

12. Whoever committed the crime...............................

13. Swimming...

14. Driving a car...

15. California...

NOTE: After you finish this exercise, reread each sentence aloud to be sure that it makes sense, and then underline each subject. Learn what a subject is.

II. Writing Simple Questions Beginning with a Verb.

Use each of the following verbs to begin a sentence in the form of a question, and complete the sentence so that it makes sense. Remember: use a question mark at the end. (Write the entire sentence on a separate piece of paper. Don't just complete it in this book.)

EXAMPLES: *Will you be here tomorrow?*

Has he been here long?

Did you see the special on television last night?

1. Are..?

2. Is..?

3. Have..........been..?

4. Did........hear...?

5. Have.......been able...?

6. Has........been able...?

7. Was...?

8. Does..........hear..?

9. Can..........hear..?

10. Will............be able..?

11. Were...?

12. Does........smell...?

NOTE: After you have completed writing these questions, read each one to yourself (aloud if you can), and make sure that it makes sense.

13

Then underline each verb, and ask yourself this question: does the verb express action, or does it express a state of being? Make sure you know what a verb is.

III. Writing Simple Commands.

Complete each command as a sentence, beginning with each of the following verbs. Use an exclamation mark at the end.

EXAMPLES: Read this book now!
Do this exercise right away!

1. Get...!
2. Stop..!
3. Hurry..!
4. Clean up..!
5. Give...!

IV. Writing Simple Sentences Using Completers.

Use each of the following completers in a simple sentence. Write the whole sentence on a separate piece of paper, and make sure that the sentence makes sense.

EXAMPLES: I love my wife.
We went to the football game last week.
Are you going to attend college?
I received some money in the mail.

1. ....a letter.
2. ....coffee.
3. ....here.
4. ....there yesterday.
5. ....New York next summer.
6. ....this exercise.
7. ....this chapter?
8. ....me.
9. ....you.
10. ....him.
11. ....her.
12. ....us.
13. ....them.

14

CHAPTER THREE

CONNECTING TWO SIMPLE SENTENCES:
THE COMPOUND SENTENCE

If you wrote nothing but simple sentences all the time, your writing would soon become very monotonous. *EXAMPLE: I love my wife. She loves me. We have been married for six years. We live in a house. The house is new.* In order to improve your style, therefore, the next thing you will learn is how to connect two simple sentences into one. Consider these two simple sentences: *I love my wife. She loves me.*

Question: How can you combine these two sentences into one?

Solution: It is very simple to combine these two sentences. Just add the word *and* between the sentences, remove the first period, and there you have it: a *longer sentence* containing the two original sentences. (*I love my wife, and she loves me.*)

NOTE: 1. The comma before *and* is optional in such a short sentence, but if you do use the comma, it comes before *and,* not after.

GROSS PUNCTUATION ERRORS. Whatever you do, you must not attempt to link two sentences together with only a comma. Such an error is called a "comma splice."

WRONG: (I love my wife, she loves me.) COMMA SPLICE. Worse yet is the fused sentence, which occurs if you run the two sentences together without any punctuation whatsoever.

WRONG: (I love my wife she loves me.) FUSED SENTENCE.

2. You may also link two simple sentences by the use of a *semicolon only.* (I love my wife; she loves me.)

3. Finally, you may link two simple sentences by using a semicolon accompanied by a strong *transitional* word such as *moreover.* (I love my wife; moreover, she loves me.)

We will now discuss each one of these methods commonly used to combine sentences.

A. USING COORDINATING CONJUNCTIONS AS CONNECTIVES.

Let us consider a similar example:
1. I can see you. You can see me.
2. *I can see you,* and *you can see me.*

What we have done here is to *compound* (pile on) one idea after the other, linking them rather securely by the word *and.* The new sentence 2 now contains two ideas which were formerly expressed as independent sentences in 1.

QUESTION: Consider the two independent sentences. Is one idea more important than the other, or are they both of equal importance?

ANSWER: Of course, they are both equally important.

QUESTION: Now consider the two ideas in sentence 2. Again, is one idea more important than the other, or are they both of equal importance?

ANSWER: Obviously, they are both equally important, because they were both of equal importance to begin with. The addition of *and* did not change their importance; it merely linked them together. If both ideas are of equal importance, they are both main ideas, and each can stand alone as an independent sentence. It follows, then, that since they are both equal or "matched" in importance, and since they go together in a sentence as a "matched" pair, just as the coordinate outfit you are probably wearing goes together (blouse and skirt, or shirt and slacks), they could be called "coordinates." The word *and* that joined them together is called a *conjunction. Conjunction* means "to bring together." Not only is *and* a conjunction, but it is a special kind of a conjunction. It is called a *coordinating conjunction* because it brings together a matched pair. Therefore, if you are married, I suppose you could call your wedding ring a *coordinating conjunction.* But you must remember this: a coordinating conjunction can only bring together a matched pair.

Note on Terminology. If you cannot remember the term "coordinating conjunction," try to remember the word "conjunction" or "connective." If you can't remember "connective," just remember "wedding ring." And if you can't remember any of these terms, it still isn't vitally important, so long as you know how to use the proper words correctly.

16

LIST OF COORDINATING CONJUNCTIONS OR CONNECTIVES
(Wedding Rings)

There are seven coordinating conjunctions or connectives (wedding rings) that you must learn now: *and, but, for, or, nor, yet, so.* Each one of these connectives can be used to join together or "marry" two simple sentences, and each should be preceded by a comma if the original simple sentences are rather long. Memorize the list now. You will soon be using it, for you will soon be writing compound sentences. As you write compound sentences, read them aloud, and you will notice that they have a certain rhythm. Truly fine writing, like poetry, does have a sense of rhythm, which makes it easy to read and easy to listen to, as well.

EXAMPLES OF COMPOUND SENTENCES FORMED
BY A COMMA
AND A COORDINATING CONJUNCTION (CONNECTIVE)

1. AND. *And* means in addition to—to add something. Do not confuse it with *but,* which means to compare or contrast something with something else.

a) I bought some milk at the store, and I also bought some bread.

b) Last week she bought a new dress, and this week she bought a new coat.

c) I boarded the plane for Chicago at noon, and I arrived there at five.

d) The plane took off on schedule, and soon we were flying over the ocean.

2. BUT. *But* indicates a contrast—something different.

a) In my right hand I have a dollar bill, but in my left hand I have a copper penny.

b) I bought some milk at the store, but I forgot to buy some bread.

c) She bought a new dress yesterday, but she returned it today.

d) We boarded the plane for Chicago at noon, but we did not take off on schedule.

3. FOR. *For* explains the reasons why. It is similar in meaning to because, but not nearly so strong.

a) I bought some milk at the store, for we were completely out of it.

b) He rushed through the crowds, for the police were chasing him.

c) The pitcher stood there completely astonished, for the rookie batter had just hit a homerun.

d) We got up early the next day, for we had a long way to travel.

4. OR. *Or* gives you an alternative. You have a choice. Often it is paired with *either* as a connective (either...or) and is then called a *correlative.*

　　a) We will visit your relatives today, or we will visit them tomorrow.

　　b) Either you will eat your vegetables, or I will not give you any dessert.

　　c) Either we will go to the opera, or we will go to the symphony.

　　d) Your car will be ready today, or it will be ready tomorrow.

5. NOR. *Nor* is the negative or opposite of *or,* and therefore it indicates no choice. It also means in addition to. Often it is paired with *neither* as a *correlative* (neither...nor).

　　a) She will not eat her vegetables, nor will she eat her dessert.

　　b) We will not visit your relatives today, nor will we visit them tomorrow.

　　c) Neither will we go to the opera, nor will we go to the symphony.

　　d) Your car will not be ready today, nor will it be ready tomorrow.

NOTE: The subject-verb order in the second part of the compound sentences is reversed when nor is used.

6. YET. *Yet* is similar in meaning to *but* (a contrast), and it is somewhat similar to *even though* (an explanation).

　　a) He does not have a job, yet he is not despondent.

　　b) We have not received the merchandise, yet we paid for it two weeks ago.

　　c) She was almost out of money, yet she bought a new dress.

　　d) He is still hungry, yet he will not eat his vegetables.

7. SO. *So* means as a result or consequence of something. It is similar in meaning to *consequently* and *therefore.*

　　a) She wanted a new dress, so she went out and bought one.

　　b) We did not want to drive there, so we took the bus.

　　c) Her dress had a large flaw, so she returned it immediately.

　　d) I am tired of studying this book, so I will put it away until later.

NOTE: A compound sentence contains two simple sentences; therefore, it must contain two subjects and *two verbs.* Do not confuse it with a simple sentence.

COMPOUND: Either we *will plant* spinach, or we *will plant* lettuce.

SIMPLE: We *will plant* either spinach or lettuce.

COMPOUND: She *bought* a new dress yesterday, but she *returned* it today.

SIMPLE: She *bought* a new dress yesterday but returned it today.

QUESTION: Since it appears that both sentences in these examples mean the same thing, which type is more effective, the simple or the compound?

ANSWER: Technically both sentences mean the same thing, and since the simple sentence uses fewer words, perhaps it is a more effective sentence. The reader gets the message, and he is not slowed down as long as he is by reading the compound sentence. On the other hand, the compound sentence repeats the subject (in these examples), thereby giving equal emphasis to the second part of the sentence. Consequently, a compound sentence is usually more emphatic than the other type.

QUESTION: Why must I learn how to write different types of sentences?

ANSWER: For the same reason that a carpenter or a mechanic must know how to use more than one type of tool. Sometimes a carpenter will use a heavy hammer instead of a light one. Why? Any hammer can pound nails and therefore get the job done. But a particular hammer (or tool) at a particular time may be more effective for a particular job, thus resulting in a better job with less effort on the part of the carpenter (or mechanic). Similarly, the more you know about writing sentences, the easier it will be for you to write, and the more effective will your writing become.

ASSIGNMENT FOR SECTION A:
USING COORDINATING CONJUNCTIONS AS CONNECTIVES.
TURN TO PAGE 23 AT THE END OF THIS CHAPTER.

B. USING STRONGER CONNECTIVES: TRANSITIONS AND SEMICOLONS

A transition (or *conjunctive adverb,* as it is sometimes called) is a word or group of words that acts as a signal and a bridge, first slowing down the reader, and then taking him smoothly from one thought to the next. It is stronger than a coordinating conjunction because it slows down the reader and in effect creates a longer pause than does a coordinating conjunction. For one thing, it is preceded by a semicolon, not a comma, and a semicolon creates a much longer pause than does a comma, at least twice as long. Furthermore, a transition usually contains two or three syllables, as compared with the one or two in the conjunction. Thus a transition, even by itself, requires more time to read than does a conjunction, thereby further slowing down the reader and in effect preparing him for the next idea or the next sentence.

19

A *transition* may be used to connect two simple sentences into a compound sentence, or it may be used to signal a change in an idea, or a reinforcement of an idea, either from one sentence to another or from one paragraph to another. Consequently, transitions are very important.

EXAMPLES: (Note the time-units or pauses: two for a semicolon, one for a comma, and one for each syllable, thus totaling *six.*)

$$2 \quad 1 \quad 1 \quad 1 \ 1= 6$$
1. She bought a new dress this week; *fur-ther-more,* she bought a new coat.

$$2 \quad 1 \quad 1 \quad 11 = 6$$
2. I received a raise last week; *how-ev-er,* inflation has offset the gain.

NOTE: Each sentence above contains six time-unit "pauses." Now compare the six time-unit with the two time-unit "pauses" created by the conjunction.

$$1 \quad 1 = 2$$
1. She bought a new dress this week, *and* she bought a new coat.

$$1 \quad 1 = 2$$
2. I received a raise last week, *but* inflation has offset the gain.

QUESTION: When should one use a conjunction, and when should one use a transition?

ANSWER: Usually, the option is up to the writer. If you, as the writer, want your reader to continue reading quickly, without pausing, or without reflecting on what he has been reading, use a conjunction. A *comma* and a *conjunction* are like an *amber light*; you slow down only momentarily, and away you go again. If, however, you want to signal your reader with a *flashing red* light and force him to stop, to reflect upon what he has been reading, and to think about what is coming next, then use a *semicolon* and a *transition.* If you really want him to stop for a longer pause, use a period before the transition—that is, write two simple sentences instead of a compound one. However, this chapter deals with compound sentences, and we shall continue talking about them. One more point: the transition does not have to be placed exactly at the connecting intersection; it may be moved to other positions in the sentence, as illustrated below. In sentences 2 and 3 the transition acts as an *interrupter,* in which case it is preceded and followed by a comma, in sentence 2, and preceded by a comma in sentence 3.

EXAMPLES OF TRANSITION USED AS A CONNECTIVE OR AN INTERRUPTER.

1. The alarm clock did not go off this morning; *therefore,* I slept in.

2. The alarm clock did not go off this morning; I, *therefore,* slept in.

3. The alarm clock did not go off this morning; I slept in, *therefore.*

NOTE: When a transition is used as a connective, it is preceded by a semicolon, which is almost as strong a punctuation mark as a period. Do not use a comma instead of a semicolon, and NEVER omit punctuation altogether.

WRONG: The alarm clock did not go off this morning, therefore I slept in.   COMMA SPLICE.

WRONG: The alarm clock did not go off this morning therefore I slept in.   FUSED SENTENCE.

LIST OF TRANSITIONS ACCORDING TO THEIR FUNCTION.

ADDITION: also, besides, in addition, in fact, furthermore, likewise, moreover.

EMPHASIS: certainly, indeed, of course, to be sure.

CONTRAST: anyway, by contrast, however, on the contrary, on the other hand, nevertheless, nonetheless.

ILLUSTRATION: for example, for instance, namely, that is, to illustrate.

CONCLUSION AND RESULT: accordingly, as a result, consequently, hence, so, therefore, to conclude, to summarize.

TIME AND SERIES: first, first of all, in the first place, to begin with, second, secondly, third, thirdly, then, further on, finally, in conclusion, to conclude.

EXAMPLES OF TRANSITIONS USED IN COMPOUND
SENTENCES

1. He had a great deal of money; *also,* he owned a lot of real estate.

2. He won the Pulitzer Prize for fiction; *in addition,* he won the Nobel Prize for literature.

3. He worked long, hard hours at the store; *furthermore,* he never even took a break.

4. The Los Angeles Rams hired a new coach in 1973; *likewise,* the Los Angeles Sharks acquired a new coach the same year.

5. This book will show you how to write correct sentences; *moreover,* it will show you how to write good paragraphs; *finally,* it will show you how to write essays.

6. He was well respected by everyone; *certainly,* nobody could deny that.

7. I am happy to be here today; *indeed,* I could hardly wait to come.

8. Many high school students are processed through their courses without learning how to write; *to be sure,* many students cannot write even one correct sentence.

9. He worked on his novel for over two years; *however,* he never completed it.

10. She had everything a person could hope for; *nevertheless,* she was not happy.

11. This book is not written for English professors; *on the contrary,* it is designed for students who want to learn how to write immediately.

12. The Cadillac gets about twelve miles per gallon; *by contrast,* the Hornet gets about twenty.

13. The winters in Canada are very severe; *for example,* the temperature often drops to fifty degrees below zero.

ASSIGNMENT FOR SECTION B: USING TRANSITIONS
AS CONNECTIVES. TURN TO PAGE 23 AT THE END
OF THE CHAPTER.

C. USING SEMICOLONS ONLY TO WRITE COMPOUND SENTENCES.

If you want to connect two simple sentences which have a very close relationship, you may want to use only a semicolon. The connection will be more abrupt than it would be with a transition, but perhaps that is the effect you want to create—a dramatized cause-and-effect relationship. Remember, though, the relationship must be very close. Examples:

1. He paid me the money; I delivered the goods.

2. He fell overboard and could not swim; he drowned.

3. The car ran out of control; it crashed.

4. I will study this book carefully; I am determined to become a good writer.

NOTE: Both parts of each sentence in these examples are of equal importance; that is, they are coordinates. They could very well be connected by a coordinating conjunction (such as *and*), or by a transition (*consequently, therefore, however,* etc.). For effect, though, the writer may wish to create a very short and abrupt break, thus dramatizing the second part of the sentence—the result.

Compare the four sentences below for effect.

1. The car ran out of control and crashed. (simple sentence, expresses an idea, but not very dramatic)

2. The car ran out of control, and it crashed. (slightly more dramatic than sentence 1)

3. The car ran out of control; *consequently,* it crashed. (transition supplies a smooth bridge, *explaining relationship*)

4. The car ran out of control; it crashed. (most dramatic of all)
NOTE: Any one of the above sentences is correct, of course; however, the fourth sentence is the most dramatic of all, and *if* that is the effect the writer is trying to achieve, then the fourth sentence, naturally, would be the most effective. Please remember, though, you as the writer have the option of choosing the most effective sentence. Good writing includes not only correct sentences, but also effective ones.
NOTE: Do not run together two sentences without any punctuation.
WRONG: The car ran out of control it crashed. (FUSED SENTENCE)
NOTE: Do not use a comma as a connective instead of a semicolon.
WRONG: The car ran out of control, it crashed. (COMMA SPLICE)

ASSIGNMENT FOR SECTION C: USING SEMICOLONS ONLY TO WRITE COMPOUND SENTENCES. TURN TO PAGE 24 AT THE END OF THE CHAPTER.

ASSIGNMENTS FOR CHAPTER THREE: WRITING COMPOUND SENTENCES.

ASSIGNMENT FOR SECTION A: USING COORDINATING CONJUNCTIONS AS CONNECTIVES.

Use *EACH* of the following *CONNECTIVES* in a compound sentence: *and, but, for, or, nor, yet, so.*
REMEMBER: You must connect two simple sentences, and each simple sentence must contain one subject and one verb.

1. *ASSIGNMENT FOR SECTION B: USING TRANSITIONS AS CONNECTIVES.*

Use fifteen different transitions (listed on page 21) to compose fifteen different compound sentences. Use a semicolon before the transition and a comma after it. NOTE: Do not use a comma before the transition.

2. ADDITIONAL ASSIGNMENT: USING TRANSITIONS AS INTERRUPTERS.

Select five of the compound sentences you have just written and rewrite them using the transition as an *interrupter*. (See examples on pages 20-21.)

Write five different compound sentences using only a semicolon.

CHAPTER FOUR

THE COMPLEX SENTENCE:
USING A MINOR IDEA TO EMPHASIZE THE MAIN ONE

REVIEW.

1. The *simple* sentence merely expresses an idea. It does not explain under what conditions the action occurred. It does not explain why. (*I entered the room.*) This is the fifth simple sentence in a row. All of these simple sentences are independent. Each one makes sense by itself.

2. The *compound* sentence merely links two simple sentences together, and both are of equal importance. The compound sentence expresses two main ideas; however, there is still no explanation for either idea. This is the third compound sentence in a row; it will be followed by a fourth. (*I entered the room, and the lights went out.*)

3. A *complex* sentence, on the other hand, explains why or under what conditions the main idea occurred. *It emphasizes only one idea*—the main one—by *explaining* it through the use of a subordinate (secondary) idea. Therefore, it *contains both* ONE MAIN IDEA and ONE MINOR ONE.

Now consider this *compound* sentence: *I entered the room, and the lights went out.* QUESTION: Which idea is the main one, the one you want to emphasize? The first idea: *I entered the room,* or the second idea: *the lights went out?*

Let us say that you want to emphasize the first idea. Can you explain why you entered the room? Can you explain under what conditions? Here is a clue: What time did I enter the room? When did I enter the room? Correct! I entered the room <u>when the lights went out.</u>

You have now written a complex sentence by explaining why, or how, or when, or under what conditions the action in the main idea occurred. You will note that the *main idea* is independent of the other idea and, therefore, can stand alone. It makes sense by itself. (*I entered the room.*) The main idea, which can be written as an independent sentence, is sometimes called a *main clause.* By contrast, the other idea cannot stand alone and make sense by itself. (When the lights went out.)

Although it expresses an idea, it is a subordinate (minor) idea and depends on the main idea to make sense. If you have difficulty in determining whether or not an idea is a main one, simply read it aloud to yourself, and then stop, as though somebody had suddenly appeared with that announcement and then abruptly left the room. If the words make sense by themselves, as a simple sentence does, they express a main idea. If they don't make sense by themselves, they are not a main idea, but rather a subordinate (secondary) idea. Try this method now. What happens?

EXAMPLES OF SECONDARY IDEAS: (Sometimes called *Subordinate Clauses).*

1. As the lights went out. (So what? What happened?)
2. When the lights went out. (So what?)
3. While the lights went out. (What happened?)

Each of the three examples above depends upon the main idea to make sense. Consequently, none of them can be written as an independent sentence, separated from the main idea. Instead, the function of such a secondary idea (or subordinate clause) is to explain why, when, or under what circumstances the action in the *main idea* occurred. In short, the minor or subordinate idea (subordinate clause) emphasizes the *main idea* (main clause) in a *complex sentence.*

SELECTING THE MAIN IDEA.

Let us consider this complex sentence again. (*I entered the room when the lights went out.*) Have you really emphasized the main idea? Let us reverse the order of the main idea and determine if it is still the major idea that you want to emphasize. (*When the lights went out, I entered the room.*) Is the fact that you entered the room really the most important idea? If that is what you want to emphasize, fine! But if you think about those two ideas for a moment, you will realize that the sentence can be more effective—certainly more dramatic— if you emphasize the other idea: *the lights went out.* You have given your reader something to think about: what will happen next? The secret of good writing is to lure your reader on, to keep him guessing about what will happen next. Examine the two sentences below now, and determine which is the most effective.

1. *The lights went out* as I entered the room.

2. As I entered the room, *the lights went out.*

PLACEMENT OF THE MAIN IDEA.

Although both sentences above are correct, and although the main idea is emphasized, you must now determine which sentence is more effective and why. Remember what I just said about dramatizing a situation, about luring your reader on. Is there any mystery in sentence 1? Perhaps. What do you remember after you have finished reading that sentence? Something about entering the room? So what? Is there any mystery, or suspense?

Now examine sentence 2. (As I entered the room, (pause)——.) Is there any suspense? Does the reader want to know what will happen next? Perhaps we can build up the suspense.

As I entered the room, and as I heard a gunshot, *the lights went out.*

Such a sentence is sometimes called a *periodic* sentence because the suspense or climax is saved until the very end, near the period. By contrast, sentence 1 below, which is sometimes called a *loose* sentence, gives the secret away immediately and leaves only the minor idea or explanation at the end. Obviously, then, the periodic sentence is more effective, or at least more dramatic, than the loose sentence. Furthermore, *the last thing you remember is usually the last thing you see.* Therefore, if you want the reader to remember the major idea, *put it at the end*—right before the *period.* That way the main idea will usually stand out in his mind longer. But in any event, if you can possibly avoid it, *do not bury the main idea in the middle.* Do you remember what you ate for lunch last Wednesday or three years ago? Of course not. Then don't expect your reader to remember something that is buried in the middle of a sentence.

In summary then, REMEMBER THESE RULES ABOUT WRITING COMPLEX SENTENCES:
1. Use a complex sentence if you want to emphasize a main idea or if you want to explain why, when, or how it occurred.
2. Be very careful that you select the most important idea as the main one. The most important idea is the most exciting one and, therefore, lures the reader on.
3. Place the main idea at the end of the sentence for dramatic effect if that is what you want to achieve. Usually this position is the most effective of all. It saves the climax for the end.
4. The beginning of the sentence is the second most effective position for placing the main idea. This beginning position gives the reader

the main idea immediately and leaves the explanation for the end.
5. The worst position of all for placing a main idea is in the middle of a sentence. Don't bury a main idea there. Nobody will remember it.
6. Above all, do not write all of your sentences in the same pattern; vary them. Variety is the spice of life.

LIST OF SUBORDINATING CONJUNCTIONS:

The following is a list of words, called *subordinating conjunctions,* which join a subordinate idea (subordinate clause) to the main one. They are also called *adverbs* because they explain the manner under which the main action occurred (when, where, how, why).

Cause of Action:	because, in that, since
Condition:	although, if, unless
Manner:	as, as though
Result:	in order that, so that
Time:	after, before, since, until, when, whenever, while

EXAMPLES OF SUBORDINATING CONJUNCTIONS IN COMPLEX SENTENCES:

1. Although it rained very hard, the roads were still open.
2. As I was walking down the street, I saw a bank robbery.
3. In order that you may become a good writer, I would like you to learn basic sentence structure.
4. He has been very busy since he received his promotion. (*Note:* A comma is unnecessary when a subordinate clause follows the main one.)
5. Exercise is important in that it keeps the body in good condition.
6. After you have read this sentence, please do the following assignment.

ASSIGNMENT FOR COMPLEX SENTENCES.
TURN TO PAGE 29.

EXERCISE 1. WRITING COMPLEX SENTENCES
Write a complex sentence for every one of the subordinating conjunctions listed on the previous page. Vary your sentence pattern; place some main ideas (main clauses) at the beginning, and place others at the end. NOTE: Use a comma if the subordinate clause introduces the main idea, as in sentences 1, 2, 3, and 5. Do not use a comma if the subordinate clause follows the main clause, as in sentence 4.
RULE:
Introductory subordinate clause, (comma) *main clause.*
Main Clause subordinate clause. (No comma necessary.)

EXERCISE 2. REVISING COMPOUND SENTENCES INTO COMPLEX SENTENCES.

Rewrite each of the following sentences subordinating one idea to emphasize the *main one.* Place the *main idea* (main clause) at the *end.*
Example: I stepped off the curb, and I fell down. (Compound)
Revised: As I stepped off the curb, *I fell down.* (Complex)

a) I was listening to the radio, and I heard the news about the World Series.
b) He worked very hard, but he did not succeed.
c) I would like to go to the beach, but it is too windy.
d) He wanted to succeed; therefore, he studied very hard.
e) She got up early, for she wanted to be on time.
NOTE: In order to subordinate an idea, use a subordinating conjunction at the beginning of the subordinate clause (minor idea). (See example above.)

EXERCISE 3.
Rewrite each of the compound sentences above as a complex sentence—with the subordinating conjunction in the middle. The *main idea* will then be at the *beginning.*
Example: I fell down as I stepped off the curb.

CHAPTER FIVE

MODIFIERS:
ADDED MATERIAL FOR INTRODUCTIONS,
CONCLUSIONS, AND EXPLANATIONS

OVERVIEW.

A modifier is a word or group of words that is used to describe something. A modifier may be vitally important to the meaning of the sentence, or it may be only added material for introductions, descriptions, explanations, or even afterthoughts. A good, well-placed modifier may mean the difference between an effective sentence and a poor one. A misplaced modifier results not only in an awkward sentence, but often in an embarrassing one. Finally, a modifier that is mistakenly written as a sentence results in an incomplete sentence—a sentence fragment—which should be avoided. This chapter will discuss modifiers as introductions, conclusions, explanations, and fragments.

I. INTRODUCTIONS.

Although a simple sentence usually begins with its subject (*I visited my brother*), there are many times when the writer introduces the subject with a word or a group of words. A group of words that describes something but does not contain a subject and a verb is called a *phrase.* (e.g. *In the beginning. Early yesterday morning.*) A group of words that contains both a subject and a verb is called a *clause. (While I was walking down the street.)*

A. Introductory Phrases.

An introductory phrase introduces the main idea (main clause). If the introductory phrase is long, or if it is very important, it should be followed by a comma so that the reader has time to pause and to concentrate, not only on the introduction, but also on the main idea (main clause). Consider the examples below in which the *introductions* are *italicized*.

1. *Yesterday* I visited my brother.
2. *Tomorrow morning* I will visit my brother.
3. *Early tomorrow morning* I will visit him again.
4. *Very early tomorrow morning* I will visit him again.
                                                    (Comma optional)
5. *Very early tomorrow morning,* I will visit him again.
6. *Very early tomorrow morning before breakfast,* I will visit him again. (Comma required after long introductory phrase)
7. *Very early tomorrow morning, just before breakfast,* I will visit him. (Comma is used to separate series of phrases)
8. *Very early tomorrow morning just before breakfast,* I will visit him. (Also correct—only one comma to separate a long introduction)

NOTE:

a) The subject of each sentence is still *I*.

b) A long introductory phrase of four or more words is usually set off from the main idea (main clause) by a comma.

c) Short introductory phrases of three words or less are usually not separated from the main idea *unless* they act as interrupters—that is, unless the writer wants the reader to pause and to think about the introduction. If the writer feels that the introduction is very important, he will want to draw attention to it by separating it with a comma from the main idea.

e.g. *Early tomorrow morning,* I will visit him again. (The writer obviously feels that the introduction is important enough to warrant the comma.)

REMEMBER, though, a comma slows down the reader. Too many commas are a nuisance and should be avoided.

Wrong: *Very early⊙ tomorrow morning⊙ before breakfast,* I will visit him. (Unnecessary commas are circled.)

d) Strong interjections (interrupters) such as *yes, no, certainly, of course,* etc. are separated by commas.

e.g. *Yes,* I will be glad to come.
     Of course, I will be happy to see you.

B. Dangling Modifiers—Avoid Them.

A modifying phrase should always refer to its grammatical subject. Certain types of phrases that contain the *-ing* form of a verb (participle) are often mistaken for subordinate clauses, which were already discussed in Chapter Four. Avoid dangling modifiers such as these participle phrases and others:

1. *While eating,* the table collapsed. (What is the subject of this sentence? Can a table eat?)

CORRECTION: While *I* was eating, the table collapsed.

2. *While swimming,* our clothes were stolen. (Were the clothes swimming?)

CORRECTION: While *we were* swimming, our clothes were stolen.

3. *Seated comfortably,* the plane took off. (Was the plane seated comfortably?)

CORRECTION: After *we were* seated comfortably, the plane took off.

4. *Built* on hills and curves, I shall always remember San Francisco. (Am I built on hills and curves?)

CORRECTION: *San Francisco,* built on hills and curves, *is* a city which I shall never forget. (OR) I shall always remember San Francisco, built on hills and curves.

5. To *swim* well, constant *practice* is required.

CORRECTION: To swim well, *one must* practice constantly.

NOTE: In order to avoid errors such as those listed above—dangling modifiers—you are advised to *rewrite* the sentence as a *complex* sentence, which contains a subordinate clause instead of a phrase.

REMEMBER: Your reader cannot communicate with you. He cannot ask what you meant, and he cannot read your mind. Do not leave him guessing. Be specific. Your sentence—*every part of it*—must be correct. Therefore, *it must be exact.* And that includes the introduction. If your introduction contains its own subject, as it will in a complex sentence, the meaning will be clear.

C. Clauses.

A clause is a group of words that contains both a subject and a verb. Clauses are of two types: *main* clauses (or *independent* clauses) that stand alone and make sense independently, and *subordinate clauses* (or dependent clauses) that cannot stand alone but must depend on the main clause to make sense. Chapter Four referred to a subordinate clause as the "minor" or "subordinate idea" that contained a subordinating conjunction (as, if, because, when, while, etc.), along with a subject and verb, and was used primarily to emphasize or explain the major idea (main clause). A subordinate clause may introduce the main idea or it may follow it. If it acts as an introduction, it is called an *introductory clause* or *introductory subordinate clause.* An introductory clause is usually separated from the main clause by a comma, particularly if the introductory clause is long or is in danger of being misread.

EXAMPLES:

1. As I was shaving, the cat ran into the room. (Comma is required to prevent misreading. *As I was shaving the cat...*)

2. While we were eating, the table collapsed. (Comma required to prevent misreading. *While we were eating the table...*)

3. While I was walking down the street, I saw a bank robbery. (Comma is useful here, but not absolutely necessary.)

4. Even though the members of the jury had deliberated long and hard, they had not been able to reach a verdict that week. (Comma is required after a long introductory clause.)

WRITING ASSIGNMENT—EXERCISE I: TURN TO PAGE 44 AT THE END OF THIS CHAPTER.

II. CONCLUSIONS.

Both phrases and clauses may be used after the main idea (main clause) as conclusions. Sometimes the conclusion should not be separated from the main idea by a comma, while at other times it should. These rules will illustrate the punctuation of conclusions.

A. No Commas.

1. If your conclusion is *short* and *unimportant,* do *not* use a comma. Why separate the conclusion from the main idea? Why slow down the reader?

e.g. a) I will visit my brother again *tomorrow morning.*

    b) I will visit my brother *very early tomorrow morning.*

2. If your conclusion is *vitally important* to the sense of the sentence and therefore *restricts* the meaning of the sentence, do *not* separate it.

e.g. a) I will go the the dance *if I can borrow five dollars.*

    b) I cannot go to the dance *unless I can borrow five dollars.*

NOTE: The first part of both sentence a) and b) above is *conditional* upon the second; that is, the introduction depends upon the conclusion for its meaning. If the conclusion is omitted, the sentence is incomplete and inaccurate.

e.g. I will go to the dance. (Not accurate)

   I cannot go to the dance. (Not accurate)

B. Use Commas.

1. If your conclusion is quite *long,* or if it contains merely *added information* (parenthetical) or description, you owe your reader the courtesy of separating it from the main idea.

a) I will visit my brother again, *very early in the month of September.* (long conclusion)

b) I will see you at noon, *when the clock strikes twelve.* (added information)

c) I plan to visit my brother again, *probably toward the end of October or November, depending upon the weather.* (long conclusion plus added information.)

2. If *both* parts of the sentence are quite long, separate them by a comma.

a) The members of the jury had been unable to reach a verdict that week, *even though they had deliberated long and hard until the very end.*

C. Comma Optional.

1. If your conclusion is fairly long (about five words), or if you want to *emphasize* it, you may want to use a comma.

a) I will visit my brother again *very early in the morning.*

(Comma optional)

b) I will visit my brother again, *very early in the morning.*

c) I saw the accident *just as we were leaving.*

(Comma optional)

d) I saw the accident, *just as we were leaving.*

WRITING ASSIGNMENT — EXERCISE II: TURN TO PAGE 44 FOR WRITING ASSIGNMENT.

35

SUMMARY: INTRODUCTIONS AND CONCLUSIONS

A. Introductions.

1. Short introductory material does not have to be followed by a comma *unless* the introduction is very important or unless there is a danger of the sentence being misread.

2. Long or important introductory material should be followed by a comma.

B. Conclusions.

1. Short conclusions should *not* be separated by a comma from the rest of the sentence.

2. Vitally important or "restrictive" conclusions (usually beginning with *if* or *unless*) should *never* be separated from the rest of the sentence.

3. Descriptive or "parenthetical" conclusions *may* be separated from the rest of the sentence—*especially* if the conclusions are long.

NOTE: The option of using a comma, both for introductions and conclusions, is almost always up to the writer except when the comma is required to prevent misreading.

III. CASUAL DESCRIPTIONS.

In addition to introducing or concluding a main idea, a modifier may also casually describe something by merely adding a certain amount of information. Such added (or thrown in) information, which is often referred to as "parenthetical," is not absolutely necessary to the sense of the sentence and, therefore, it should be enclosed by commas. If this added information (or description) is removed, it will not drastically alter the meaning of the sentence. The purpose of this type of modifier is to *describe,* to bring additional information to the main idea. The purpose of the commas is to separate such additional information from the main idea. For example, consider this sentence: *All students, who are only human, are sometimes lazy.*

QUESTION: What happens when we remove the phrase *who are only human?* Does the sentence still make sense?

ANSWER: Of course it does. (*All students are sometimes lazy.*) We have removed only a modifier that supplied additional information. The added information was merely a casual description. It was not vitally necessary to the sense of the sentence.

Now consider this sentence: *My father works very hard.*

QUESTION: Can you describe your father? What does he do? Where does he live? Can you rewrite the sentence supplying additional information?

REVISION: 1. My father, *a farmer,* works very hard.
2. My father, *a farmer in Illinois,* works very hard.
3. My father, *a grain farmer in Illinois,* works very hard.
4. My father, *who is a grain farmer in Illinois, works very hard.*

SUGGESTION: Memorize the examples above, and then study the examples below so that you will know how to supply additional information by adding group modifiers.

MAIN IDEA: *Mr. Bell is a detective.* Now describe him. What is he wearing?

A. Add a Group Modifier: A Phrase or a Clause.

1. Mr. Bell, *in a blue suit,* is a detective. (Phrase)
2. Mr. Bell, *wearing a blue suit,* is a detective. (Phrase)
3. Mr. Bell, *who is wearing a blue suit,* is a detective. (Clause)

(OR)

4. Mr. Bell, *in the doorway,* is a detective. (Phrase)
5. Mr. Bell, *standing in the doorway,* is a detective (Phrase)
6. Mr. Bell, *who is standing in the doorway,* is a detective. (Clause)

QUESTION: Which sentences in Group A are the least effective?

ANSWER: The ones containing the most "deadwood." Do the words *who is* add anything vitally important to the description? Of course not. The pronoun *who* merely emphasizes the identification, but it is really extra wordage. Therefore, sentences 3 and 6 are the least effective. As a rule, the fewer words you use to express an idea, the better.

NOTE: Because the group modifier in sentences 1 and 4 is so short, it does not necessarily have to be set off by a comma. (See Section B-2 below.) As a rule, though, whenever you add a group modifier that contains only description, you should set it off with a comma.

B. Add Linking Group Modifiers.

1. Mr. Bell, *in a blue suit, who is standing in the doorway,* is a detective.

2. Mr Bell *in a blue suit, who is standing in the doorway,* is a detective.

3. Mr. Bell, *wearing a blue suit and standing in the doorway,* is a detective.

4. Mr. Bell, *who is wearing a blue suit and who is standing in the doorway,* is a detective.

5. Mr. Bell, *standing in the doorway and wearing a blue suit,* is a detective.

37

6. Mr. Bell, *the tall man with the bald head, who is standing in the doorway and wearing a blue suit,* is a detective.

C. But Avoid Awkward and Unclear References Through Misplaced Modifiers.

1. Mr. Bell, in a blue *suit standing* in the doorway, is a detective. (Is the suit standing in the doorway?)
2. Mr. Bell, standing in the *doorway wearing* a blue suit, is a detective. (Is the doorway wearing a blue suit?)

RULE: To avoid awkward sentences like these, place the modifiers as close as possible to the words they are supposed to modify.

D. Other Examples of Group Modifiers to Add Information.

(Main idea) My uncle John is my favorite uncle.
1. My uncle John, *who lives in Long Beach, in a beautiful apartment, with a view of the ocean, near the pier,* is my favorite uncle.

(OR)

2. My uncle John, *who lives in a beautiful apartment with a view of the ocean, near the pier in Long Beach,* is my favorite uncle.
3. Uncle John, *who drives forty miles to work every day and ninety miles to visit our family every weekend,* is my favorite uncle.
4. The province of British Columbia, *which has hundreds of rivers and glacier-fed lakes, as well as thousands of towering mountain peaks,* is one of the most beautiful provinces in Canada.

(OR)

5. The province of British Columbia, *with hundreds of rivers and glacier-fed lakes and thousands of towering mountain peaks,* is one of the most beautiful provinces in Canada.
6. Her car, *which cost only $500.00,* runs well.

WRITING ASSIGNMENT — EXERCISE III: TURN TO PAGE 44 AT THE END OF THIS CHAPTER.

IV. VITAL EXPLANATIONS: RESTRICTIVE (REQUIRED) MODIFIERS.

Certain modifiers are absolutely essential to the meaning of the sentence and, therefore, cannot be removed. Such "required" or *restrictive* modifiers should *never* be separated by commas. Group modifiers beginning with the word *that* are almost always *restrictive* (required) because they *point out* a particular thing.

Examples of Restrictive Modifiers to Supply Vital Information.

1. The car *that is parked in the red zone* has a ticket.
2. The car *that is parked in the green zone* does not have a ticket.

QUESTION: Are we referring to a particular car in both sentences?
ANSWER: Of course!
NOTE: Therefore, we do not separate the modifiers by commas, because the modifiers are absolutely necessary to the sense of the sentence.

3. The car *that is parked in the red zone* has a ticket, but the car *that is parked in the green zone* does not have a ticket.

QUESTION: What would happen if we removed the modifiers in any of the examples above?
ANSWER: We wouldn't know which car the writer is talking about, and the sentence therefore wouldn't make sense. (The car has a ticket, but the car does not have a ticket.)

Other Examples.

4. The car *which is parked in the red zone* has a ticket.
5. The car *parked in the red zone* has a ticket.
6. The car *in the red zone* has a ticket.

Also Consider These:

7. The patient *who had a heart attack* died, but the patient *who had an ulcer* was released from the hospital.

QUESTION: What would happen if we removed the modifiers?
ANSWER: The sentence wouldn't make sense.
(The patient died, but the patient was released from the hospital.)

And These:

8. All students *who earn at least a "D"* will pass this course, but all students *who do not earn at least a "D"* will fail.
9. All students *receiving at least a "D"* will pass, but all students *receiving less than a "D"* will fail.
10. All students *that earn at least a "D"* will pass, but all students *that do not earn at least a "D"* will fail.

QUESTION: Again, what would happen if we removed the restrictive modifier?

39

ANSWER: Again, the sentence wouldn't make sense.
(All students will pass, but all students will fail.)
SUGGESTION: Memorize sentence 3, 7, or 8 so that you will always remember what a restrictive modifier is.

NOTE ON RELATIVE PRONOUNS.

A pronoun renames or substitutes for a *noun* (a person, place, or thing). Certain pronouns refer only to persons, others only to non-humans or things, and one particular pronoun refers to both humans and non-humans.

1. *Who* and *whom* refer *only* to *persons. Who* is a *subject; whom* is an *object. That* may refer to persons, *either* as a subject or object.

(The man *who* owes me money is here.)	(subject)
(The man *that* owes me money is here.)	(subject)
(The man *whom* I wanted to see is here.)	(object)
(The man *that* I wanted to see is here.)	(object)

2. *Which* refers to *non-humans* and to *non-living things. That* also refers to non-humans and to non-living things.
(The dog *which* howls every night is outside.)
(The dog *that* howls every night is outside.)
(The book *which* I spoke to you about is on my desk.)
3. *Whose* indicates ownership and usually refers to humans, but it may also refer to non-humans and to non-living things.
(That man *whose* daughter I know visited me.)
(The book *whose* pages are torn is on my desk.) *Stilted:* The book, *the pages of which* are torn, is on my desk. This sentence contains too much deadwood (e.g. "the pages of which"). If one word does the job of two or more words, it is more effective and should be used.

WRITING ASSIGNMENT — EXERCISE IV: TURN TO PAGE
45 AT THE END OF THIS CHAPTER.

SUMMARY OF PUNCTUATION FOR MODIFIERS: ADDED DESCRIPTIONS AND VITAL EXPLANATIONS:
Group modifiers supplying merely *additional information* (parenthetical) require commas both before and after the modifier.
e.g. All students, *who are only human,* are sometimes lazy.

Group modifiers supplying *vital* (required) explanations that are necessary for the meaning of the sentence should *not* be punctuated.
e.g. All students *who do not earn at least a "D"* will fail the course.

V. MISPLACED AND SQUINTING MODIFIERS.

A modifier should be placed as close as possible to the word it modifies; otherwise, the sentence may lose its meaning entirely.

ERROR. My wife gave some cookies to my friends *with nuts in them.* (Do my friends have nuts in them?)

CORRECTION. My wife gave some cookies *with nuts in them* to my friends.

ERROR. He wore an expensive leather jacket with fancy buttons *that cost $150.* (Do the buttons cost $150?)

CORRECTION. He wore an expensive leather jacket *that cost $150* and that contained fancy buttons.

IMPROVEMENT. His expensive leather jacket, which cost $150, contained fancy buttons.

ERROR. You can see the sign *driving down the road.* (Can a sign drive?)

UNCLEAR. She *almost* won two hundred dollars worth of prizes. (Did she win any prizes? Apparently not.)

CLEAR. She won *almost* two hundred dollars worth of prizes. (Her prizes amounted to over $190.00.)

WRITING ASSIGNMENT — EXERCISE V: TURN TO PAGE 45 AT THE END OF THIS CHAPTER.

VI. AVOIDING MODIFIERS, SUBJECTS, AND PREDICATES AS SENTENCE FRAGMENTS.

Very often instead of completing a sentence, the inexperienced writer *breaks it in two* by putting a period where it does *not* belong: in the middle of a sentence. In his desire to emphasize a part of the sentence—usually the modifier—he puts a period at the introductory modifier and therefore writes it as a sentence, or he breaks off the concluding modifier from the main clause with a period, writing the conclusion also in the form of a sentence.

At other times he simply breaks the sentence in two, splitting the subject-group of words from the verb and its object (predicate). This mistake usually results in two fragments, since both a subject and verb are required in a sentence.

Finally, in his attempt to emphasize an object—the result of an action—he may split the object from the rest of the sentence, by writing only a noun clause.

All of these "incomplete sentence" errors, which are very serious,

41

are called *sentence fragments,* or simply *fragments.* A fragment is a piece of something, a splinter. A piece of a sentence, therefore, is also a fragment. Although fragments are used occasionally in fiction, sometimes with effect, and in commercial advertising, usually with less effect, they are not only grammatically incorrect, but they also slow down the reader unnecessarily and often cause confusion. Therefore, they should be avoided. *Do not write fragments.*

You can AVOID WRITING FRAGMENTS simply by *reading each sentence* to yourself, and then asking yourself this question: *Does this "sentence" make sense as it is written?* If it depends for its meaning on the sentence to follow, it certainly is not a complete sentence. If it depends for its meaning on the previous sentence, again it is a fragment. The only exceptions to this rule are these: Certain *sentences that begin with coordinating conjunctions* (and, but, or, etc.) or with conjunctive adverbs or *transitions* (however, therefore, moreover, etc.) depend slightly on the previous sentence for complete meaning. (e.g. I cannot swim. However, I would like to learn how.) By comparison, fragments depend entirely on another sentence for meaning.

A. Fragments at the Beginning of a Sentence.

1. *Early yesterday morning. Just before breakfast.* I visited my brother. (Introductory modifiers are incorrectly written as sentences.)
CORRECTION: Early yesterday morning just before breakfast, I visited my brother. OR: Early yesterday morning, just before breakfast, I visited my brother.
2. *Late in the afternoon. Just before the sun set. As we were driving to the beach.* We saw the accident. (Introductory modifiers are fragments.)
CORRECTION: Late in the afternoon just before the sun set, as we were driving to the beach, we saw the accident.
ALSO CORRECT: Late in the afternoon, just before the sun set, as we were driving to the beach, we saw the accident.
3. *Although she was the best qualified candidate and worked very hard to get elected.* She lost.(Long introductory clause is incorrectly written as a sentence.)
CORRECTION: Although she was the best qualified candidate and worked very hard to get elected, she lost.
4. *The tall man who is standing outside, next to the telephone booth. Is my uncle.* (Subject-group of words plus modifiers are written as an incomplete sentence. Likewise, the completer appears as a fragment.)

CORRECTION: The tall man who is standing outside, next to the telephone booth, is my uncle.

B. Fragments at the Tail End of the Sentence.

NOTE: Of all fragment errors, these types, at the tail end of the sentence, appear most often.

1. I wanted to clean up my room. *Before my mother came home.* (Subordinate clause as the conclusion is incorrectly punctuated as a sentence.)

CORRECTION: I wanted to clean up my room before my mother came home.

2. He spent ten years working on his greatest novel. *Which won the Nobel Prize.* (Concluding modifier appears as a fragment.)

CORRECTION: He spent ten years working on his greatest novel, which won the Nobel Prize.

3. My uncle John lives in Long Beach. *In a beautiful apartment. With a view. Of the ocean. Near the pier.* (Four concluding modifiers, in the form of prepositional phrases, are incorrectly written as sentences.)

CORRECTION: My uncle John lives in Long Beach, in a beautiful apartment with a view of the ocean, near the pier.

ALSO CORRECT: My uncle John lives in Long Beach, in a beautiful apartment, with a view of the ocean, near the pier.

4. I felt that I had done a good job in my classroom. *That I had communicated with my students. And that I had taught them well.* (Two incorrectly punctuated noun clauses, conclusions, appear as fragments.)

CORRECTION: I felt that I had done a good job in my classroom, that I had communicated with my students, and that I had taught them well.

SPECIAL NOTE: To avoid fragments, please remember this rule: If your hand becomes tired, put your pencil or pen down on the desk and take a rest, but *don't* put a period where it doesn't belong—*in the middle of a sentence.* If you want to emphasize a conclusion, as I have just done in the sentence above, you may use a dash—a long one— or you may use a comma, which is also effective, because both punctuations create a pause. If you really want to emphasize a point, write it as a separate sentence. Write it as a *complete* sentence. But *do not write fragments.* Remember: a fragment is only part of a sentence.

WRITING ASSIGNMENT — EXERCISE VI: TURN TO PAGE 46.

ASSIGNMENTS FOR CHAPTER FIVE: MODIFIERS.

Exercise I. Writing Modifiers as Introductions.

Write a simple sentence. (Example: We are going to the football game.) Now *enlarge* your sentence by adding introductory modifiers, beginning with one word or two (e.g. On Tuesday), and gradually increase your introduction by a long phrase or series of phrases or clauses.

Example:

a) *On Tuesday,* we are going to the football game.

b) *Early on Tuesday evening,* we are going to the football game.

c) *Early on Tuesday evening, just after dinner,* we are going to the football game.

Remember: write the entire sentence each time, and use correct punctuation.

Exercise II. Writing Modifiers as Conclusions.

Write the same simple sentence that you have written for Exercise I. Now instead of adding introductions, *add the concluding modifiers,* beginning with one or two words, and gradually increase the conclusion by a long phrase or series of phrases and clauses. You may use the same introductions you used in Exercise I for your conclusions in Exercise II. But *write* the *entire sentence each time, and use correct punctuation.*

Exercise III. Modifiers as Casual Descriptions (Parenthetical).

Below is a list of simple sentences, each containing an *italicized* word or words. *Rewrite each sentence* using *each* of the following types of modifiers:

a) one group modifier after the italicized word

b) a series of group modifiers.

Note: You will have to rewrite each sentence, therefore, two different ways. (List begins on page 45)

SIMPLE SENTENCES

1. *Mrs. Clark* is my teacher.
2. *My aunt Martha* is my favorite aunt.
3. *Our car* runs well.
4. *Our television* is out of order.
5. *My bike* is the best one I have ever owned.
6. *Our state* (or province) is the best one in the country.
7. *This handbook* is mine.
8. *This assignment* is almost finished.

Exercise IV. Vital Explanations—Restrictive (Required) Modifiers.

Rewrite each of the sentences below, using a group modifier that supplies vital information—that is, a restrictive modifier. The nouns to be modified are *italicized.*

1. The *bicycle* belongs to me, but the *bicycle* belongs to you.
2. The *man* is my uncle, but the *man* is not my uncle.
3. The *classroom* is where I just came from, but the *classroom* is where I am headed for.
4. Mr. *Brown* is my friend, but Mr. *Brown* is not my friend.
5. The *girl* won the beauty contest, but the *girl* lost the contest.
6. The *football game* was won by the Rams, but the *football game* was won by the Vikings.

Exercise V. Misplaced and Squinting Modifiers.

Each of the following sentences contains a misplaced or squinting modifier. *Rewrite each sentence,* placing the modifier as close as possible to whatever it is supposed to be modifying.

1. Mary saw a blouse in the window of a department store that she liked.
2. She bought a ribbon for her hair that cost fifty cents.
3. The plane took off from the runway with all seats full.
4. I borrowed an egg from my sister that was rotten.
5. We have a bird in a cage that never sings.
6. You can see the sign driving down the road.
7. My mother gave some chocolates to our neighbor that she bought at a candy store.
8. She almost made the Honor Roll four times.

9. Her uncle just arrived here two months ago.

10. On arrival in the Soviet Union, a Russian immigration officer searched me.

11. While cycling through the park, some blackbirds ate our lunch.

Exercise VI. Sentence Fragments.

Each of the following groups of sentences contains at least one fragment. *Rewrite* each group, using correct punctuation to eliminate the fragments.

1. Before I go home this evening. I will have to finish this work.

2. Late yesterday afternoon. Just as we were getting out of school. I lost my pocketbook.

3. That beautiful set of bedroom furniture. Which was on display all last week. At Sears. Is no longer there. Because it was sold.

4. The new Chevy. Which goes on display next week. Probably on Friday. Will cost over $6,000. Which is a lot of money. Even in these days. Of spiraling inflation.

5. I watched the news on television. As soon as I got home.

6. We were detained last summer. During our trip to the Soviet Union. Because our papers were not in order.

7. When I graduate from high school. I intend to go on to college. Even though I may have to work my way through.

8. I believed her story. That she had traveled a great distance. Without funds. And that she hadn't eaten in two days. Which is a long time. To go without food.

9. After I finish this assignment. On fragments. I am going to put my book down. And take a break. Before I continue with the next chapter. Which is a very long chapter. Because it deals with all the rules. Of grammar and usage. That one should know. If he wants to be a good writer.

PART THREE

HANDBOOK OF GRAMMAR AND USAGE

CHAPTER SIX

HANDBOOK OF GRAMMAR AND USAGE

This chapter will acquaint the reader with the basic rules of grammar and usage, and will point out the most common errors that should be avoided by the writer. The chapter will be concise and must therefore use basic grammar terminology. However, brief examples will illustrate the major points discussed. For the benefit of the teacher, abbreviated symbols, which he may want to use on his students' papers, will be supplied in parenthesis.

1. ADJECTIVES and ADVERBS (ad)

Do not confuse adjectives with adverbs.

A. Adjectives.

Adjectives modify only nouns. (He is a *slow* driver. He is a *good* writer. His writing is *good*. She is an *excellent* cook. Her meals are *good*. Her meals always taste *good*.)

B. Adverbs.

Adverbs modify not only verbs, but also adjectives and other adverbs. Usually adverbs end in —y or in —ly. They frequently explain how or in what manner something happened, or else they bring additional information to explain other modifiers. (He drives *slowly*. He writes *well*. She cooks *well*. He is a *very* slow driver. He is *really* a *very* slow driver.)

NOTE: Avoid excessive use of both adjectives and adverbs, because overuse tends to make your writing seem padded. Instead, use a more appropriate noun or a stronger verb. A noun and a verb constitute the heart of the sentence; everything else acts as a completer.

PADDED WRITING: He was truly a tall man.

IMPROVED: He towered above everyone else.

2. AGREEMENT (AGR)

A. Subject-Verb.

A verb always agrees with its subject in number. A singular subject requires a singular verb; a plural subject requires a plural verb. This rule applies regardless of tense. NOTE that the tense of the verb changes only in the *past* and *present*, not in the future, and that the *difficulty* with tenses usually lies in the *third person singular,* which is often confused with the first person singular. (See section 27, tense) REMEMBER: The *third person singular* (he, she, the car, it) is *singular;* the third person plural (the people, the cars, they) is plural.

1. SINGULAR: The *man is* here. *He was* here. *She was* here. The *car was* here. *It was* here. The *car has been* here. *It has been* here.

2. PLURAL: The *men are* here. The *women were* here. The *cars are* here. *They are* here. *They have been* here. *They were* here. *They are* gone.

3. GROSS ERROR: SINGULAR: The engine *run.* It *run.* He *don't* care.

CORRECTION: The engine *runs.* It *runs.* He *doesn't* care.

4. GROSS ERROR: PLURAL: You *was* there. We *was* there. They *was* there.

CORRECTION: You *were* there. We *were* there. They *were* there.

5. INTERVENING SOUNDS: Do not confuse intervening words with the subject. Always determine what the subject is, and make the verb agree with it.
WRONG: The *report* of the incidents *were* recorded.
CORRECT: The *report* of the incidents *was* recorded. (Subject is *report.)*
WRONG: The reports of the hearing *was* recorded.
CORRECT: The *reports* of the hearing *were* recorded.

6. COMPOUND SUBJECTS are usually considered to be plural. (A dog and a cat are good pets. Paper and pen are required.)

7. SINGULAR AND COMPOUND SUBJECT JOINED BY COORDINATING CONJUNCTION AND CORRELATIVE (EITHER-OR — NEITHER-NOR): If one subject is singular and the other is plural, the verb agrees with the *nearer* one. (Neither John nor his *sisters were* here. Neither his sisters nor *John was* here.)

B. Pronouns as Subjects.

1. SINGULAR PRONOUNS require SINGULAR VERBS. These

pronouns are singular: *anyone, everyone, each, nobody, somebody, something,* etc. (Everyone is here. Nobody was here. Nothing has changed.)

2. PLURAL PRONOUNS require PLURAL VERBS. These pronouns are usually plural: *all, more, most, some. Both* is always plural. (Both John and Mary are here. All of my friends are here.)

3. SINGULAR OR PLURAL PRONOUNS take SINGULAR OR PLURAL VERBS depending on the context. Note these pronouns which may take singular or plural verbs: *none, any, more, most,* and sometimes *all.* (None of the evidence is ready. None of my friends are here. None of my friends is here. All of the evidence is here. Most of the evidence is here. Most of my friends are here.)

4. RELATIVE PRONOUNS require a singular verb when the antecedent (the thing referred to) is singular, but they require a plural verb when the antecedent is plural. Always determine the antecedent.

SINGULAR: Jane is *the only one* who *is* here. (*Who* clearly refers to the only one.)

Jane is *the only one* of the girls *who* is here. (There is *only one* girl who is here, and *who* refers to her—the only one.)

PLURAL: There are many *girls* who *are* here.

Jane is one of many *girls* who *are* here.

Jane is one of the many girls *who* are here.

Jane is one of the *girls* who *are* here.

C. Pronoun-Antecedent:

As in rule B-4, a pronoun agrees with its antecedent. Use singular pronouns to refer to singular antecedents, and use plural pronouns to refer to plural antecedents. In *formal [standard] English, the following antecedents* are SINGULAR: *any, anyone, anybody, each, every, everyone, everybody, either, neither, nobody, man, woman, person, someone, somebody.*

FORMAL: Will everyone pick up *his* pencil? (Everyone means every *single one*—individually; it does not mean all of the people in the group.)

INFORMAL: Will everyone pick up *their* pencil?

FORMAL: Everybody had lost his keys and nobody could get into his car.

FORMAL (Plural): All of the people had lost their keys, and they could not get into their cars.

D. Collective Nouns.

Collective nouns are usually considered singular. The reference is usually to a unit. (General Motors gave *its* employees a raise. American Airlines was considerate of *its* employees. The jury reached *its* verdict.) NOTE: There is only *one* General Motors Corporation. If collective nouns are considered as individual members, a plural pronoun is used.

PLURAL: The employees of General Motors received their raise.
The members of the jury reached their verdict.

E. Demonstrative Adjectives.

Demonstrative adjectives (this, that, these, those) must agree in number with the noun they modify.

WRONG: This kind of vegetables tastes good.
These kind of vegetables tastes good.

CORRECT: This kind of vegetable tastes good.
These kinds of vegetables taste good.

3. ABBREVIATIONS (ab)

A. CONTRACTIONS: Although this rule is gradually changing, certain contractions such as *can't, don't, isn't, won't,* etc., are not acceptable in formal writing. The grammar purists, however, are dying.

B. SHORTHAND SYMBOLS: Avoid symbols such as these in your writing: ¢, #, @, and especially &. Furthermore, never make up your own abbreviations: (WRONG: Ger. took Eng. at col.) Write what you mean. (CORRECT: Gerald took English at college.)

C. NUMBERS: Do not use Arabic in formal writing unless the number requires more than two words.

WRONG: 9, 95.

CORRECT: nine, ninety-five, 101.

SPELL OUT numbers at the beginning of a sentence. (One hundred and twenty-nine pounds were eaten.)

4. CAPITALS (CAP)

Although capital letters are not used nearly so often as they were a century ago, they must still be used in three major instances:

a) to *begin* every sentence or line of poetry (This is a sentence. Roses are red.)

b) to spell the pronoun *I* under all circumstances (Yesterday *I* awoke.)
c) to spell all *proper nouns,* whether abbreviated or not (I studied *English* under *Dr. Purcell.*).

NOTE: A *proper noun* names a *specific* person, place, or thing. By contrast, a *common* noun, which does not require capitals, merely indicates *any* person, place, or thing *of any category;* consequently, a common noun can only generalize; it cannot be specific.

COMMON NOUNS: man, college, degree, doctor.

PROPER NOUNS: Lynol L. Israels, University of Manitoba, Doctor of Medicine.

Note that the word *doctor* can refer to any category of doctors. The title *Doctor of Medicine* is very specific, however, and so is the *name* Dr. Lynol L. Israels. The title *president* could refer to *any* such classification, which is very general. The President of the United States, or even *the* President (if the reference is understood) is a *specific* title—a proper noun—and must be capitalized.

PROPER NOUNS AND ADJECTIVES REQUIRING CAPITALS

A. A person's name, any address, city, county, state, country, continent, or specific geographic location:

Mrs. Raymond Gonzales, a native of the West, is originally from Adams County in Colorado. She now resides at 345 North Holly Avenue, Garden City, Nevada. She has traveled extensively throughout the United States and Canada, and next year she intends to fly south to Mexico for an extended vacation, which will also include a visit to South America. (Note that the *West* is a geographic area, whereas flying south is merely a general direction.)

B. Any language whatsoever, nationality, religion, or religious reference:

Father Flanagan, who is quite proud of his Irish ancestry, is well versed not only in Catholicism, but also in other Christian denominations, as well as in other religions, including Judaism and Islam. Furthermore, he is a noted linguist, fluent in Italian, Spanish, German, Hebrew, and of course English.

C. Any particular movement or organization or affiliation:

In his youth he was a member of the Boy Scouts of America. Later he joined the United States Army and saw action with the 101st Airborne Division. Upon his discharge he became politically active in the Republican Party.

D. Any date, holiday, historical event, special event, or proclamation:

Although Washington's Birthday is celebrated as a national holiday in the United States, the date often varies from state to state. On the other hand, Independence Day, celebrated on July 4, never varies.

E. Any important title or honorary distinction whether abbreviated or not:

Mr. H. Harvey is Chairman of the Board of Allied Inventions. His brother, Dr. M. Harvey, is a dentist, and his cousin, Senator Atkins, is on the influential Ways and Means Committee in the California Senate. Mr. Harvey's son Charlie is a right-winger for the Atlanta Flames and was given the Clarence Campbell Award last year for being the National Hockey League's most valuable player.

F. Any title of any piece of writing or work of art, any particular newspaper, magazine, or book:

I just read the chapter "All our Sins," from Johnny Alger's new novel, *Five in the Iron Horse,* which is now appearing in an abridged form published by *Reader's Digest.*

G. Any particular manufactured item that is given a particular name, such as a ship, a particular car or airplane; and any particular thing that is in a class by itself:

Years ago he crossed the Atlantic in five days on the *Queen Mary;* last week the crossing took less than five hours on the supersonic Concorde. Yet the drive from Kennedy Airport to downtown New

York, even in a Cadillac, requires at least an hour and sometimes two. NOTE: General courses of study — unless they are languages — are not capitalized. (I will study music, not English.)

Specific courses are always capitalized. (I enjoy Music 11.)

Honorary distinctions are capitalized when they are referred to by title. (Have you seen Mother? No, I have not seen your mother.) NOTE: *English is always capitalized.*

5. CASE: PRONOUNS (CA)

Pronouns have three cases which indicate whether they are subjects or objects or whether they show possession. Use the correct pronoun case. Do not say,"Me and him were there," or "She gave it to I." And do not write,"The gopher ran down it's hole," or "That is your's."

Personal Pronouns

	SUBJECTIVE CASE	OBJECTIVE CASE	POSSESSIVE CASE
		(Singular)	
First Person	I	me	my, mine
Second Person	you	you	your, yours
Third Person	he, she, it	him, her, it	his, her, hers, it
		(Plural)	
First Person	we	us	our, ours
Second Person	you	you	your, yours
Third Person	they	them	their, theirs

Relative and Interrogative Pronouns

Singular	who	whom	whose
Plural	who	whom	whose

53

A. Subjective (or) Nominative Case.

These pronouns *name* the *subject;* therefore, they are *subjects* of verbs, *not objects.* Multiple pronouns do not change case. If you are in doubt about whether they are subjects or not, use only one such pronoun in a sentence and determine its case that way. (Him and me were there. Could you say, *"Me was there"?* No. Could you say, *"Him was there"?* No. Obviously, then, you are using the wrong case. Now substitute subjects for the objects you have mistakenly used. Could you say, "He was there"? Yes. Could you say, "I was there"? Yes. Then you obviously say, "He and I were there," and you would be correct.)

NOTE: *subjects* that act as *complements* (renaming the subject) are still subjects. Although such expressions as, "It is me," and "It is us," are widely used in everyday speech, they are *not correct* in formal English.

SUBJECT COMPLEMENTS:

It is I. (*I* and *it* are one and the same. *I* am *it. Both are subjects.* Each is equal and each can be substituted for the other. Therefore, the object *me* would be *incorrect* if it were substituted for a *subject.*)

CORRECT: I am *he.* It was *she* who called. Was it *he* who called? It was *they.*

Comparisons:

Subject pronouns do not change case when they are compared.

WRONG: He is taller than me. I am taller than him.

CORRECT: He is taller than *I* (am tall). I am taller than *he.*

WHO and *WHOEVER* are subjects, whether they act as the subject of a sentence or the subject of their own clause.

WRONG: Whom should I say called? Give it to whomever is here.

CORRECT: *Who* called? *Who* should I say called? Whoever is here, give it to that person. Give it to *whoever* is here.

B. Objective Case.

If an object is an object, do not try to make it over into a subject. Objects have their place and must be used, and they must be used correctly.

WRONG: I saw *she.* We gave it to *they.* He gave it to *I.*

CORRECT: I saw *her.* We gave it to *them.* He gave it to *me.*

NOTE: An object pronoun may be the object of a verb, expressed or implied, or the object of a preposition.

Object of a verb. I love *her.* I like *him* and *her.* I saw *them.*
Object of an implied verb: Mary likes you more than (she likes) me.
Mary likes you as well as (she likes) me.
Object of a preposition: I wrote to her. This message is intended for
them—for *him* and *her.*

WHOM AND WHOMEVER ARE ALWAYS OBJECTS.
WRONG: *Who* are you looking for? I will vote for *whoever* I
choose.
CORRECT: *Whom* are you looking for? I will vote for *whomever* I
choose.

NOTE: *Whom* is used in formal writing, as illustrated above;
whomever is used in very formal writing, but in actuality it is rarely
used.

C. Possessive Case.

The possessive case shows possession. Possessive pronouns
precede a gerund (a verbal noun ending in -ing).

NOTE: *Its, his,* and *hers,* as well as *ours,* are all possessive pronouns
and, therefore, already indicate possession. They do *not require* an
apostrophe, as do nouns which show possession. (This is John's hat.
This is *his* hat. The gopher ran down *its* hole.)

Examples of possessive pronouns:

This is *my* book. It is *mine.* It is *her* book. It is *hers. Her* singing is
excellent. I enjoy *her* singing. I enjoy *his* singing. *Whose* book is this?
Do you know *whose* book this is?
NOTE: I enjoy *his* singing. (Correct)
       I enjoy *him* singing. (Wrong)

6. COLLOQUIALISM AND SLANG (coll)

Avoid colloquial and slang expressions in formal writing.
WRONG: He is a neat guy. She is green off the farm. He took off like
a shot out of hell. I dig that kinda music.
CORRECT: He is a likeable person. She is naive. He left in a terrible
hurry. I love that kind of music.

7. COHERENCE (COH)

Coherence involves the unity within a sentence itself, the unity
between sentences, and finally the unity between paragraphs
themselves as well as their relationship to the entire essay. In short,

coherence means the sticking together of the same thing; it is the glue that keeps a piece of writing unified.

Coherence as it involves paragraphs and essays will be dealt with in detail in Part IV of this book.

A. Sentence Unity: (U)

In order for a sentence to make sense, its parts must be related in a logical manner. Do not mix horses with apples unless you show how they are related. *Do not write illogical sentences* like these:

1. Mr. Sklove is a history teacher, and his wife cooks excellent spaghetti every Friday night.
2. My car broke down but I passed the exam.
3. He could never be a good governor because he isn't handsome enough.

QUESTION: What does one part of the sentence have to do with the other?

ANSWER: Obviously nothing. If you intend to show a cause-and-effect relationship, *you must show it;* you cannot leave it to the reader's imagination. REMEMBER: He does not know what you are thinking.

IMPROVEMENT: 1. The Skloves have different fields of specialization. Mr. Sklove is a history teacher, but his wife is a gourmet cook. One of her specialties is spaghetti, which she prepares every Friday night.
2. While driving to college to take my exam, my car broke down. Fortunately, however, I was still able to get to class on time. I took the exam and passed it.
3. It is unlikely that he will receive enough votes to get elected as governor because he lacks the handsome, stereotype image that seems to attract the largest number of votes.

NOTE: The original sentence is illogical because looks have nothing to do with one's performance in public office.

B. Misplaced Parts: (MM) or (MIS-Part)

Your modifiers should be as close as possible to what they are supposed to modify. Do not separate them needlessly. (See Chapter Five.) *Do not split verb phrases* if you can avoid it, and do not separate a subject from its object needlessly.

WRONG: On his car there was a sign that had a flat tire, which read, "For Sale."

I would, if I have time, like, at your convenience, to see you.

CORRECT: On his car, which had a flat tire, there was a sign that read, "For Sale."

If I have time, I would like to see you at your convenience.

C. Dangling Modifiers: (DGL) (See Chapter Five.)

The introductory phrase must refer to its grammatical subject. Do not omit the subject if it is required in the introduction.

WRONG: While hiking in the mountains, the sun came up. (Was the sun hiking in the mountains?)

CORRECT: While *we* were hiking in the mountains, the sun came up.

D. Transitions: (Trans;) (See Chapter Three and Chapter Four.)

Use transitions when they are required to show clear sentence relationships.

VAGUE: He worked very hard at his job. He was fired.

CORRECT: *Although* he worked very hard at his job, he was fired.

He worked very hard at his job; *nevertheless,* he was fired.

NOTE: The correct use of transitions will not only ensure coherence in your writing, but it will also provide a certain rhythm in your sentences, thus giving them a euphonious (pleasant sounding) effect. Remember: good writing not only makes sense but also reads well and sounds well.

8. Comma Splice (C/S)

One of the worst and most common punctuation errors is the comma splice; that is, *the use of a comma instead of a period* OR instead of a *semicolon* OR instead of another construction such as a *coordinating conjunction* or *semicolon and* a *transition. Do not link two sentences together with a mere comma.* Instead, write two simple sentences or a compound sentence or a complex sentence.

WRONG (C/S): She bought a coat this week, she also bought a dress.

CORRECTION: a) Use a period, thereby writing two simple sentences. (She bought a coat this week. She also bought a dress.)

b) Use a semicolon instead of a period, thereby writing a compound sentence. (She bought a coat this week; she also bought a dress.)

c) Use a semicolon plus a transition as a connective, thereby writing a compound sentence. (See page 21 for transitions.) (She bought a coat this week; in addition, she bought a dress.)

d) Use a comma and a coordinating conjunction, thereby writing a compound sentence. (See page 17 for coordinating conjunctions.) (She bought a coat this week, and she also bought a dress.)

e) Use a subordinating conjunction to write a complex sentence. (p. 28) (Although she bought a coat this week, she also bought a dress.)

NOTE: *Do not use a comma in front of a transition that connects two simple sentences;* instead, *use a semicolon, or* rewrite the sentence as a complex sentence or as two simple sentences. (Note sentence c above, as well as the examples below.)

WRONG (C/S): He worked very hard, however, he still lost his job.
CORRECT: a) He worked very hard; however, he still lost his job.
b) Although he worked very hard, he still lost his job.
c) He worked very hard. However, he still lost his job.

9. COMPARISONS AND OMISSIONS (COMP, OM, or Λ)

A. Comparisons.

Avoid illogical or *incomplete comparisons.* You cannot compare an apple with a horse, nor can you compare the temperature with a particular date on a calendar. Likewise, students cannot be compared with a college, nor can wine be compared with a particular state.

WRONG:
1. It is warmer today than yesterday.
2. The students at Compton College are more friendly than any other college.
3. California's wine is better than any other state.
4. California produces better wine than any other state.
5. He is taller.

CORRECTIONS:
1. *It is* warmer today than *it was* yesterday.
2. The *students* at Compton College are more friendly than *students* at any other college. OR...more friendly than *those* of any other college.
3. *California's wine* is better than *that* of any other state.
4. California *produces* better wine than any other state *does.*
5. He is taller *than I am.* OR...taller *than Fred.*

58

B. Adjectives and Adverbs Compared.

Adjectives and adverbs show degrees of comparison through their forms:

1. Positive: (no degree of comparison)
   John is a *slow* driver. John drives *slowly*.

2. Comparative: (compares *two* items)
   John is a *slower* driver than Fred (is). John drives *more* slowly than Fred does.

3. Superlative: (expresses the ultimate degree of comparison among three or more items)
   John is *the slowest* driver among us (three). (OR) John is *the slowest* driver of all. John drives *the most slowly* of anyone.

NOTE: Certain items cannot be compared, because their definition indicates an exact degree in itself. Note particularly such items as these: *perfect, round, flat, straight, unique, dead.*
WRONG: This book is very *unique*. (Unique means unlike anything else. Either the book is unique or it isn't.)
CORRECT: This book is unique.
WRONG: His artistry is more perfect than yours. (Perfection is perfect.)
CORRECT: His artistry is more nearly perfect than yours. (Artistry may approach perfection, or may equal it, but nothing can exceed perfection.)

C. Omissions of Words.

Do not omit *any* words either through carelessness or through ignorance. Articles, conjunctions, and prepositions all have their place in certain sentences. If they are required, do not omit them.

WRONG: 1. He gave letter to John.
2. I saw him month ago.
3. He hurried was late.
4. She heard the speaker was absent.
5. Sundays we stay home.
6. This type sentence is wrong.

CORRECT: 1. He gave *the* letter to John.
            2. I saw him *a* month ago.
            3. He hurried *but* was late.
            4. She heard *that* the speaker was absent.
            5. *On* Sundays we stay home.
            6. This type *of* sentence is right.

10. DICTION or WORD CHOICE (d)

Use appropriate diction. If you are in doubt about the meaning of a word, consult a dictionary. Also, make use of a thesaurus for synonyms (words that have similar meanings). REMEMBER: The only tools you have are the words you use. If your choice of words is ineffective, or worse yet, incorrect, your finished product—your writing—will suffer proportionately. Avoid words with nebulous meanings such as *this* or *thing* or *you know what I mean*. Be specific. Paint a picture with your words. Let your reader know *how you feel* about your topic. Use concrete nouns—proper nouns if possible—and strong verbs instead of a series of adjectives and adverbs. Make your writing live, and you will be proud of it.

11. FRAGMENT (Frag)

(NOTE: See Chapter Five, Section VI, for a discussion of sentence fragments.)

A fragment is a broken-off piece of a sentence, usually at the beginning or at the tail end of a sentence. Fragments are not acceptable in formal writing. Do not use a period instead of a comma, simply because your wrist is tired or because you want to emphasize a point.
Complete the sentence.

WRONG: *While we were waiting. For the bus.* We saw the accident. (Fragments are mistakenly written for sentences at the *beginning*.)

CORRECT: While we were waiting for the bus, we saw the accident.

WRONG: We saw the accident. *While we were waiting for the bus.* (Fragment occurs at the *tail end* of the sentence—the most common occurrence.)

CORRECT: We saw the accident while we were waiting for the bus.

12. FUSED SENTENCES (FS)

(NOTE: *See page 15 for* a discussion of *fused sentences.*)

Do not run two sentences together without any punctuation. Such a gross error is probably the worst of all sentence structure errors, particularly where punctuation is involved, and indicates that its writer has virtually no concept of what a sentence is.

REMEMBER: A sentence MUST end with a period, question mark, or exclamation mark. Fused sentences can be *eliminated by* writing *two simple sentences,* OR by writing a *compound sentence,* OR by writing a *complex sentence.*

WRONG: I ran to the store for milk the store was already closed. (FS)
CORRECTION:

a) Write *two simple sentences.* (I ran to the store for milk. The store was already closed.)

b) Write a *compound sentence* by using:

      1. a comma and a coordinating conjunction (I ran to the store for milk, *but* the store was already closed.)

      2. a semicolon and a transition (I ran to the store for milk; *however,* the store was already closed.)

      3. a semicolon alone (I ran to the store for milk; the store was already closed.)

c) Revise the sentence as a *complex sentence.* (*Although* I ran to the store for milk, the store was already closed.)

NOTE: If you have studied Chapter Two and learned what a simple sentence is, and if you have also studied Chapters Three and Four, which dealt with compound and complex sentences, you will know what a sentence is and what it is not. REMEMBER: A fused sentence is *not* a sentence, and it is not two sentences. It is a gross error.

Do not mistakenly write a fused sentence in place of a compound sentence.

WRONG: I ran to the store for milk however the store was already closed.

NOTE: Transitions (however, therefore, etc.) *must be preceded* either by a *semicolon* OR a *period.*
CORRECTION:

1) I ran to the store for milk; however, the store was already closed.
2) I ran to the store for milk. However, the store was already closed.

13. ITALICS (ital) or ———

In order to *italicize* words, underline them. Italics are used mainly to underscore foreign words, complete titles of books or works of art, as well as newspapers and magazines. Italics are also used for names of ships and for words spoken as words.

EXAMPLES:

a) The *Queen Mary* is in Long Beach.

b) The title of this book is *You Can Learn to Write.*

c) The Los Angeles *Times* is one of the country's prestigious newspapers.

d) In French *il est possible* means it is possible.

e) The English do not pronounce the *h* as we do in words like *hotel* and *hard.*

NOTE: Use italics sparingly. Do not underline titles of articles; use quote marks instead.

14. MIXED CONSTRUCTIONS, PARALLELISM, and BALANCE (MIX, //)

A room has four walls, two of which are equally paired; a car has four wheels, all of which are equally balanced. Likewise, your writing should match certain pairs and balance the others. Do not mix horses with bacon or stones with lettuce. In a series of two or more items, *do not mix* different forms of speech, particularly verbs, or *different types of modifiers* such as phrases and clauses. Balance your sentence with the same parts if possible so that the sentence not only makes sense but also reads well.

WRONG: (Mixed and unbalanced parts are *italicized.*)

a) He likes to fish, to swim, and *surfing.*

b) He likes fishing, swimming, and *to surf.*

c) He is a teacher *and* who is interested in his students.

d) For dinner my wife served me salad, potatoes, and *she fried chicken.*

e) He has *neither* a job and he has no money.

f) Either you will give me your wallet *because it will be taken* away.

g) She is not only a good housekeeper, but *she cooks* well.

CORRECTION: (Completion of balanced parts is *italicized.*)

a) He likes to fish, to swim, and *to surf.*

b) He likes fishing, swimming, and *surfing.*

c) He is a *teacher who* is interested in his students.

d) For dinner my wife served me salad, potatoes, and *fried chicken.*

e) *Neither* does he have a job, *nor* does he have any money.

f) *Either you will give* me your money, *or I will take* it away.

g) She *is not only* a *good housekeeper,* but she *is also a good cook.*

NOTE: CORRELATIVES COMMONLY USED IN PAIRS: both . . .

and; either . . . or; neither . . . nor; not only . . . but also; so . . . as; whether . . . or.

NOTE: 1. Do not mix *phrases and clauses* with correlatives.

2. Do not mix the wrong verb form with correlatives.

WRONG: 1. *She is* not only *a good housekeeper* but also *in her cooking.*

2. Either *you will give* me your wallet, or *it will be taken* away.

CORRECT: 1. *She is* not only a good housekeeper, but *she is* also *a* good cook. (OR) Not only is she a good housekeeper, but she is also a good cook. (NOTE: Two clauses are now matched instead of the previously mixed phrase and clause.)

2. Either *you will give* me your wallet, or *I will take* it away. (NOTE: Two parallel, future tenses, both in the active voice, replace the mixed construction. See items 16 B and C.)

15. NOT CLEAR: NOT COMMUNICATING (NC)

Do not presume that your reader can read your mind. He can't. He can read your writing, but if it isn't exact, if it isn't clear, he may not understand what you intended to say. In fact, he may misinterpret your intention altogether. Communication involves the *transfer* of a message from one point to another. Always imagine that your reader is on the moon, and that the only way you can communicate with him is by the written word. *Be exact.* Be particularly careful with vague pronoun references (item 20) and with omissions (item 9).

16. POINT OF VIEW SHIFTS (P/V)

Do not shift point of view from one subject to another, from one tense to another, from one voice to another, or from one mood to another. Be consistent.

A. Subject Persons.

Do not shift from one person to another. Be particularly wary of shifting to the second person singular "you."

WRONG: (Shift from *I* to *you.*) I will explain how I write. The first thing *you* do is . . . CORRECT: The first thing *I* do is . . .

WRONG: (Shift from *third* person to *you*) It is very easy today for *a person* to become a professional football player. The first thing *you* do is . . .

WRONG: (Addressing an implied reader as *you*) It is very easy today *for you* to become a professional football player.

NOTE: Such sentences addressed to me, the reader, are obviously incorrect. Because of my age and lack of physical stamina, I can never become a professional athlete of any sort, especially a football player. To avoid such incorrect and sometimes absurd sentences, DO NOT ADDRESS THE READER AS YOU UNLESS YOU MEAN HIM OR HER SPECIFICALLY.

CORRECT: It is very easy today for a person to become a professional football player. The first thing he does is . . .

NOTE: The indefinite *one* may also be used instead of *he*. The first thing *one* does is . . .

WRONG: (Shift from *singular* to *plural*) *Everyone* in class brought *their* books.

CORRECTION: Everyone in class brought *his* books. (See Section 2 Agreement, item C: Pronoun-Antecedent).

WRONG: If a *student* studies hard, *they* will succeed.

CORRECT: If a *student* studies hard, *he* will succeed.

WRONG: (Shift from *plural* to *singular*) If all the black *people* united, the black *man* could influence legislation.

CORRECT: If all the black *people* united, *they* could influence legislation.

B. Tense. (P/V t)

Do not shift from one tense to another within the same sentence, and *avoid shifts between sentences* unless the shifts are vital.

WRONG: (Past to present) She *stood* up and *cooks* dinner.

CORRECT: She *stood* up and *cooked* dinner.

WRONG: (Present to past) She *begins* to read and then *put* the book down.

CORRECT: She *begins* to read and then *puts* the book down.

WRONG: (Future to past) I *will go* to the game if you *came* on time.

CORRECT: I *will go* to the game if you will *come* on time.

C. Voice. (P/V v)

Do not shift voice within a sentence, either *from active to passive* or *from passive to active.*

WRONG: (Active to passive) First *he dug* the garden, and then the vegetables *were planted by* him.

CORRECT: First he dug the garden, and then *he planted* the vegetables.

WRONG: (Passive to active) The ball *was thrown by* the quarterback,

64

and the receiver *caught it.*

CORRECT: The ball *was thrown by* the quarterback, and it *was caught by* the receiver.

D. Mood. (P/V m)

Do not shift mood within a sentence, either from the indicative to the imperative or *from the imperative to the indicative.*

WRONG: (Indicative to imperative) First of all, you *should dig* your garden, and then *plant* your vegetables.

CORRECT: First of all, *you should dig* your garden, and then *you should plant* your vegetables.

WRONG: (Imperative to indicative) *Dig* your garden and then *you should plant* your vegetables.

CORRECT: *Dig* your garden and then *plant* your vegetables.

NOTE: *Consistency in point of view contributes toward a unified sentence.*

REMEMBER: A unified sentence is easy to read and easy to understand. A sentence or a larger piece of writing that is not unified will almost certainly cause confusion in the reader's mind. Therefore, strive for unity in your writing. If you are writing about a person, *do not shift pronouns,* and *do not shift tenses.* Also, try not to shift voice or mood, although these shifts are not so confusing as are the shifts between subject persons and pronouns or between tenses.

17. POOR TOPIC SENTENCE (PTS)

Use an effective topic sentence in each paragraph, preferably at the very beginning. A topic sentence clearly expresses the writer's *attitude* toward a *particular,* rather narrow *topic.* This point will be dealt with at length in Chapter 10 of this book.

18. PUNCTUATION (P)

Punctuation marks are extremely important. They create breath *pauses* or *stops* of various durations, thereby giving the reader time to pause and to think about what he has read or to prepare him for what he is about to read. A punctuation error, either one that is omitted or one that is unnecessarily inserted, not only can create confusion in the reader's mind, but also can change the entire meaning of the sentence. Consequently, lawyers pay particular attention to punctuation because it may emphasize the meaning or lack of meaning in a sentence, and obviously the meaning or interpretation of a sentence may very well affect the outcome of their case. Even the beginning writer usually tries to pay attention to punctuation because he wants to communicate; he wants his reader to understand what he (the writer) is trying to say.

Although there are many, many rules for correct punctuation, these rules can be simplified if you remember the following analogy between *punctuation marks* and various kinds of *traffic signals:*

a) A *comma* is like a *flashing amber* light, at which you *momentarily slow down,* without stopping, look around briefly, and then if there is no oncoming traffic, you resume full speed ahead.

b) A *semicolon* is like a *flashing red* light; you *actually stop* for a second or two; you look around very carefully to make sure there is no oncoming traffic; then and only then do you proceed on your way.

c) A *period* or a *question mark* is like a *red stop light.* You must *actually stop* and *wait. You must stop and wait for a long time until* the light changes to green. Then and only then can you proceed on your way.

NOTE: A *semicolon* is *almost* like a period within a sentence; only the pause is slightly shorter for a semicolon.

d) A double or long dash — not to be confused with a hyphen — is like a *traffic bump* that suddenly jars you awake so that you will concentrate very carefully on what is happening in between the traffic bumps.

NOTE: Traffic bumps are usually installed in school parking lots for a very good reason — to slow down the driver. Unnecessary traffic bumps, however, are nothing but a nuisance, and therefore should be avoided. The same rule applies to your writing.

e) A *parenthesis* is like an *extra road sign* (or two) that brings you additional information (or directions) to ensure that you take the right road. Parentheses (plural) act as a back seat driver does when he *whispers* in your ear, just to make sure that you are on the right road.

A. THE COMMA (,)

A comma is used within a sentence to indicate the least possible separation in thought. A comma indicates a short breath pause and forces the reader to slow down and to take notice, much as a driver must slow down for an amber light.

A comma is used in each of the following instances:

1. TO SEPARATE MAIN CLAUSES CONNECTED BY A COORD-INATING CONJUNCTION, SUCH AS *and, but, for, or, nor,* and *yet (See pages 16-18.)*

EXAMPLES:

a) The plane took off on schedule, and we were soon flying over Chicago.

b) I simply stood there captivated, for in front of me stood a very beautiful girl.

c) Classical music lives for all time, but popular music is often forgotten overnight.

d) Either you will eat your vegetables, or I will not give you any dessert.

e) He will not eat his vegetables, nor will he eat his dessert.

f) She was almost out of money, yet she bought a new dress.

NOTE: A comma is *not required* for a compound verb in a *simple sentence.*

FAULTY: I dived into the water, and swam toward shore. (Simple sentence)

CORRECT: I dived into the water and swam toward shore.

CORRECT: I dived into the water, and I swam toward shore. (Compound sentence)

2. AFTER A LONG INTRODUCTORY CLAUSE OR PHRASE OR WHEN THE CLAUSE OR PHRASE IS IN DANGER OF BEING MISREAD

EXAMPLES:

a) *Long Clause:* As I was walking down Santa Monica Boulevard toward the ocean, I saw a large camera crew filming a movie.

b) *Misreading:* When we entered, the dog jumped up to greet us.

While I was shaving, the cat ran into the room.

As we were eating, the table collapsed.

c) *Verbal Phrase:* After being without a job in Los Angeles for almost ten weeks, I decided to return to my home in Rhode Island.

d) *Long Phrase:* With such an extremely large group of well trained athletes, our college should be able to win practically all the games.

Early tomorrow morning before breakfast, I will visit my brother.

CAUTION: Usually a comma is *not used* after a *short introductory* phrase or clause.

EXAMPLES:

a) *Short Phrase:* In the beginning God created the heaven and the earth.

b) *Short Clause:* If you work hard you will succeed.

NOTE: You would not *necessarily* be wrong if you used a comma in the examples above; however, the introductory material is so short that a comma is really unnecessary. It slows down the reader.

3. TO SET OFF NON-RESTRICTIVE MODIFIERS (WORDS, PHRASES, AND CLAUSES)

DEFINITION: A non-restrictive modifier is *additional information* which is *not absolutely necessary* in the sentence; that is, if it is removed, it will not appreciably change the sense of the sentence. (See Chapter 5, III.)

In Chapter Five of this book the non-restrictive modifier is referred to as a *casual description*. A restrictive modifier, on the other hand, which is referred to as a *vital explanation* (Ch. 5, Sec. IV), is *absolutely necessary* to the sense of the sentence and should not be separated.

EXAMPLES:

Non-Restrictive: a) All students, who are only human, are sometimes lazy.

b) My car, which cost me only $2,000.00, is better than a Cadillac.

c) My wife, whom I first met in a library, teaches school.

NOTE: These sentences will *still make sense* if the non-restrictive modifier (casual description) is removed.

EXAMPLES: a) All students are sometimes lazy.

b) My car is better than a Cadillac.

c) My wife teaches school.

Restrictive or *Vital Modifiers* cannot be removed from the sentence without completely altering its meaning. Such modifiers must *not* be enclosed by commas.

EXAMPLES:

CORRECT: All students *who earn at least a D* will pass this course.

WRONG: All students will pass this course.

CORRECT: The car *that is parked in the red zone* has a ticket, but the car *that is parked in the green zone* has no ticket.

WRONG: The car has a ticket but the car has no ticket.

NOTE: Modifiers, particularly non-restrictive (casual descriptions), also act as introductions and conclusions, in which cases they are still separated from the main clause by a comma. (See Chapter Five.)

EXAMPLES: Exhausted, I was rushed to the hospital.

I was rushed to the hospital, exhausted.

4. TO MARK A CONTRAST OR TO SET OFF A STRONG EXPRESSION OR A CHANGE IN THOUGHT

EXAMPLES:

a) I called Jim, not Harry.

b) He swam quietly, yet quickly.

c) He worked very hard, but failed miserably.

5. TO SET OFF SENTENCE MODIFIERS OR INTERRUPTERS WITH WORDS LIKE THESE:

accordingly, then, therefore, on the other hand, in the first place, yes, no, well, indeed, certainly, finally, perhaps, in fact, etc.

NOTE: These words often mark a *transition* or *summary,* or they direct the reader's attention to a turn in the thought of the paragraph.

EXAMPLES:

a) The best football players, *of course,* end up in the professional leagues.

b) *Of course,* the best basketball players are the first to be drafted.

c) My luck held, *however,* and I was able to make it to shore.

d) Yes, I am eager to begin my new job.

e) *Certainly,* I would love to come.

f) Consider, *for example,* the alternate solution.

g) *To summarize,* the comma is used to set off interrupters.

NOTE: Interrupters may be removed without altering the meaning of the sentence.

6. TO SET OFF ABSOLUTE PHRASES (a noun or pronoun plus a participle)

EXAMPLES:

a) *The time being up,* we all went back to our class.

b) *My board having been lost* in the surf, I found myself swimming to shore.

c) *His assignment having been completed,* he put his books away.

7. TO SET OFF A NON-RESTRICTIVE APPOSITIVE: A NOUN OR NOUN-SUBSTITUTE THAT HELPS CLARIFY ANOTHER NOUN (OR NOUN-SUBSTITUTE) JUST MENTIONED

NOTE: The italicized modifier (non-restrictive appositive), which *brings additional information* to the sentence but is not absolutely necessary, can be removed without altering the meaning of the sentence.

EXAMPLES:

a) He is very fond of my favorite author, *Herman Melville.*

Still Correct: (He is very fond of my favorite author.)

b) Bernard Malamud, *an author of deep insight,* wrote some very serious novels.

Still Correct: (Bernard Malamud wrote some very serious novels.)

c) One of James Jones's novels, *From Here to Eternity,* has been widely read.

Still Correct: (One of James Jones's novels has been widely read.)

d) Two of my three sisters, *Merle and Sylvia,* live in Long Beach.

Still Correct: (Two of my three sisters live in Long Beach.)

e) One of my teachers, *Mr. Ponnech,* is in his office now.

Still Correct: (One of my teachers is in his office now.)

NOTE: A RESTRICTIVE APPOSITIVE OR MODIFIER POINTS OUT A PARTICULAR THING AND IS THEREFORE ABSOLUTELY ESSENTIAL FOR THE MEANING OF THE SENTENCE. A RESTRICTIVE MODIFIER MUST NOT BE SET OFF BY A COMMA.

EXAMPLES:

a) James Jones's novel *From Here to Eternity* has been widely read, but the rest of his novels have not been so widely read.

b) My sisters *Merle and Sylvia* live in Long Beach, but my sister *Etta* lives in Lakewood.

c) The idea *that you are qualified* is unwarranted.

NOTE: INTRODUCTION OF APPOSITIVES

When *namely, that is, viz,* and *i.e.* introduce an appositive or an explanation, they are preceded and followed by a comma.

(I have only one favorite sport, *namely,* football.)

When *such as, as, especially, e.g.,* and *for example* introduce an example or a series of examples, they should be preceded by a comma, but not followed by one.

(I love many sports, *especially* swimming, surfing, and tennis.)

When *such as* is restrictive, a comma is not used in front of it.

(A serious grammatical error *such as* the one you just made is not acceptable in standard English.)

8. TO SET OFF DATES AND GEOGRAPHICAL EXPRESSIONS AND INITIALS OR TITLES FOLLOWING A PERSONAL NAME

EXAMPLES:

a) On Tuesday, *June 2,* we left for San Francisco.

b) July 4, *1776,* was an important date in history.

c) Long Beach, *California,* is the new home of the *Queen Mary.*

d) Charles Brooks, *A.B., M.A., Ph.D.,* was my composition teacher.

NOTE: RESTRICTIVE DATES SHOULD NOT BE ENCLOSED BY COMMAS

(The year 1939 is significant to my generation.)

(He departed on January 20th.)

9. TO SET OFF WORDS IN DIRECT ADDRESS (VOCATIVES)

a) Please turn off the television, *Mary.*

b) You realize, *Mr. Brown,* that your insurance policy has lapsed.

10. AFTER A MILD INTERJECTION

a) *Oh,* I suppose it's all right.

b) *Well,* if you must know the truth, I shall tell you.

11. TO SEPARATE A SERIES OF COORDINATES (TWO OR MORE WORDS, PHRASES, OR CLAUSES OF EQUAL IMPORTANCE)

NOTE: Coordinates can be *interchanged* with one another, and they can also be separated by *and* instead of by a comma. If they cannot meet either of these two tests, they are not coordinates and should not be separated by a comma.

EXAMPLES:

A. Two or more WORDS:

(NOUNS) 1. For Baltimore the players were *Smith, Jones,* and *Hollman.*(OR) For Baltimore the players were *Jones, Hollman,* and *Smith.* OR...the players were Hollman and Jones and Smith.

2. For breakfast I had juice, toast, and bacon and eggs.

NOTE: *Bacon and eggs* is considered as a unit; therefore, it is not separated by a comma. In all *other series,* a *comma precedes and.*

(ADJECTIVES) 3. He was a *tired, old* man. (OR) He was an *old, tired* man. OR...tired and old man. Or...old and tired man.

4. We entered the *dark, dingy, dusty, dirty* railroad station. OR... dingy and dusty and dirty and dark railroad station.

NOTE: *Railroad station* is a noun even though *railroad* may be considered as an adjective by some grammarians. In the sentence, however, *railroad* acts as part of the noun and therefore cannot be interchanged with any other adjective. Consequently, it is not a coordinate.

B. Two or more PHRASES:

1. I often encountered him *on the freeway, on the parking lot, in the library,* and *at the beach.*

2. *Very early in the morning, on my way to the bus stop,* I met Marilyn.

C. Two or more CLAUSES:

(Subordinate Clauses) 1. *As I was driving down the road, before I even got to the intersection, just as I ran out of gas,* my car got a flat tire.

(Main Clauses) 2. *I sorted out the clothes, I took out the trash,* and *I brought in the paper.*

NOTE: If the entire series consist of main clauses that are not separated by a coordinating conjunction (and, but, etc.), *semicolons* must be used.

I sorted out the clothes; I took out the trash; I brought in the paper.

REMEMBER: A comma precedes *and* in a series; it does not follow *and.*

WRONG: The colors of the flag are red, white, and, blue.

CORRECT: The colors of the flag are red, white, and blue.

11. TO PREVENT MISREADING OR DELAY IN READING

a) Ever since, I have read many historical novels.

b) To Fred, Hanson announced his plans.

c) As I was eating, the table collapsed.

d) Inside, the room was almost in darkness.

c) What kind of girl she is, is hard to say.

12. TO SET OFF *he said, she replied,* and SIMILAR DIRECT QUOTATIONS.

a) "We are ready to go," he said.

b) "I didn't hear you," she replied.

B. UNNECESSARY COMMAS ⊙

1. Do *not* use a comma to *separate* the *subject from its verb,* the *verb from its object,* or *an adjective from the noun it immediately precedes.*

NOTE: In the following sentences the encircled commas should be omitted:

a) My lifelong *friends* from Napa⊙ *will be* visiting us soon. (No comma between *subject* and *verb*)

b) My instructor *said*⊙ *that the freshman composition course was vitally important.* (No comma between *verb* and *object*)

The new automobile engines *produce*⊙ *much less exhaust emissions* than did the previous engines.

c) She was a charming, intelligent, *beautiful*⊙ woman. (No comma between *adjective* and *its noun*)

2. Do *not* use a comma to *separate two words or two phrases joined by a coordinating conjunction.*

a) He really *likes* to swim⊙and *loves* to surf. (*And* joins two verbs in a simple sentence; therefore, a comma is unnecessary.)

b) The bird flew *up to the tree*⊙ *and* then *down to the garden.* (*And* joins two phrases.)

3. Do *not* use a comma to *separate restrictive* (vitally important) *clauses, phrases,* or *appositives.*

a) All students⊙ *who do not earn at least a D*⊙will fail the course. (Restrictive clause)

b) The car⊙*parked in the red zone*⊙has a ticket. (Restrictive phrase)

c) My uncle⊙ *John*⊙ lives in Long Beach, but my uncle⊙ *Bill*⊙ lives in Santa Monica. (Restrictive appositive)

4. In a *series,* do *not* use a comma *before the first item, after the last* item, or *after a coordinating conjunction.*

a) For lunch we had⊙soup, salad, and rolls. (No comma before the first item)

b) Fruit salad, cottage cheese, and rolls⊙ were all we had for lunch.(No comma after the last item)

c. For lunch we had soup, salad, and⌒ rolls. (No comma after a coordinating conjunction)

5. Do not use a comma to set off *very short introductions.*

a) Yesterday⌒I went to the game.

b) Last night⌒I went to the game.

c) Perhaps⌒you had better leave.

d) Yet⌒he never gave up hope.

NOTE: The general rule regarding the use of the comma is this: *When in doubt, leave it out.*

C. The Semicolon (;)

The semicolon can be compared to a flashing red light; both are signals which require an actual stop before proceeding any farther. A semicolon, therefore, creates a much longer pause than that of a comma, but a much shorter pause than that of a period; however, its effect is almost like that of a period because it separates one complete thought from another, or it joins one complete thought to another, as the case may be.

The semicolon is used in the following instances: one, to link two closely-related sentences that do not contain any other connective; two, to link two closely-related sentences that already contain a connective, such as a coordinating conjunction, a conjunctive adverb (however, therefore, nevertheless, etc.), or a transitional phrase (on the other hand, to summarize, etc.); to separate the main breaks in a series of compound sentences which already contain coordinating conjunctions; and finally, to separate the main breaks in a long sentence such as this, which already contains internal punctuation. Remember: The semicolon acts as a period does; it marks off one complete thought from another. (See Chapter Three.)

EXAMPLES:

1. A semicolon is used *alone* to link *two closely-related sentences.*

a) He worked very hard on the project; he wanted to succeed.

b) Although he worked very hard on his project, he never succeeded; there were simply too many unforeseen obstacles that got in his way.

2. A semicolon is used *along with* another connective, such as a *conjunctive adverb* or *transition,* to link two closely-related sentences.

a) He worked very hard at his job; *however,* he never succeeded.

b) The evidence that confronts us is overwhelming; *in short,* an advanced civilization has already been here.

3. A semicolon is used to *separate* the *main breaks in* a series of

73

compound sentences that already contain coordinating conjunctions.
a) Some of the engineers assigned to the project worked very hard, but others seemed to loaf all day; yet the project had to be completed on time, for the government contract would expire soon.

4. A semicolon is used to separate the *main breaks* in a *long sentence* that already contains extensive internal punctuation.
a) We had three distinct menus: to begin with, there was breakfast, which included juice, eggs, toast, and coffee; then there was lunch, which consisted of soup, salad, fruit, and rolls; and finally there was dinner, which included not only cocktails and hors d'oeuvres, but also steak, wine, and a liqueur.

REMEMBER: A semicolon indicates very strong punctuation, almost (but not quite) as strong as a period. Compare these three sentences for effect.
1. He worked very hard on his novel. But he never completed it.
(The period marks an *emphatic, long pause* between two simple sentences.)
2. He worked very hard on his novel; yet he never completed it.
(The semicolon marks a *slightly* shorter and *less emphatic* pause than does the comma; however, the connection between the two main clauses is still *very strong.*)
3. He worked very hard on his novel, but he never completed it.
(The comma indicates a *short breath pause* that smoothly connects the two main clauses, leaving almost no emphasis in the pause.)

NOTE: Although you should use the correct punctuation mark, you should also use the most effective punctuation for a particular piece of writing.

D. The Colon (:)

The colon acts as an *introducer.* It points out *material* that *will follow.* A colon is used in the following instances:
1. to formally *introduce* a *series* (I need the following material: a hammer, a pair of pliers, and a screwdriver.)
2. to formally introduce a quotation (The Department of Finance puts it this way: "We must save money.")
3. to formally introduce a summary (She had only one desire in life: to get married.) NOTE: The introduction explains the summary.
4. to formally introduce an appositive (Practically all of the work was done by one man: Richard Matador.)
5. to substitute as a period between two main clauses when the second clause explains the first (One's goal in life should be more than merely to succeed: one should try to help his fellow man.)

NOTE: The beginning word in the second main clause may be capitalized, or it may be a lower case letter. The option is up to the writer.

6. to introduce a formal salutation (Dear Sir:)
7. to mark certain conventional separations
      a) hours from minutes (9:15 P.M.)
      b) chapter from verse (Kings 15:2)
      c) volume from page (*Time* 103: 11-15.)
      d) title from subtitle (*Bernadine: A Revolutionist*)
      e) city from publisher (New York: Finley Press).

E. Terminal Punctuation:
Periods, Question Marks, and Exclamation Points.

1. THE PERIOD (.) A period is used at the end of every sentence that makes a statement, gives a declarative or mildly imperative opinion, or poses an indirect question. In addition, a period is *often* used for abbreviations *such as* A.M., C.O.D., and U.C.L.A., although it need not be used for such abbreviations; it is always used for other common abbreviations such as Dr., Mr., and Mrs.; and it is also used as an ellipsis (three spaced periods. . .) to indicate an omission of at least one word within a quoted passage.

NOTE the use of the period to terminate these different types of sentences.

a) *Statement.* This sentence is a statement of fact.
b) *Declarative opinion.* Written communication is vitally important.
c) *Mildly imperative.* Please learn how to write properly.
d) *Indirect question.* She asked me if she could learn how to write.

2. THE QUESTION MARK (?) A question mark is used after direct questions and after sentences phrased as a question. The question mark terminates the sentences, but it may also be used between or among the parts of a series.

a) *Direct question.* Did you see the movie?
b) *Declarative question.* You saw the movie?
c) *Between parts of a series.* Did you read the book? see the movie? or attend the play?

NOTE: Do not use a comma after a question mark.

3. THE EXCLAMATION POINT (!) The exclamation point is used as terminal punctuation after an emphatic interjection or expression of great surprise or emotion, as well as after a command.

a) *Emotion.* Oh! What a dreadful sight! How terrible!
b) *Command.* Get out of here! Immediately!

NOTE: Use the exclamation point very sparingly. Instead, use a comma after most interjections, and use a period to conclude most declarative and mildly exclamatory sentences.

F. Other Punctuation:
Parentheses, Dashes, and Brackets

1. PARENTHESES ( ) Use parentheses sparingly, to supply additional information or illustrations that may be required to clarify a particular point. The effect of parentheses could be compared to that of an additional road sign or a back seat driver whispering in the driver's ear. If the reader, like the driver, is not quite certain about the meaning (or clarification) of a sentence, parentheses (like a back seat driver) will explain.
EXAMPLE: The federal government (in Washington) is concerned with matters of national importance.

2. DASHES — A double dash used in typing or a long, single dash used in handwriting creates an *abrupt break* within a sentence so that the writer can *summarize* an idea *or* bring *additional information* to a sentence immediately and emphatically, without rewriting the sentence. If parentheses could be compared to a whispering back seat driver, the *dash*—if it is used in the *middle* of a sentence like this—could then be compared with a *shouting* back seat driver. The dash is generally used for abrupt changes in thought, as illustrated in the previous sentence. However, it is also used in place of a colon to briefly summarize an idea or to set off an appositive.
(Dash replacing colon) She had only one desire—to get married
There was only one outstanding player—Hull.
NOTE: Use the dash sparingly in formal writing.

3. BRACKETS [ ] Brackets are used to indicate editorial corrections or to interpolate quoted matter. They must be used sparingly.
"He believe [*sic*] the President would speak." "He arrived [on] Sunday."
NOTE: a bracketed *sic*—meaning "thus it is written in the original"—indicates that the error appeared in the original quotation.

19. QUOTED MATTER AND RESTATEMENTS (" ")

Use quote marks correctly when quoting somebody else's words or when indicating a selection within a book or magazine. Remember to close your quote marks. Also remember that all punctuation except semicolons goes *inside* the quote marks, not outside. Quotes within quotes are indicated by single marks.

A. Selection Within a Book:

Jack Kates, "Chapter Three: Connecting Two Simple Sentences: The Compound Sentence," *You Can Learn To Write.*

B. Formal Quote:

John Smith, in his recent book *Property,* states his theory thus: "I believe the public must have a firm respect for the rights of others. There is, in my opinion, no alternative. For unless we have 'law and order,' we may ultimately reach the point where we will have chaos." (NOTE the quote within quotes indicated by a single mark in this *direct quotation.*)

C. Informal Direct Quote:

According to the author of *Property,* John Smith, "The public must have a firm respect for the rights of others."

D. Formal or Informal Quote:

John Smith states: "The public must have a firm respect for the rights of others." (Formal)
John Smith states, "The public must have a firm respect for the rights of others." (Informal—introduced by comma)

E. Restatement:

John Smith believes that unless the public respects individual rights, it may find itself in a chaotic condition.
(NOTE: A restatement involves a summary in the writer's own words of what somebody else said. Do not use the original words in your own summary because that involves plagiarism: an unlawful copy of somebody else's material. If you must use the original phrase or sentences, use quotation marks.)

F. Informal Quote Introduced by Restatement:

John Smith believes that "the public must have a firm respect for the rights of others." "There is," in his opinion, "no alternative." "For unless we have 'law and order,' " he emphasizes, "we may ultimately reach the point where we will have chaos." (NOTE that all punctuation goes inside the quote marks in this *indirect quote.*)

G. Ellipsis: Omission of less than one sentence:

"I believe the public must have a firm respect for the rights of others.

There is . . . no alternative. For unless we have 'law and order,' we may . . . have chaos." (NOTE: An ellipsis is three spaced periods and is used only in a quotation to indicate that some of the author's original words have been omitted.)

H. Ellipsis Including Period:
Omission of at least one sentence:

John Smith states that "the public must have a firm respect for the rights of others. . . . For unless we have 'law and order,' we may . . . have chaos."

I. Editorial Corrections:

David Bruce states that "almost everyone believe [sic] the President is not telling the truth." (NOTE: When quoting somebody else's words, quote them *exactly* as they are written, but insert a bracketed *sic*—meaning "thus it is written in the original"—to indicate the original error.

20. REFERENCES: PRONOUNS (Ref)

One of the most careless and common errors committed in writing is the use of vague and often missing references for pronouns. Every pronoun should refer clearly to a particular antecedent (reference), without causing any confusion or guessing whatsoever. The reader should not have to waste his time trying to figure out what the pronoun refers to. Therefore, be especially wary of using *it, he, they, this, that,* and *which* without a clear reference.

Note the following *examples* of *vague references.*

A. WRONG: He sat on a park bench all day, working on his writing assignment. *It* was hard. (What was hard, the bench or the assignment?)

CORRECT: The bench was hard. (OR) The assignment was hard.

B. WRONG: Mary told Helen that *she* had not been telling the truth. (Who was not telling the truth, Mary or Helen?)

CORRECT: 1. Mary admitted to Helen that she had not been telling the truth.

(OR) 2. Mary accused Helen of not telling the truth.

(OR) 3. Mary told Helen that she (Mary) had not been telling the truth. (OR) . . . that she (Helen) had not been telling the truth.

(OR) 4. Mary said to Helen, "I have not been telling the truth."

C. WRONG: I was speeding on the freeway and *they* gave me a ticket. (Who did?) I didn't like *it*. (Like what?) *He* shouldn't have done *that*. (Who shouldn't have done what?) *Which* reminds me, I've got to be *there* to take care of it *then* because *that's* the third *one* this year. (What does <u>which</u> refer to, where is <u>there</u>, when is <u>then</u>, and what is <u>that</u>?)

CORRECT: I was speeding on the freeway, and the policeman gave me a ticket. I didn't like receiving the citation. He shouldn't have given me one. The incident reminds me that I've got to be in court next week because that is the third such moving violation I have been cited for this year.

D. WRONG: *They* make good wine in California. (Who does?)
CORRECT: 1. The vintners make good wine in California.
   (OR)   2. California produces good wine.
   (OR)   3. Good wine is produced in California.

E. WRONG: She was interested in drama, and she wanted to become *one* someday. (Become what?)
CORRECT: She was interested in drama, and she wanted to become an actress someday.

F. WRONG: Community colleges in California are notorious for exploiting their part-time faculty. *This* is wrong. (What is wrong?)
CORRECT: 1. This type of exploitation is wrong.
   (OR)   2. Such exploitation is wrong.

NOTE: Use extreme caution in beginning a sentence with *this,* because the demonstrative pronoun *this* should *not* refer to a preceding idea within a sentence or to a complete sentence unless—and only unless—the reference is crystal clear. *This* should never refer to a whole paragraph. *This* by itself should not refer to the title of an article or a book. In short, *this* should point out a *particular* person or thing, like *this sentence,* or *this word,* or *this book,* etc.

G. WRONG: *This* was very interesting. I enjoyed the plot.
CORRECT: *Bernadine* was a very interesting novel. I enjoyed the plot.

21. SENTENCE SENSE (SS)

For a number of reasons, most of which have already been discussed, your sentence may not make sense. Read every sentence to yourself, aloud if possible, to make sure that it is a sentence—that it makes sense. If it doesn't make sense to you, how do you expect it to make sense to somebody else? Rewrite it until it does make sense.

22. SPELLING AND POSSESSIVES (Sp, /')

A. Spelling.

Although spelling rules or lists will not be included in this book, and although I, personally, have had enormous difficulty with spelling for most of my life, I would strongly advise students to do as I have done in recent years: make liberal use of a good dictionary and a good speller. If you can't afford a good dictionary, buy a paperback version, but use one. Spellers, such as *20,000 Words and 30,000 Words,* are also extremely helpful, especially if you are in a hurry and have weak eyesight. In addition, try to learn a *basic list* of the most common words that you misspell. Use a little notebook to jot them down in alphabetical order; then learn them. Finally, ask somebody who is a good speller to proofread your writing. I always have somebody proofread mine. You will be pleasantly surprised at how this advice will help you if you follow it.

B. Possessives.

The possessive case for pronouns was discussed on pages 53 and 55 in this chapter. The following rules for *possessives in nouns* should be noted and learned. (REMEMBER: THE POSSESSIVE CASE INDICATES OWNERSHIP.)

1. Form the possessive case of all SINGULAR NOUNS and INDEFINITE PRONOUNS (anyone, everyone, somebody, etc.) by adding *'s* to the ending *regardless* of the final consonant (sound) or the number of syllables contained *unless* there are more than two syllables.

EXAMPLES: (the boy's shirt, Charles's home, the fox's tail, Katz's rule, Uris's novel, his mistress's address, Mrs. Holmes's cake)

EXCEPTIONS: *Usage suggests* that if a noun contains *more* than *two* syllables and already ends in an *-s* or *-z* sound, the addition of the final *-s* might be *unpronounceable* and, therefore, a mere apostrophe (') added to the ending *is sufficient.*

EXAMPLES: a. (Aristophanes' plays, Ulysses' strength, Mr. Gonzales' store, Achilles' heel, Xerxes' strategy.)

   b. (Ancient biblical references, such as, for conscience' sake, for righteousness' sake, Moses' laws.)

NOTE: Some of these biblical references are often rewritten: The laws of Moses.

2. Form the possessive case for ALL PLURAL NOUNS *that already end in s* by adding only an apostrophe (').

EXAMPLES: (the ladies' powder room, the girls' cloakroom, the boys' locker room.)

3. Form the possessive case for all IRREGULAR PLURAL NOUNS by adding *'s*.

EXAMPLES: (the men's room, the geese's pond, the alumni's gathering)

4. To indicate JOINT OR COLLECTIVE OWNERSHIP, add *'s* to the LAST NOUN—or ' if the last noun is plural.

EXAMPLES: (Gilbert and Sullivan's operettas, mothers and daughters' tea, students and teachers' meeting.)

NOTE THE OMISSION OF AN APOSTROPHE IN THESE CASES:

1. *Inanimate objects* indicate possession by dropping either the 's or by converting to an *of phrase* or other similar modifier.

EXAMPLES: (the tree trunk OR the trunk of the tree, the table legs OR the legs of the table, the building entrance OR the entrance to the building)

2. Organizations often omit the apostrophe.

EXAMPLES: (California State University System, California Teachers Association).

23. SUBORDINATION (Sub)

The subordination of minor ideas was discussed in Chapter Four (pages 26-29), which dealt with complex sentences. REMEMBER: all ideas are not of equal importance. The *major idea* should be *emphasized* by expressing it in a simple sentence, which stands alone, *or* by placing it in the *main clause* of a *compound sentence,* which *subordinates ideas of lesser importance* by using them to explain the main idea.

EXAMPLE OF COORDINATION: BOTH IDEAS EQUALLY IMPORTANT (He could not get along with his wife, and *they got a divorce.*)

EXAMPLE OF SUBORDINATION TO EMPHASIZE THE MAIN IDEA: (Since he could not get along with his wife, *they got a divorce.*)

REMEMBER THIS LIST OF SUBORDINATING CONJUNCTIONS: *as, as if, as though, after, although, before, because, in order that, in that, if, even though, until, unless, since, when, whenever, while, so that.*

Remember: Subordinating conjunctions introduce subordinate clauses which cannot stand alone but instead depend for their meaning on the main clause, which can stand alone. Use subordination effectively by placing the main idea either at the very end of the sentence or at the very beginning. Use subordination when it is needed to emphasize a main idea. But do not overuse subordination. Nothing is more monotonous to read than the same sentence pattern over and over and over again.

24. VARIETY (Var)

Review chapters two, three, and four so that you will be familiar with various sentence patterns, which you will soon be using in your writing. Remember to use a variety of sentence patterns because they not only are effective in expressing ideas clearly, but they also are effective in adding a certain rhythm to your writing, all of which makes your writing enjoyable to read. In summary, fine writing, like poetry, not only reads well, but also sounds well.

25. VERBS (V):

Function (F), Tense (t), Helping and Linking Verbs (L), Voice (vo), Mood (m)

A. Function:(F)

1. DEFINITION: A verb is a word (threw) or a group of words (might have thrown) that expresses *action* (a happening), *existence* (a state of being), or a *condition*. A verb describes the subject by telling the reader what the subject does (action), where or what the subject is (existence), or what condition the subject is in. A verb, therefore, makes an *assertion* or statement about the subject, telling the reader *what is happening*. And since something must happen in a sentence, or something must be somewhere, or something must be in a particular condition, *a verb is absolutely essential in the sentence.* In short, a *verb* is the *heart of* the *sentence.* Without a verb, the only sentence possible—if it can be called a sentence—is an exclamation (Oh, how terrible! What a tragedy!).

2. ASSERTIONS: Verbs make the following assertions about the subject and express the following conditions:
a) Verbs show *what the subject does—direct action.*
    1) The pitcher *throws* the ball.
    2) The pitcher *has thrown* the ball.
    3) She *should have taken* his advice.
b) Verbs show *what happens to the subject—passive action.*
    1) The ball *was thrown* by the pitcher.
    2) The book *should have been read* by the student.
c) Verbs show *who,* or *what,* or *where* the subject is—*existence.*
    1) John *is* the closest friend I have.

2) John *is* the name of my closest friend.
3) John *may become* a doctor.
4) John *was* outside.
d) Verbs show *how* the *subject is described—particular condition.*
1) My friend *is* tired.
2) My friend *is* tall.
3) My friend *seems* tired.
4) Roses *smell* sweet.

3. PLACEMENT:

a) Verbs almost always *follow* their *subject* in declarative sentences (statements).
1) The pitcher *threw* the ball.
2) Five people *are* in the room.
b) When the "expletive" (filler) *there* is used, the order is reversed.
1) There *are* five people in the room.
2) There *is* the pitcher.

NOTE: *There* is not a subject; it is an expletive or filler and does not contribute to effective writing. Eliminate it, if at all possible.

c) If the sentence is in the form of a *question,* the *verb*—or part of the verb phrase—*follows* the subject.
1) *Did* the pitcher *throw* the ball?
2) *Have* you *been able* to read the book?

B. Tense: (t)

1. DEFINITION: Since the verb tells what is happening, it obviously must tell *when* the action occurred—past, present, or future. This expression of *time* is called *tense.* In addition to these three *basic* or *simple* tenses, which are used most of all, there are three additional tenses, sometimes called *compound* tenses, that express exact divisions of a particular time. These *compound tenses* are formed by using a *helping* or *linking* verb—a form of "to be" or "to have."
Examples: (I have seen him. I had seen him. I will have seen him.)
2. FORMS OF A VERB: The three major forms of a verb, which are *always* listed in a dictionary, are these:
a) *Present Tense:* be have see swim write love
b) *Past Tense:* was had saw swam wrote loved
c) *Past Participle:* been had seen swum written loved
3. SIMPLE TENSES:
a) *Present Tense:* The pitcher *throws* the ball to the catcher.

(Continuous action occurs at the present moment.)

b) *Past Tense:* The pitcher *threw* the ball two minutes ago.

(Past action has already occurred.)

c) *Future Tense:* The pitcher *will throw* the ball two minutes from now.

(Future action will occur.)

4. COMPOUND TENSES: (Note the exact division of time.)

a) *Present Perfect Tense:* The pitcher *has thrown* the ball, just this very instant.

(This tense requires *have* or *has* and indicates that the action extends to the present time.)

b) *Past Perfect Tense:* The pitcher *had thrown* the ball before the umpire arrived.

(This tense requires *had* and indicates that the action *already was completed* before some other past action occurred.)

c) *Future Perfect Tense:* The pitcher *will have thrown* the ball by the time we arrive.

(*Shall have* or *will have* are required in this tense, which indicates that the action will be completed before some designated time in the future.)

5. PROGRESSIVE TENSE FORMS: (These tense forms indicate a *continuous* or progressive action.)

a) *Present Progressive:* He *is throwing* the ball.

b) *Past:* He *was throwing* the ball.

c) *Future:* He *will be throwing* the ball.

d) *Present Perfect:* He *has been throwing* the ball.

e) *Past Perfect:* He *had been throwing* the ball.

f) *Future Perfect:* He *will have been throwing* the ball.

NOTE: All of these various forms express nuances or delicate shades of meaning, and although they are helpful for very accurate writing, they are not absolutely essential for the beginning writer. However, you should know the *basic parts* of the verb: plain or infinitive form (swim), past tense (swam), and past participle (swum). When in doubt, you should consult the dictionary. Finally—and this is most important—you should know the changes in *verb endings,* both in the *past* and *present* tense.

6. CHANGES IN VERB FORM: Verbs change form, usually through their endings (inflections), both in the past tense and in the third person singular of the present tense. Frequently, the past participle also changes.

a) *Past Tense and Past Participle:*

1) With *regular* verbs the past tense and past participle are formed simply by *adding —ed, —d,* or *—t* to the plain form (infinitive), which is also called the stem.

EXAMPLES: to *walk,* walked, walked; *shave,* shaved, shaved, *deal,* dealt, dealt.

2) With *irregular* verbs, which are sometimes called *strong* verbs, a vowel is changed within the stem.

EXAMPLES: swim, swam, swum; see, saw, seen; begin, began, begun.

3) Sometimes only a consonant is changed.

EXAMPLES: build, built, built.

4) Some verbs do not change their form in the past tense.

EXAMPLES: burst, cost, set.

5) When in doubt, consult the dictionary.

b) *Present Tense—Third Person Singular:* Verbs change their form in the third person singular, present tense, by adding *—s.* This is the *only change* in the present tense, yet many people forget to use it. Learn it now, and remember it.

EXAMPLES: I walk, you walk, he *walks,* we walk, you walk, they walk.

I run, he *runs;* I cook, she *cooks;* they speak, he *speaks;* he *lives,* she *lives,* it *lives.*

NOTE ON MAJOR ERRORS IN TENSE COMMITTED BY STUDENTS: Two of the most common tense errors committed by students are explained in 6 a) and 6 b) above: the failure to add the *tense ending* to the *past tense,* particularly in verbs such as *use* and *accustom* (He *used* to go, not use to go; I was *accustomed* to reading, not accustom.); and the failure to change the ending to *—s* in the *third person singular* of the *present tense.* (He *speaks,* not speak; the engine *runs,* not run.). Since these errors are too common, you should not only be aware of them, but more importantly, you should avoid them.

C. Helping and Linking Verbs: (I)

1. HELPING (AUXILIARY) VERBS: Forms of to *be* and to *have* may stand alone or may help to form *verb phrases* and *compound tenses.*

a) *To be:* am, are, is, was, were, been. (He has been here.)

b) *To have:* have, has, had. (He *had been seeing* her.)

2. LINKING VERBS link the subject with descriptive words, called "complements," that follow the verb. The following are

linking verbs: *be, seem, become, appear,* as well as verbs that describe the five senses, *look, smell, taste, sound,* and *feel.*

EXAMPLES: a) He *appears* calm.
b) The cake *tastes* sweet.
c) The music *sounds* loud.

NOTE: *adjectives,* not adverbs, follow linking verbs, because the adjective acts as a complement, thus completing the meaning of the sentence.

D. Voice: (vo)

Use the *active* voice whenever possible rather than the *passive voice.*

1. Active Voice shows what the subject does; that is, the *subject acts* and thereby *performs* the *action.*
EXAMPLES: The pitcher *threw* the ball, and the batter *hit* a home run.

2. Passive Voice shows what has happened to the subject; that is, the *subject* instead of acting *is acted upon.*
EXAMPLES: The ball *was thrown by* the pitcher, and a home run *was made by* the batter.

NOTE that the active voice seems alive whereas the passive voice seems dead. Some types of writing such as scientific or police reports demand the passive voice because the emphasis is upon objectivity. However, such writing, although very necessary, is terribly dull. Therefore, whenever possible, avoid using the passive voice.

E. Mood: (m)

Mood expresses the writer's attitude toward his sentence, indicating whether he is stating a *fact* or asking a question, making a *supposition,* or issuing a *command.* These are the *three moods:*

1. Indicative Mood: expresses a *statement* of *fact* or *asks* a *question.*
EXAMPLES: I *am* here. *Are* you here? This book *is* new.

2. Imperative Mood: expresses a *command* or a *request.*
EXAMPLES: *Get* out of here! Please *hand* me that note.

3. Subjunctive Mood: expresses a *condition contrary to fact,* a *resolution,* a *wish,* a *doubt,* a *concession,* or a *probability.*
EXAMPLES: If I *were* an elephant, I would eat peanuts. I move that the meeting *be* adjourned. I wish I *were* a millionaire. I doubt that she

will be here. If he *be* condemned without a fair trial, we will all be to blame. She looks as if she *were* guilty.

26. WORDINESS (W)

Avoid "padding" in your writing. Use active verbs and vivid nouns instead of multitudes of modifiers. Avoid stilted language such as this: They conveyed the gentleman to his abode of residence, in a highly intoxicated condition. Instead, use concise, effective language such as this: They carried the drunk man home. If one word can do the work of three, use it.

CHAPTER SEVEN

GLOSSARY OF DICTION AND USAGE

The words and phrases discussed in this chapter are often misused both in everyday speech and in written communication. Although the list is far from complete, it includes the most common errors. If the word or phrase you are looking for, however, is not included, or if you would like more information about any word listed, consult a good dictionary. Also, usage does change over a long period of time. Nothing remains the same forever.

The three levels of usage described in the glossary are as follows:

Formal

refers to words or expressions in the standard English vocabulary, listed in the most respected dictionaries, without special usage labels. Formal English is used by the most educated writers and speakers and is accepted as *the* standard in both high school and college writing. It is therefore the highest level of usage.

Informal

These words or expressions are labeled *Informal* or *Colloquial* in dictionaries, yet they are widely used in informal conversation, even by some educated speakers. In writing, however, especially in high school and college writing, informal usage should be avoided. Remember: informal usage is a level below formal usage.

Substandard

refers to *illiterate* expressions, as well as to *slang*, and should be avoided not only in speech, but particularly in writing. The main problem with substandard usage is that it is understood only by a particular class of people in a particular region in a particular era. For example, slang expressions may change meaning from one month to the next, even among a particular group. Such expressions, therefore, cannot communicate meaning among people in general.

A, AN: Use *a* before a consonant sound (*a* book, *a* heavy load, *a* one-page theme).

Use *an* before a vowel sound (*an* apple, *an* honest girl, *an* umpire, *an* orange).

Exception: Use *a* before certain vowel sounds like *uniform, u*niverse, *u*tility company.

ABOUT: Do not use *at about* instead of about, and do not substitute *as to* for about.

Wordy—He arrived at about midnight.

Formal—He arrived about midnight. (OR) He arrived at midnight.

Substandard—He spoke as to his idea.

Formal—He spoke about his idea.

ACCEPT, EXCEPT: The verb *accept* means "to receive." (John *accepted* the gift.)

Except means "with the exception of." (She likes everything *except* spinach.)

AD is an informal shortening of *advertisement.* Use the complete word in formal writing.

ADVICE, ADVISE: *Advice* is a noun. (The teacher gave me some advice.)

Advise is a verb. (I will do what my teachers *advise.* I *advise* you to follow my advice.)

AFFECT, EFFECT: *Affect* is a verb meaning "to influence." (The drought will *affect* the crops.)

Effect may function as a verb, meaning "to bring about, to achieve." (The legislators *effected* some reforms.)

Effect usually functions as a noun, meaning "the result." (The *effect* of the drought on the crops is disastrous.)

AIN'T is an illiterate contraction of *am not,* avoided by educated people except for humorous effect.

ALIBI is a legal term used informally for *excuse*.
    Formal—He had an *excuse* for his absence.
    Informal—He had an *alibi* for his absence.

ALL, ALL OF: *All* followed by a *noun* is more concise than *all of* (*all* the people, *all* the money, *all* the work).
    The *of* is often retained before a *pronoun* or a *proper* noun (*all of* them, *all of* Canada).

ALL RIGHT, ALRIGHT: *All right* is still the preferred spelling.

ALLUDE, REFER: *Allude* means "to refer indirectly." (His speech *alluded* to his earlier campaign without specifically mentioning it.)
    Refer means "to direct attention to." (I *refer* you to Chapter V.)

ALLUSION, ILLUSION: *Allusion* means "an indirect reference."(He made an *allusion* to his opponent.)
    Illusion means a "misleading image" or "false impression." (The desert heat produced an *illusion* of a lake.)

ALMOST, MOST: *Most* is sometimes used as an informal substitute for *almost*.
Formal—*Almost* all teachers are conscientious.
Informal—*Most* all teachers are conscientious.

ALOT should be written as two words—*a lot*.

ALREADY, ALL READY: *Already* is an adverb meaning "previously." (When she arrived home, dinner was *already* on the table.)
    All ready means "completely prepared." (Dinner will be *all ready* when you get home.)

ALTOGETHER, ALL TOGETHER: *Altogether* means "wholly, complete." (That noise is *altogether* unnecessary.)
    All together means "in group." (We were *all together*.)

ALUMNUS, ALUMNA, ALUMNI: An *alumnus* is a male graduate (plural—*alumni*); an *alumna* is a female graduate (plural—*alumnae*); *alumni* refers to male and female graduates grouped together.

A.M., P.M.,(or AM, PM) or a.m., p.m.: Use these only with figures.

(We arrived at 8:30 A.M. and left at 4:30 P.M.)
(We arrived at half-past eight in the morning and left at half-past four in the afternoon.)

AMONG, BETWEEN: *Among* implies more than two. (She divided the cake *among* her four children.)

Between implies only two. (She *divided* the cake between the two.) However, *between* is now used to express a reciprocal relationship or the relationship of one thing to several things. (An agreement was reached *between* the three corporations; the difference between the *three* proposals was so slight that it was negligible.)

AMOUNT, NUMBER: *Amount* refers to things in bulk or mass. (That farm produces a huge *amount* of grain.)

Number refers to countable objects. (Last year that ranch raised a large *number* of cattle.)

AN, A — See A, AN.

AND, ETC: *Et Cetera* (Latin means "and the rest of"; therefore, the contraction (*etc.*) does not require an *and*. (She caught several kinds of fish, including halibut, trout, snapper, etc.)

AND/OR: Except in legal or commercial writing, this expression is inappropriate and distracting.

ANGLE is *slang* for *point of view* or *aspect*. (What's your *angle?*)
Correct—What is your *reasoning?*
Correct—The pilot banked his plane at a sharp *angle.*

ANY is used informally in the sense of "at all" in negative or interrogative sentences. (It hasn't snowed *any*. Did the needle hurt *any?*)

ANYONE, ANY ONE: *Anyone* means "anybody" or "any person at all."(*Anyone* can learn to write.)

Any one means any "specific" person or thing in a group.
(*Any one* of those students will qualify; *any one* of those books is interesting.)

Similar forms are *everyone, every one; someone, some one.*

ANYWAYS, ANYWHERES: These are substandard for *anyway, anywhere.*

ANYPLACE is informal for *anywhere.*

APT, LIKELY: *Apt* refers to a natural ability. (She is apt at swimming.) But it is often used *informally* as a synonym for *likely.*
Formal—The course is *likely* to be interesting.
Informal—The course is *apt* to be interesting.

AROUND is often used informally to mean *about* or *near.*
Formal—He left *about* noon.
Informal—He left *around* noon.
Formal—She liked to be *near* her friends.
Informal—She liked to be *around* her friends.

AS: In formal writing, avoid using *as* instead of *that* or *whether,* and do not substitute *as* for *because, for, since, while, who,* or *which* in introducing subordinate clauses.
Formal—I am not sure *that* I should do it.
Informal—I am not sure *as* I should do it.
Formal—*Because* it was foggy, the airport was closed.
Informal—*As* it was foggy, the airport was closed.
(See also LIKE, AS, AS IF.)
Formal—*Because* his brakes didn't work, he had an accident.

AS TO is an inexact substitute for *about.*
Formal—I questioned her *about* her work.
Informal—I questioned her *as to* her work.

AS...AS, SO...AS: Formal usage prefers *so...as* to *as...as* in negative comparisons, but both are correct.
Formal—She is not *so* old *as* she looks.
Informal—She is not *as* old *as* she looks.
Formal—She is as old as she looks.

AT: Although *from* after *where* is standard (*Where* are you *from?*), *at* after *where* is redundant and substandard.
Formal—Where do you live?
Substandard—Where do you live *at?*
Formal—Where is she eating?
Substandard—Where is she eating *at?*

AT ABOUT: See ABOUT.

AWHILE, A WHILE: *Awhile* is an adverb. (Let us rest *awhile* before continuing.)

A while is an article and a noun. (Let us rest for *a while* before continuing.)

AWFUL, AWFULLY: These are informally used as vague intensifiers. (I am *awfully* sorry.) But they are inappropriate in formal writing. Use a more exact word. (I am *extremely* sorry.)

BAD, BADLY: Although both are now standard in the sense of "ill" or "sorry," writers usually prefer *bad* after such verbs as *feel* or *look*.
> He plays *badly*.
> She feels *bad*.
> You look *bad*.

BALANCE: Do not substitute this word for "the rest of" or "the remainder."
Formal—She remained home for *the rest of* the day.
Informal—She remained home the *balance* of the day.

BANK ON, TAKE STOCK IN are informal expressions for *rely on* and *trust in*.

BEING THAT, BEING AS HOW are substandard substitutes for subordinating conjunctions *as, because, since*.

BECAUSE: See REASON...BECAUSE

BESIDE, BESIDES: Both words are interchangeable when meaning "except." (There is nobody here *beside* you; there is nobody here *besides* you.)
Beside is also used as a preposition meaning "by the side of." (She sat down *beside* him.)
Besides is generally used as an adverb meaning "moreover," "in addition to." (He receives a bonus *besides* his regular income.)

BETTER: See HAD BETTER, HAD RATHER, WOULD RATHER.

BETWEEN, AMONG: See AMONG.

BUG is informal for *germ* or *defect* and slang for *enthusiast*.
Formal—He caught the *flu*; his *germs* are contagious.
Informal—He caught the *bug*; his *bugs* are catching.
Formal—My television still has some *defects*.

94

Informal—My television still has some *bugs.*
Formal—He is a swimming *enthusiast.*
Slang—He is a swimming *bug.*

BURST, BURSTED, BUST, BUSTED: The principal parts of *burst* are *burst, burst, burst. Bursted, bust,* and *busted* are not standard.

BUT HARDLY, SCARCELY: *Can't help but* is now standard, but the double negatives *can't hardly* and *don't scarcely* are still nonstandard.
Formal—I *can't help but* laugh. (OR) I *can't help* laughing.
Formal—I *can hardly* see. (OR) I *can scarcely* see.

BUT WHAT is informal for *that* in negative expressions.
Formal—She has no doubt *that* she will pass.
Informal—She has no doubt *but what* she will pass.

CALCULATE, GUESS, RECKON: These are substandard terms for think or expect.

CAN, MAY: In formal usage *can* means "to be able." (I *can* swim.)
   May means "to have permission." (*May* I go swimming?)

CAN'T HARDLY: See BUT HARDLY, SCARCELY. Use *can hardly,* instead.

CASE, LINE are often used unnecessarily.
Wordy—In your *case,* I believe you.
Improved—I believe you.
Wordy—She wants something in the *line* of a new dress.
Improved—She wants a new dress.

CENTER AROUND, CENTER ABOUT: These common expressions are illogical.
Informal—The argument *centered around* the President's speech.
Formal—The argument *centered on* the President's speech.

COMPARE TO, COMPARE WITH: *Compare to* is used to liken two objects as the same in some way. (He *compared* a bicycle *to* a motorcycle.)
Compare with is used to examine objects in order to discover their similarities and differences. (She *compared* her latest essay *with* her

earlier one.)

COMPLECTED is a dialect form for *complexioned.*
Formal—She is dark *complexioned.*
Substandard—She is dark *complected.*

CONSENSUS OF OPINION is redundant. Omit "of opinion" because consensus means "a general agreement of opinion."

CONSIDERABLE is standard as an adjective meaning "amount" and is often used informally as a noun. It is substandard as an adverb meaning *considerably* or *very.*
Formal—They earned a *considerable* amount of money.
Formal—They gained *considerable* wealth.
Informal—They gained *considerable* in the stock market.
Substandard—The market dropped *considerable.*

CONTACT: In formal writing use a more specific word such as *meet, interview, consult, talk to,* or *write to* when you mean "to meet or talk with."

CONTINUAL, CONTINUOUS: *Continual* means "frequently repeated." (He made continual errors.)
   Continuous means "without interruption." (The storm was *continuous.)*

CONTINUE ON: This expression is redundant. Omit *on.*

COULD OF is a substandard form of *could have.*

CREDIBLE, CREDULOUS: *Credible* means "believable, reliable." (His story was *credible.)*
   Credulous means "inclined to believe on slight evidence." (A *credulous* person often believes anything he hears.)

CUTE is too trite and vague a word to use in reference to *approval.*

DEAL is used informally to mean *"business transaction,"* but it is often overworked in place of more exact words such as *agreement, bargain, plan,* or *secret agreement.*

DIFFERENT FROM, DIFFERENT THAN: American writers usually

prefer *different from,* whereas, the preference in England is *different than.* Both expressions are now generally accepted.

The decision was *different from* what I had expected. (OR) The decision was *different than* what I had expected.

Formal—My tastes are *different from* yours.

Informal—My tastes are *different than* yours.

DIFFER FROM, DIFFER WITH: *Differ from* means "to stand apart because of unlikeness." (My tastes *differ from* yours.)

Differ with means "to disagree." (I *differ with* you on your choice.)

DONE is standard as an adjective and as the past participle of the verb do. (My essay is *done;* I have *done* the work.)

It is substandard as an adverb or a substitute for *did.*

Substandard—My essay is *done* written; I *done* the work.

DON'T is a contraction of *do not.* (I *don't* know you; they *don't* know you.) Don't write *don't* for *does not.*

Illiterate—He *don't* work here anymore.

DUE TO: The prepositional use of *due to* is now appropriate except in the most formal writing.

Formal—She arrived late *because* of an unavoidable delay.

Also accepted—She arrived late *due to* an unavoidable delay.

Due as an adjective—Her success was *due to* her persistence.

EACH AND EVERY is redundant.

EACH OTHER, ONE ANOTHER can be used interchangeably. Some writers still prefer *each other* when referring to only two, but *one another* when referring to more than two.

EFFECT, AFFECT: See AFFECT, EFFECT.

EITHER, NEITHER: Both are singular subjects used to refer to one or the other of two. (*Either* John or Mary will come; *neither* John nor Mary wants to come.)

EMIGRATE, IMMIGRATE: *Emigrate* means "to move *from* a country."

Immigrate means "to move *into* a country."

They *emigrated* from Ireland.

They *immigrated* to the United States.

EMINENT, IMMINENT: *Eminent* means "distinguished." (He is an eminent doctor.) *Imminent* means "threatening" or "about to happen." (Death seemed *imminent.*)

ENTHUSE, ENTHUSED: *Enthuse* is used informally as a verb meaning to show enthusiasm. *Enthused* is used informally as a synonym for *enthusiastic.*
Formal—She was *enthusiastic* about her trip.
Informal—She was *enthused* about her trip.

EQUALLY AS GOOD: The *as* is unnecessary. *Equally good* is correct.

ETC. This Latin abbreviation for *et cetera* ("and the rest") is appropriate for business and informal writing and may be used sparingly in formal writing if its meaning is clear. Do *not* place *and* before etc., because the *and* then becomes redundant.

EVER SO OFTEN means "very often, frequently."

EVERY SO OFTEN means "occasionally, every now and then."

EVERYONE, EVERY ONE: See ANYONE, ANY ONE.

EVERYPLACE is informally used as an adverb meaning *everywhere.*

EVERYWHERES is substandard for *everywhere.*

EXAM: informal abbreviation of *examination.* In formal writing use the complete word.

EXCEPT, ACCEPT: See ACCEPT, EXCEPT.

EXPECT: Informally used for *suppose* or *think.*
Formal—I *suppose* I should go to bed.
Informal—I *expect* I should go to bed.

EXTRA: Some writers object to using *extra* as an adverb meaning "unusually."
Formal—Yesterday was an *unusually* cold day.
Informal—Yesterday was an *extra* cold day.

FABULOUS is informal for *very good* or *pleasing*.
Formal—Your dinner was *very good* (or *excellent)*.
Informal—Your dinner was *fabulous*.

FACT, THE FACT THAT: These words are often unnecessary when using the word *that*.
Formal—She was aware *that* he had gone home.
Wordy—She was aware of *the fact that* he had gone home.

FARTHER, FURTHER: *Farther* is used in formal writing when referring to distance; and *further* when referring to degree, quantity, or time.
Formal—Our destination is two miles *farther*.
Formal—We need *further* information for our research.
Formal—Summer is only two months *further*.

FAZE is informal for *disconcert, bother,* or *daunt*.
  Formal—The challenge did not *daunt* him (or *bother* him).
  Informal—The challenge did not *faze* him.

FELLOW is informal when used to mean *person*.

FEWER, LESS: Although these words are often used interchangeably, in formal usage *less* refers to value, degree or amount; and *fewer* refers to number or the countable.
Formal—She is *less* critical than she used to be.
Formal—She now spends *fewer* hours at home.
Informal—*Less* than fifteen people were present.

FIELD is an overworked and often redundant word.
Formal—He majored *in* chemistry.
Wordy—He majored *in the field of* chemistry.

FIGURE is often used informally for *think, expect, suppose,* or *believe*.

FINE is a vague and overused adjective to express approval (a *fine* teacher). As an adverb it means *well* in informal usage. (The car *runs* fine.)

FLUNK is informal for *fail*.

FOLKS is informal for *parents,* or *relatives*. It is used in formal usage to mean "people in general" or a "specified group." (The *old folks* will gather here.)

FORMER, LATTER: Former refers to the first-named of two, but if three or more items are named, *first* and *last* are used.
Formal—The Kings and Seals are the two National Hockey League teams in California; the *former* is in Los Angeles and the *latter* in Oakland.
Formal—We always eat three meals a day: breakfast, luncheon, and dinner; the *first* in the morning, and the *last* in the evening.

FUNNY is used informally to mean *strange, queer,* or *odd*. Use a more exact word.

FURTHER, FARTHER: See FARTHER, FURTHER.

GET is used in many informal and substandard expressions that are inappropriate in formal usage. Avoid these expressions: *get going, get to go, get at it, get wise to, get away with*. It is commonly used, however, in such standard idioms as *get along with* (a person), *get the better of* (somebody), *get at* (information), and *get over* (an illness).

GOOD is almost always used as an *adjective*. (She is a *good* teacher.) It is considered informal when used as an adverb. (She teaches *good*.)
Formal—She teaches *well*.

GOOD AND is informal in such expressions as *good and hot, good and ready*. Avoid such expressions in formal writing.

GOT, GOTTEN are both past participles of *get* and are both appropriate in formal writing. (I have just got a raise. (OR) I have just gotten a raise.) Writers in England, however, consider *gotten* old fashioned.

GRAND, GREAT, WONDERFUL are inexact and overworked adjectives meaning "excellent."

GUY is informal for man or boy.

GYM is an abbreviation used informally for *gymnasium*.

HAD BETTER, HAD RATHER, WOULD RATHER are all standard idioms used to express advisability (with *better*) or preference (with *rather*). *Better* alone is informal. *Ought* or *should* is more formal than the idiom *had better*.
Formal—She *had better* see the doctor.
Informal—She *better* see the doctor.
Most formal—She *ought* to see the doctor. (OR) She *should* see the doctor.

HAD OF, HAD OUGHT are both substandard for *had, ought*.
Formal—I wish I *had* (not *had of*) been there.

HALF A, A HALF, A HALF A: Both *half a* and *a half* are acceptable, but avoid the redundant *a half a*.
Formal—She worked *half a* week (OR) *a half* week.
Redundant—She worked *a half a* week.

HANGED, HUNG are often used interchangeably in informal usage. However, formal usage prefers *hanged* in reference to executions (The prisoner was *hanged*) and *hung* in reference to objects (The picture was *hung* on the wall).

HARDLY: See BUT, HARDLY, SCARCELY.

HAVE GOT is used informally. (I *have got* a toothache.) However, formal usage prefers have. (I *have* a toothache.)

HAVE OF: See OF, HAVE.

HEALTHFUL, HEALTHY: *Healthful* means "giving health." (Vitamins are *healthful*.)
    Healthy means "having health." (She is *healthy*.)
Both, however, are standard words meaning "conducive to health."
Standard—Arizona has a *healthy* climate.
Standard—Arizona has a *healthful* climate.

HIMSELF, MYSELF, YOURSELF: See MYSELF, YOURSELF, HIMSELF.

HISSELF is substandard for *himself*.

IDEA is often vague for *belief, conjecture, intention, plan,* or *theory*. Use a more specific noun whenever possible.

Vague—The coach explained his *idea.*
Exact—The coach explained his *plan* for the game.

IF, WHETHER are used interchangeably after such words as *say, ask, know, doubt, see, wonder,* and *understand.* (Ask *if* (OR) ask *whether* she can go; I *wonder if* (OR) I *wonder whether* it will rain.) If an *alternative* is expressed, formal usage prefers *whether.* (He doesn't know *whether* or not he can come.)

ILLUSION, ALLUSION: See ALLUSION, ILLUSION.

IMMIGRATE, EMIGRATE: See EMIGRATE, IMMIGRATE.

IMMINENT, EMINENT: See EMINENT, IMMINENT.

IMPLY, INFER: *Imply* means, "to hint" or "to suggest." (The author *implied* that the government was corrupt.)
    Infer means "to draw a conclusion from evidence."
(The reader *inferred* from the book that the government was corrupt.)

IN, INTO: In formal usage *in* generally indicates location. (We met *in* the classroom.)
    Into indicates motion or direction. (We walked *into* the classroom. I fell *into* the lake.)
    Although both *in* and *into* are used interchangeably in informal usage, the formal rule is more logical in sentences like these:
Logical—He drove in a Chevy, but I drove *in* another car.
Illogical—He drove in a Chevy, but I drove *into* another car.

IN BACK OF, IN BEHIND, IN BETWEEN are all wordy expressions for *back of, behind, between.*

INCREDIBLE, INCREDULOUS: *Incredible* means "too extraordinary to admit belief." (The defendant's story seemed *incredible.*)
    Incredulous means "not inclined to believe." (The defendant's story made the judge *incredulous.*)

INDIVIDUAL, PARTY, PERSON: *Individual* refers to a particular person, or thing, as distinguished from a group. (John is an *individual.* Each person has an *individual* set of fingerprints.)
Party refers to a group of people, except in legal or political language. (We made reservations for a *party* of four.)

102

Person refers to a human being. (Mary is the only *person* here.)

INDULGE means "to be tolerant toward" or "to gratify one's desire." It does not mean "to take part."
Formal—The mother *indulged* (tolerated) her mischievous child.
Formal—They *indulged* in feasting (gratified their desires).
Inaccurate—They *indulged* (took part in) a feast.

INFER, IMPLY: See IMPLY, INFER.

INFERIOR THAN is substandard for *inferior to* or *worse than.*

INGENIOUS, INGENUOUS: *Ingenious* means "clever" or "resourceful." (Jim's invention is ingenious.)
    Ingenuous means "open" "frank" or "naive." (Jim was too *ingenuous* to investigate the copyright law.)

IN REGARDS TO is substandard for *in regard to* or *as regards.*

INSIDE OF, OUTSIDE OF: Often the *of* is unnecessary when *inside* or *outside* are used as prepositions. (I stayed *inside* [not *inside of*] the room.) *Inside of* is informal for *within,* and *outside of* is informal for *except, besides.*
Formal—I will see you *within* two weeks.
Informal—I will see you *inside of* two weeks.
Formal—She has no friends *except* her classmates.
Informal—She has no friends *outside of* her classmates.

IRREGARDLESS is substandard for *regardless.*

IS WHEN, IS WHERE: In giving definitions, do not use *when* and *where* after is.
Awkward—A goal *is when* the puck enters the net.
Formal—A goal *is scored* when the puck enters the net.
Awkward—A university *is where* students go for higher education.
Formal—A university *is an institution* for higher education.

ITS, IT'S: These are two of the most common spelling errors.
Its is a *possessive* pronoun and has no apostrophe. (The cat ate *its* food.)
It's is a *contraction* of *it is* or *it has.(It's* cold today.)

KIND, SORT are *singular* forms. (*This kind* of food; *this sort* of desk.) *Plural* forms are *these kinds* and *these sorts*.

KIND OF, SORT OF are both informal when they mean *somewhat or rather*.
Formal—He is *somewhat* angry. He is *rather* sad.
Informal—He is *kind of* angry. He is *sort of* sad.

KIND OF A, SORT OF A: Omit the *a* in formal usage.
Formal—She wanted some *kind of* book.
Informal—She wanted some *kind of a* book.

LATER, LATTER: *Later* refers to time. (It is *later* than you realize.) *Latter* refers to the last named of only two. (See FORMER, LATTER.)

LAY, LIE: The principal parts of LAY are *lay, laid, laid.*
The principal parts of LIE are *lie, lay, lain.*
If you can substitute a form of "to be," *to lie* is correct. (After dinner I *lie* (am) down.) If "to place" or "to put" makes sense, *to lay* is correct. (I will *lay* the book down; the chicken *laid* an egg.)

LEARN, TEACH: *Learn* means "to gain knowledge." (I *learned* from my teacher.)
Teach means "to impart knowledge." (She will *teach* me how to write.)

LEAVE, LET: *Leave* means "to depart." (I must *leave* the room.)
Let means "to allow." (Please *let* [not leave] me go.)

LESS, FEWER: See FEWER, LESS.

LIKE, AS, AS IF: In formal usage, *like* is used to compare two *objects.* (*This* book is *like* that one. He looks *like me.*)
When comparing two *actions* (verbs), however, *as* or *as if* should be used formally. (He plays *as* a professional does; he plays *as if* he were a professional.)
Formal—She talks *as if* she were angry.
Informal—She talks *like* she was angry.

LIKELY, APT: See APT, LIKELY.

LIKELY, LIABLE: In formal usage *likely* means "probable." (The movie is *likely* to begin on time.) *Liable* means "legally responsible" or "susceptible to something unpleasant." (The window cleaners are *liable* to have an accident, and the contractors then will be held *liable*.)

LINE, CASE: See CASE, LINE.

LITERALLY means "without exaggeration" and is therefore the opposite in meaning of *figuratively*. (She *literally* swam the English Channel.) Avoid confusing or illogical sentences like these: *He literally lifted the train with one hand. She literally died when he surprised her.*

LOCATE should not be used to mean "settle."
Formal—They *settled* in Canada.
Informal— They *located* in Canada.

LOOSE, LOSE: *Lose* means "to cease having." (Did you *lose* your key?) The verb *loose* means "to set free." (He set the prisoner *loose*.) The adjective *loose* means "free, not fastened." (My keys are *loose*.)

LOTS, LOTS OF are informally used for *much* or *a great deal*.
Formal—We had a *great deal* of time, and there was *much* to see.
Informal—We had *lots of* time, (OR *a lot of*) and there was a lot to see.

MAD is informal when used as a substitute for *angry* or *enthusiastic*.

MAY, CAN: See CAN, MAY.

MAY BE, MAYBE: Note the difference between the verb form *may be* and the adverb *maybe*, meaning "perhaps."
    She *may be* the best teacher I will ever have.
    Maybe we will go to the mountains next week.

MAY OF is substandard for *may have*.

MIGHTY means "powerful, strong." (The Peace is a *mighty* river in Canada.) Avoid the informal use for *very, exceedingly*.
Informal—That suit is *mighty* expensive. They are *mighty* good people.

MORAL, MORALE: *Moral* as a noun means "lesson, maxim"; as an adjective it means "ethical" or "correct conduct." (The *moral* of the story is that one should strive toward *moral* behavior.)

Morale means "a cheerful or confident state of mind." (The students' *morale* in this school is excellent.)

MOST, ALMOST: See ALMOST, MOST.

MR.: American usage always requires a period after this male title and never writes it out except for humor. No marital status is specified.

MS.: This title, *Ms.*, is a recently adopted abbreviation for salutations and letters directed either to a single or married woman and, therefore, does not designate the marital status of the woman. Its use is now standard.

MUST OF is substandard for *must have.*

MYSELF, YOURSELF, HIMSELF: These are *intensive* pronouns. (I *myself* will go; you *yourself* must do it; he *himself* will be there.) In formal usage they are inappropriate for the personal pronouns *I, you, him,* as well as for the objective pronouns *me, you,* and *him.*
Formal—Mary and *I* will be there.
Informal—Mary and *myself* will be there.
Formal—Everyone, *I* included, will be there.
Informal—Everyone, *myself* included, will be there.
Formal—Everyone, *I myself* included, will be there.
Formal—He gave it to Allan and *me.*
Informal—He gave it to Allan and *myself.*

NEITHER, EITHER: See EITHER, NEITHER.

NICE is an overworked and vague word of approval. Use it sparingly.

NO ACCOUNT, NO GOOD are informal words for *worthless, useless.*

NO HOW is substandard for *not at all.*

NO WHERES is substandard for *nowhere.*

NOPLACE is substandard for nowhere.

106

NOWHERE NEAR is informal for *not nearly*.

NUMBER, AMOUNT: See AMOUNT, NUMBER.

OF, HAVE: The preposition *of* is substandard when substituted for the verb form *have*.
Formal—Bill could *have* (would *have,* may *have,* might *have,* must *have,* ought to *have*) been here.
Informal—Bill should *of* (would *of,* may *of,* might *of,* must *of,* ought to *of*) been here.

OFF OF: The *of* is unnecessary. (I fell *off* [not *off of*] the ladder.)

OK, O.K., OKAY are used informally for *all right* or *correct.* In *formal* usage, however, replace OK with a more *specific* word.

ONE AND THE SAME are trite for *the same*.

ONE ANOTHER, EACH OTHER: See EACH OTHER, ONE ANOTHER.

ON THE AVERAGE OF is trite for *about* or *almost*.

OUGHT TO OF is substandard for *ought to have*.

OUT LOUD is informal for *aloud*.

OUTSIDE OF: See INSIDE OF, OUTSIDE OF.

OVER WITH is informal for *over, ended*.
Formal—Our vacation is *over* (or *ended*).
Informal—Our vacation is *over with*.

PARTY, PERSON, INDIVIDUAL: See INDIVIDUAL, PARTY, PERSON.

PER is used in commercial expressions, such as *two dollars per hour, forty hours per week,* or in phrases of Latin origin, such as *per capita* and *per diem.* In ordinary writing use *a* or *an: twice a week, eighty cents a pound, fifty miles an hour*.

PERCENT is an abbreviation meaning "by the hundred." It is not

followed by a period and may be written as one or two words. In formal usage, *percent* follows a numeral (50 *percent*) and is not used as a substitute for *portion* or *part;* instead use *percentage.*
Formal—A large *part* (or *portion*) of the movie was boring.
Formal—A large *percentage* of the audience was restless.
Informal—A large *percent* of the movie was boring; a large *percent* of the audience was restless.

PERSON, PARTY, INDIVIDUAL: See INDIVIDUAL, PARTY, PERSON.

PHONE is informal for *telephone.* Use the full word in your formal writing.

PHOTO is informal for *photograph.* Use the full word in your formal writing.

PLAN ON is informal and redundant in phrases such as *plan on going* and *plan on seeing;* instead use "plan to go" and "plan to see."

PLENTY is informal when used as an adverb meaning *very* or *amply.*
Formal—The work was *very* hard.
Informal—The work was *plenty* hard.

P.M., A.M.: See A.M., P.M.

PRINCIPAL, PRINCIPLE: *Principal* is an adjective or noun meaning "chief" or "main official," but *principle* is a noun meaning "fundamental truth." (The *principal* reason our school *principal* is so successful is that he believes in the *principle* of equality.)

PROPOSITION is informal in the sense of dealing with a matter or person, as in, *"Closing the school is a bad proposition."*

PROVEN as the past participle of the verb *prove* is used less often than *proved.*

PUT ACROSS, PUT OVER, PUT IN: *Put across* and *put over* are informal for "to accomplish something against opposition." *Put in* is informal for spend.
Formal—The politician was *successful* in his campaign.
Informal—The politician *put across* his campaign.

Formal—We *spent* an entire day at school.
Informal—We *put in* an entire day at school.

QUITE A FEW, QUITE A LITTLE, QUITE A BIT are informal for *many, more than a little, a considerable amount.*

RAISE, RISE: *Raise, raised, raised* are forms of the verbs *raise.*
(I *raise* corn; I *raised* corn; I *have raised* corn.)
Rise, rose, risen are forms of the verb *rise.*
(I *rise* at dawn; I *rose* at dawn; I *have risen* at dawn.)
(The bread *will rise;* the bread *rose;* the bread *has risen.*)

REAL is informal for *really* or *very.*
Formal—My wife works *really* (or *very*) hard.
Informal—My wife works *real* hard.

REASON IS BECAUSE is an informal redundancy. Use *that* instead of *because* or rewrite the sentence.
Formal—The reason he is late is *that* he overslept.
Informal—The reason he is late is *because* he overslept.
Formal—The reason why I am here is *that* I was invited. (OR) I am here because I was invited.
Informal—The reason why I am here is *because* I was invited.

RECKON is informal for *calculate, guess, think.*

RELIGION is not a synonym for *cult, denomination, sect.*
Accurate—She belongs to the Protestant *denomination.*
Accurate—She belongs to the Christian *religion.*
Inaccurate—She belongs to the Protestant *religion.*

RIGHT: *Right* is informal for *very* or *directly.*
Formal—Being *very* alert, he drove *directly* to the police station.
Informal—Being *right* alert, he drove *right* to the police station.

RIGHT ALONG and RIGHT AWAY are informal for *continuously* and *immediately.*
Formal—We drove *continuously* (OR) *without interruption.*
Informal—We drove *right along.*
Formal—Come home *immediately.*
Informal—Come home *right away.*

RISE, RAISE: See RAISE, RISE.

SAID as an adjective (*the said party, the said document*) is a legal term, inappropriate in formal writing.

SAYS, SAID are not interchangeable. *Says* is present tense; *said,* past.
Formal—She *walks* in and *says,* "hello"; she *walked* in and *said,* "hello."
Substandard—She *walks* in and *said,* "hello"; she *walked* in and *says,* "hello."

SCARCELY: See BUT, HARDLY, SCARCELY.

SELDOM EVER: Use *seldom, seldom if ever,* or *hardly ever.*

SELDOM OR EVER: Use *seldom or never.*

SHALL, WILL: *Will* is now standard in all persons except in expressions of extreme emphasis or obligation. (You *shall* hang by your neck until you are dead.)

SHOULD, WOULD: *Should* is used for all persons to express conditions and obligations. (I *should* go home now; if you *should* decide to come, please phone ahead of time.)
Would is used for all persons to express a customary action of desire. (He *would* wake up at the slightest sound; *would* that I could sleep in!)

SHAPE is informal for *condition.*

SHAPE UP is informal for *to behave properly* or *to develop favorably.*

SHOULD OF is substandard for *should have.*

SHOW UP is informal for *appear* and *prove.*
Formal—John did not *appear* at the meeting; our team *proved* better than yours.
Informal—John did not *show up* at the office; our team *showed up* better than yours.

SIZE UP is informal for *estimate* or *judge.*

Formal—I *judged* the situation as desperate.
Informal—I *sized* up the situation as desperate.

SO, SO THAT: In clauses of purposes, *so that* is preferred to *so*.
Formal—She turned out the lights *so that* I could sleep.
Informal—She turned out the lights *so* I could sleep.
So meaning *very* is informal and often overused.
Formal—She is *very* efficient.
Informal—She is *so* efficient.

SOME is informal for *extraordinary, remarkable,* or *striking.*
Formal—He is a *remarkable* writer.
Informal—He is *some* writer!

SOMEONE, SOME ONE: See ANYONE, ANY ONE.

SOMEPLACE is informal for *somewhere.*

SOMETHING, SOMEWHAT are informal for *slightly.*
Formal—He is *slightly* overweight.
Informal—He is *somewhat* overweight.

SOMETIME, SOME TIME: *Sometime* is used in the sense of an *occasion* or *some other time; some time* means a *period* of time. (*Sometime* you will visit us and we will spend *some time* together.)

SOMEWHERES is substandard for *somewhere.*

SORT, KIND: See KIND, SORT.

SORT OF A: Omit the *a.*

SORT OF, KIND OF: See KIND OF, SORT OF.

STOP is informal as a substitute for *stay.*
Formal—We *stayed* at a motel.
Informal—We *stopped* at a motel.

STATIONARY, STATIONERY: *Stationary* means "in a fixed position." (The car remained *stationary.*)
 Stationery refers to paper and writing supplies. (We bought

some stationery.) Note that the spelling of *stationery* contains an *e,* as in envelope.

SUCH is informal when used as an intensifier.
Formal—We saw a *very* exciting movie.
Informal—We saw *such* an exciting movie.
No such a is substandard for *no such.* (There is *no such* rule (NOT) *no such a* rule.)

SURE is informal for *certainly* or *surely.*

SUPPOSED TO: Remember to add the *—d* when writing these expressions: I was *supposed* to be there; I *used* to attend his class.

SURE AND is informal for *sure to.*

SWELL is substandard for *very good.*

TAKE: Avoid such informal expressions as *take it out on, take up with.*
Formal—Do not *get angry at* her; do not *vent your anger* on her.
Formal—I would like to *become friendly with* her.

TEACH, LEARN: See LEARN, TEACH.

THAN, THEN: Do not confuse *than* (used for comparisons) with *then* (used to denote time).
He is taller *than* John.
We will eat dinner; *then* we will go to a movie.

THEIR, THERE, THEY'RE are three of the most commonly confused words.
Their is a possessive pronoun. (We went to *their* home.)
There is an adverb or expletive. (*There* are five people in that room. Where? Over *there.*) Note: *There* and *where* both indicate direction and are very similar in spelling—*ere.*
They're is a contraction of *they are. (They're* here now.)

THEIRSELF, THEIRSELVES are both substandard for *themselves.*

THESE KIND, THESE SORT, THOSE KIND, THOSE SORT: See KIND, SORT.

112

THIS HERE, THAT THERE, THESE HERE, THEM THERE are all substandard expressions. Use *this, that, these, those.*

THING is too vague a word to be used in effective writing. Whenever possible, replace it with a more specific word.

TO, TOO, TWO are another group of the most commonly misspelled words.

To is a preposition indicating *direction* and *can* sometimes be *pronounced* with a short vowel sound of "u" as in "up" and "rug." (I am going *to* the store.)

Too is an adverb which functions not only as a modifier (It is *too* hot in here), but as an intensifier meaning "also." (He owes me some money *too*.) *Too* cannot be pronounced with a short vowel but must be pronounced with the double "oo" as in "moon."

Two is a numeral. (I have *two* dollars.) It also is pronounced with the double "oo." Note, therefore, that *to* is the *only* one that can possibly be pronounced with a *short* vowel.

TRY AND, SURE AND are informal for *try to, sure to.*
Formal—*Try to* get some sleep.
Informal—*Try and* get some sleep.
Formal—Be *sure to* get some sleep.
Informal—Be *sure and* get some sleep.

THROUGH is not quite so accurate a word as *finished.*
Formal—He is *finished* reading.
Informal—He is *through* reading.

TYPE is informal for *type of.*
Formal—What *type of* book are you reading?
Informal—What *type* book are you reading?

UNINTERESTED means "bored." (I was *uninterested* in his story.)

UNIQUE, like several other adjectives (*complete, perfect, round, straight*), describes qualities that do not vary and, therefore, they cannot be compared logically. If something is *unique,* there is nothing else like it. Logically, then, one could not write *this is the most unique thing I have ever seen.* Instead, one should write *this is the most nearly unique thing.* Likewise, one should write *more nearly round* or *more nearly perfect.*

113

USED TO: Be sure to add the—*d*.

WAIT ON is substandard for *wait for*.
Formal—I am *waiting for* my mother to arrive.
Substandard—I am *waiting on* my mother to arrive.
Correct—The waitress *waited on* her customer; the nurse *waited on* the patient.

WANT IN, OUT, DOWN, UP, OFF, THROUGH are informal expressions for *want to come* (or *want to come in*), *out*, *down*, *up*, *off*, and *through*.

WANT THAT is substandard in a sentence such as *I want that he should come*. Instead write "I want him to come."

WEATHER, WHETHER: *Weather* refers to climate. (The *weather* is cold.)
    Whether is which of two. (I don't know *whether* I should go or stay.) See WHETHER.

WAYS is informal for *way* in reference to distance.
Formal—Denver is a long *way* from here.
Informal—Denver is a long *ways* from here.

WHERE is informal for *that*.
Formal—I read *that* the President won the election.
Informal—I read *where* the President won the election.

WHERE...AT is redundant and substandard. Omit the *at*.
Formal—*Where* does he live? *Where* is his car?
Substandard—*Where* does he live *at*? *Where* is his car *at*?

WHICH, WHO, THAT: *Which* refers to things or animals; *who* refers only to persons; *that* refers to persons, things, animals.

WHETHER, IF: See IF, WHETHER.

WHILE should not be used or substituted for *and* or *but*. *While* refers to "time."

WHO, WHICH: See WHICH, WHO.

114

WILL: See SHALL.

WORST WAY is informal for *very much*.
Formal—I wanted *very much* to see her. (OR) I wanted to see her *very much*.
Informal—I wanted to see her *in the worst way*.

WOULD OF is substandard for *would have*.

WOULD RATHER: See HAD BETTER, HAD RATHER, WOULD RATHER.

WONDERFUL is an overused, vague word of approval.

YOU: Do not use *you* as an indefinite pronoun. Instead use *one* or a *person*.
Formal—*One* (or *a person*) must practice constantly in order to become a ballerina.
Informal—*You* must practice constantly in order to become a ballerina.

YOU WAS is substandard for *you were*.

YOUR, YOU'RE: *Your* is a pronoun showing possession. (I like *your* coat.)
    You're is a contraction of *you are*. (*You're* too excited.)

YOURSELF, MYSELF, HIMSELF: See HIMSELF, MYSELF, YOURSELF.

PART FOUR

HOW TO WRITE THEMES: PARAGRAPHS AND ESSAYS

CHAPTER EIGHT

OVERVIEW OF PART FOUR:
PARAGRAPHS AND ESSAYS

A. DEFINITION.

If you have studied the previous chapters and done all of the assignments, you should now be able to write effective sentences. If you have read Chapter Six, you will realize that there are many fine points to be mastered in writing, some of which you should have already mastered and others which you should master soon. Although you are not expected to learn all of the grammar and usage explained in the Handbook, you should remember what the Handbook deals with and where you can look up any grammatical problem that you might encounter. Remember: the Handbook is a reference. Do not be afraid to use it.

By now you should have enough confidence in yourself and in this book to attempt larger compositions: paragraphs and essays. A written composition may consist of anything from a sentence to a volume of books. A sentence, as you realize, is a group of words that usually deals with only one idea. A paragraph is merely a series of closely related sentences explaining a particular, rather narrow topic; thus it merely elaborates on a particular idea. In effect, a paragraph is a miniature essay, for an essay is merely a series of closely related paragraphs dealing with a particular topic. An essay, therefore, provides a more detailed explanation of a topic than does a paragraph, because it encompasses a broader scope. However, both the paragraph and the essay are very similar in organization. Each contains a central idea, usually in the form of a topic sentence, supported by a detailed explanation. The paragraph explains one very narrow part of the topic; the essay explains the whole topic. Once you learn how to write a paragraph, you will very easily learn how to write an essay. Neither one is difficult to master provided that you follow some organizational pattern such as the ones which will be explained shortly.

Please remember, though: *you cannot learn to write unless you, yourself, write.* I know dozens of high school and college instructors who think they are doing a marvelous job of teaching, because they assign reading material to their students, they explain the material to their students, and they even quiz the students on the material. There is only one thing missing: the students are not required to write. Consequently, the students never do learn how to write. Although they have learned the rules, they cannot apply them. That is one of the major reasons why the writing illiteracy rate in this country is so high. Students cannot write because they have not been required to write.

To illustrate how important practice is in the mastering of a skill, I would like you to imagine for a moment that you are a coach of a professional football team. Would you hire a quarterback merely on the basis of the quarterback's ability to memorize the football rules and plays? Of course not! The idea it absurd. Nobody can possibly acquire the skills demanded of a quarterback merely by memorizing rules and plays. One must get out on the field and practice the game. In fact, one must play under pressure, time and time again, before he is any good. Any skill requires constant practice. There is no other way to learn it. And since writing is a skill, you obviously must practice the skill before you can become competent at it. To summarize, there are no short cuts. You must do the writing that is assigned.

After you have done each assignment, read your writing aloud, sentence by sentence, to make sure that each sentence makes sense and is grammatically correct. Bracket or circle any errors that you make, and then rewrite each assignment at least once. Good writing, I again emphasize, does not come easily. Rather, it is the result of "improvement." Before you can improve anything, however, you must first study it in order to determine its strengths and weaknesses. That's what *criticism* is: an analysis of something in order to determine its strengths and weaknesses, so that the original something may be improved, or at least better understood. Hopefully, I feel that anything can be improved after it is studied and better understood.

Since I cannot critique your paper personally, you as the reader and critic are playing a dual role: one, as the writer; and two, as the critic. Consequently, you must be honest with yourself and with me. For we can't afford deception. It's too late for that now.

118

B. OVERVIEW.

This section will deal with a particular type of writing, often referred to as *expository* writing or *exposition,* which means the type of writing used for *explanations.* Although there are other types of writing, such as dialogue, narration, and poetry, to name but a few, there is one particular type of writing used in business letters, exams, essays, reports, and research papers. This particular type of writing requires the writer to *explain* something in *an organized manner, to prove his point.* Obviously, then, explanatory writing is extremely important.

Just as there is more than one way to write a sentence in order to express an idea or two, there is more than one way to write a longer composition—a paragraph or essay—in order to explain or prove a point. Sometimes, however, one method is more effective than others. This entire section will emphasize the *most basic* organizational pattern in all explanatory writing, one that has been widely used since the ancient Greeks, approximately 2,400 years ago, first devised and practiced "rhetoric," which they referred to as the "art of persuasion," and which they used to present information and to persuade audiences at assembly meetings and law courts. This basic pattern of explanation, which requires a thesis statement and supporting evidence, is called the *thesis-and-support* argument (or explanation), and it will be used in five types of themes or essays: *process analysis, persuasion* by *examples, classification, comparison* and *contrast,* and *definition.*

One chapter will be devoted to each type of theme. To be sure, these organizational patterns overlap and cannot be isolated from each other in the strict sense of the word. Nevertheless, each type of theme mentioned above is organized in a slightly different manner from the others and is effective in its own way. Therefore, the more of these organizational patterns you know, the more effective will be your writing. In short, the previously mentioned analogy of the carpenter and his tools is still valid. The more tools you have at your command, the easier it is for you to do a superior job.

Even more important than the instructions in each chapter are the model themes, for they illustrate how to organize and write a particular paragraph or essay. Most important of all, however, is the written assignment at the end of each chapter. Remember, then, first study the instructions; then study the model themes; and finally do the written assignments.

CHAPTER NINE

PROCESS ANALYSIS

A. Definition.

Process analysis is a type of analysis that explains *how* something is done or how something happened. The organization in a process analysis theme provides *detailed* directions or instructions on a particular topic, explaining in *exact* chronological order a particular procedure. The steps involved, therefore, must be in exact sequence—from beginning to end. Any recipe, for example, is a form of process analysis, because the reader is given detailed and precise directions on what ingredients to use and *how to use* them, in order to prepare a particular food or drink. A recipe, therefore, is a type of organization that explains a particular procedure or process from beginning to end. Any instructions or directions that come with "How-to-do-it-yourself" kits are also forms of process analysis. The instructions are very orderly and they are precise. Detailed directions on how to reach a particular destination are also a form of process analysis. Even a historical or scientific description of how something occurred is also a form of process analysis. In short, *any detailed, systematic explanation of how something happened or how something can happen is a form of process analysis.* And since something is usually happening in a chronological order, process analysis, obviously, is a very important type of organization.

In its simplest form, process analysis involves giving elementary directions. For example, if I were to ask you how to get to Long Beach from Los Angeles International Airport, you might reply, "Take the Pacific Coast Highway south." Although such a vague answer does not provide any detail, it is, nonetheless, a form of process analysis; it has given orderly directions.

Let us now elaborate on these directions by supplying more

detail and by including the *purpose* or *central idea:* to provide precise directions that will enable anyone to drive to Long Beach from Los Angeles International Airport. These directions are to be handed out to all passengers arriving at Los Angeles Airport, even though they may never have heard of Long Beach.

The *purpose* or central idea of your writing must be stated in the handout; otherwise your reader won't know what the handout is all about. The purpose could be in the form of a title or headline: *Highway Directions from Los Angeles International Airport to Long Beach.* Then you could proceed with the directions. The purpose could also be stated in the form of a complete sentence, at the beginning of the directions, thus: *This handout will provide directions for driving to Long Beach from Los Angeles International Airport.* Finally, your purpose could be more subtly integrated in the writing itself, thus: *In order to drive to Long Beach from Los Angeles International Airport, you must travel east from the airport, past the control tower, until you reach Sepulveda Boulevard, and then turn south.* Regardless of how you state your purpose or central idea, it must be stated clearly so that the reader knows why you are trying to communicate with him and what your communication involves. If you do not state the purpose or central idea in your writing, whatever you write may be as meaningless to the reader as the windswept sands of the desert.

Now that you have crystallized the purpose of your writing, let us resume with your *detailed* explanation of road directions to Long Beach. Perhaps your writing might read something like this:

MODEL 1

In order to drive to Long Beach from Los Angeles International Airport, you must first travel east for about a mile, past the control tower, until you reach Sepulveda Boulevard. At the Sepulveda Boulevard intersection, there is a three-way stop light, in addition to clearly marked traffic lanes, which facilitate the easy flow of traffic in three directions, both for oncoming traffic and outgoing traffic. Get into the right-hand lane so that you can turn right—that is, south—onto Sepulveda, which at this point has merged with the Pacific Coast Highway, also known as Highway I. Turn right (south) and stay on Highway I until you reach Long Beach, about twenty miles away. A road sign will indicate the city limits.

The paragraph above is a series of closely related sentences about one topic or *one central idea:* road directions to Long

Beach from Los Angeles International Airport. Although there is more than one way to get to Long Beach from the Los Angeles Airport, the paragraph explains *one method* and one method only. In short, the paragraph is *unified;* and it deals with only *one aspect* of a topic.

Such a paragraph—or any paragraph for that matter—is easy to write provided that you follow certain simple rules.

B. RULES FOR WRITING A PARAGRAPH.

1. Define your topic.
2. Narrow your topic so that you write about only one aspect of it.
3. State your central idea or purpose as a topic sentence at the very beginning.
4. Support or explain your topic sentence by one or more closely related sentences, which are arranged in a logical sequence and which deal only with your topic.
5. Provide transitions or repeat key words and phrases to make your paragraph coherent—stick together. (See page 125)
6. Conclude your paragraph with a sentence that once more relates to the topic sentence.

WRITING ASSIGNMENT No.1—Turn to Page 141.

C. DEFINITION OF TERMS.

Although many of the terms already mentioned will be explained in the next chapter, you should be familiar with some of these terms right now. Consequently, they will be explained briefly, below.

1. Topic

A topic is a rather narrow part of a general subject. (Some grammarians might reverse the order and call a subject part of a topic, while other grammarians use the terms interchangeably. It really doesn't make any difference, so long as the topic—what you are going to write about—is limited in scope. This book will refer to the broad, overall subject as a "subject," and to the narrow portion of the subject as a "topic." Education, for example, is a broad, general subject. A particular college course, therefore, could be considered as a topic. A particular class section taught by a particular instructor would be a fairly narrow topic. A further *narrowing* of the *topic* would focus on a *particular aspect* of that particular class. Remember, then, the more narrow is your topic, the more vivid will be your writing, because the more specific will be your explanation. Equally important, a narrow topic facilitates unity—a oneness of purpose.

2. Thesis Statement.

The word "thesis" means a position, proposition, or belief. A thesis statement is an unproved statement of the writer's position or his belief about a particular topic. Since the thesis statement *summarizes* the *central idea,* it obviously is the *most important* sentence of all, for it tells the reader what the essay is all about. Moreover, it gives the *purpose* for the particular piece of writing, and expresses the writer's *attitude* toward his topic. Every essay, therefore, should have a thesis statement. If there is no thesis statement, there will almost certainly be no unity, and the reader might as well go around in circles as read the essay. The thesis statement is usually most effective if it is placed in the opening paragraph of the essay. Also, it is most effective as the first sentence in the paragraph or as the second or final sentence in the paragraph. Whatever you do, though, do not bury it in the middle. It is a sign post; it gives the reader directions. Let him see it right away, if at all possible.

3. Topic Sentence.

Many teachers use the terms "thesis statement" and "topic sentence" interchangeably. A topic sentence is merely a thesis statement for a particular paragraph. Therefore, the same rules apply. Remember, then, *the topic sentence, like the thesis statement, gives the writing purpose and unity by providing a road sign which states the central idea.* If at all possible, place the topic sentence at the beginning of the paragraph.

4. Coherence.

The property of similar things sticking together is called coherence. In writing, coherence is achieved by one sentence leading into the next, either *logically* or by means of *transitions, reiterations,* (repetition), or *explanations.* The same definition applies to paragraphs. One of the most common and effective methods of achieving coherence is by repeating key words and phrases, and by supplying transitions—words like *and, but, however, therefore, etc.,* which have already been discussed in earlier chapters (3-5). For your convenience, however, here is a list of the most commonly used connectives and transitions.

LIST OF CONNECTIVES AND TRANSITIONS SIGNALING:

A. ADDITIONAL FACTS (SERIES): again, also, and, another, besides, but also, equally important, finally, first, further, furthermore, in addition, initially, in the first place, last, lastly, likewise, moreover, next, plus, secondly, to begin with, then too, thirdly, too.

B. SERIES: (Note: *This particular list is invaluable for writing a process analysis.*)
   1) initially, first, first of all, to begin with;
   2) second, secondly;
   3) third, thirdly;
   4) next, after that, afterwards;
   5) to conclude, in conclusion, finally.

C. COMPARISON (SIMILARITIES): as, as with, as though, also, by comparison, in like manner, in the same way, likewise, or, similarly.

D. CONTRAST OR CHANGE OR CONDITION: although, anyhow, any way, at the same time, but, by contrast, despite, either, even though, for all that, however, if, in any event, in contrast, in spite of, instead, nevertheless, neither, nonetheless, nor, notwithstanding, on the contrary, on the other hand, or, otherwise, still, unless, yet.

E. PLACE: above, across, among, adjacent, below, beneath, beside, between, beyond, farther, here, in, into, nearby, nearer, on, opposite to, over, there, under.

F. CAUSE OR PURPOSE: all things considered, because, for, for this purpose, if, in order to, with this object in mind, since, toward this end.

G. RESULT: accordingly, as a result, because, consequently, for this reason, hence, obviously, since, so, then, therefore, thus.

H. REPETITION: all of this means, as has been noted, as has been stated, finally, in brief, in conclusion, in essence, in other words, in short, on the whole, that is to say, to conclude, to summarize.

I. SPECIFIC EXAMPLES: a few of these are, especially, for example, for instance, in particular, let us consider an example, the following will illustrate, to illustrate, specifically.

J. EMPHASIS: basically, essentially, certainly, in fact, indeed, of course, truly.

K . TIME: after, afterward, at last, at length, as soon as, at present, before, currently, finally, immediately, in the meantime, later, meanwhile, now, not long after, since, soon, then, until, when, whenever, while.

L . AMOUNT: all, few, fewer than, greater, less than, more than, most, none, over, under, several, smaller, some.

5. Unity.

Unity means a "oneness" of purpose and subject. A unified sentence expresses one idea. A *unified paragraph explains one idea* by dealing with only one aspect of a narrow topic in one tense from one point of view. Unity can be achieved, therefore, by narrowing the topic, by maintaining a consistent point of view both in tense and person, and by eliminating any sentence that does not deal directly with the topic. (See section 16, Point of View Shifts, in the Handbook, pages 63-65.)

6. Development.

The development of a paragraph involves supplying *detailed explanations* or *examples* which support the topic sentence. Since the topic sentence is usually framed as a generalization that demands proof, it must be supported by *specific evidence* or detailed explanations. The more detailed is the support, the more developed will be the paragraph. Likewise, an essay requires development. A well developed essay will contain several well developed paragraphs, all of which support the topic sentence in the essay.

D. ORGANIZING THE PROCESS BY ANALYZING ITS PARTS.

Before you even begin to write a process theme, you must first think of a particular process that you wish to describe. Secondly, you must divide the process into a series of *very detailed steps* in their *exact sequence*. If the steps are not in order, the whole paragraph, or even the whole essay, will be disorganized because it will be incoherent. Thirdly, you must arrange the steps into broad categories that will later become paragraphs. Then, and only then, should you attempt to write the essay.

To illustrate, let us think of a very simple process: *getting up in the morning*. Let us first list some steps without bothering to place them in their proper order.

1. Shut off alarm clock.
2. Get dressed.
3. Take a shower.
4. Eat breakfast.
5. Get out of bed.
6. Cook breakfast.
7. Shave or put on makeup.
8. Wake up.

If you were to write a paragraph now using the sequence of steps listed above, your sentences would be incoherent. They would not make sense because they would not relate to one another. Consequently, the whole paragraph as such would be incoherent. To illustrate such incoherence, let us examine the example below.

(EXAMPLE OF INCOHERENT PARAGRAPH)
I get dressed. I shut off the alarm clock. I take a shower. I eat breakfast. I get out of bed. I cook breakfast. I shave. I wake up.

Such a series of disorganized sentences illustrate what could happen if one were to attempt to write a paragraph without thinking about any sequence or organization. To say the least, the arrangement of such sentences out of sequence is absurd. One does not get dressed before he showers, nor does one eat breakfast until he has first cooked it. Obviously, therefore, *every properly written paragraph must be organized.* The sentences must follow each other in their proper sequence, from beginning to end.

E. DETERMINING THE PROPER SEQUENCE OF STEPS FOR COHERENCE.

Let us now correct the sequence, listing first things first.

1. Wake up.
2. Shut off alarm clock.
3. Get out of bed.
4. Take a shower.
5. Get dressed.
6. Cook breakfast.
7. Eat breakfast.

Let us now attempt to write a brief paragraph by writing sentences in their *proper order* as listed above.

MODEL 2

I wake up. I shut off the alarm clock. I get out of bed. I take a shower. I get dressed. I cook breakfast. I eat breakfast.

To be sure, we have written seven sentences, all of which make sense, and all of which are arranged in their proper sequence. However, they certainly do not read well. They are much too abrupt, and their effect on the reader could be compared to the effect on a driver bumping along a gravel, washboard road. What they need is something to *smoothen* the effect, to glue them together so that they *flow* into one another. Obviously, then, they need revision, which must include a variety of sentence patterns. Moreover, the sentences need transitions so that the connection between them is smooth and natural.

Let us, therefore, rewrite the paragraph by revising the sentences themselves and by supplying transitions. Finally—and most importantly—let us begin the paragraph with a *topic sentence* that tells the reader what the paragraph is all about.

F. SUPPLYING A TOPIC SENTENCE AND TRANSITIONS FOR COHERENCE.

MODEL 3

Every morning I follow a certain procedure in getting up. **First of all, after** the alarm clock rings, I wake up **and** turn it off. **Secondly, I** get out of bed, take a shower, shave, **then** get dressed. **After** I am dressed, I cook breakfast, and **finally** I eat.

The brief, forty-nine word paragraph above now contains only four sentences instead of seven, yet it explains clearly and smoothly the particular procedure of getting up in the morning. Note the transitions (in bold face) which smoothen the sentences and help them stick together, thus providing coherence. The paragraph, therefore, is an improvement over the previous ones because of the revised sentence structure, which not only combines several steps into one—still in their proper sequence—but also smoothens the effect through transitions.

G. DETAIL FOR DEVELOPMENT.

Even though the paragraph above is coherent and reads well,

and even though it is unified—since it describes only one thing (getting up in the morning)—it is still rather brief for a paragraph. What it needs now is more development—that is, more detail which would explain a little more fully the process of getting up. Let us, therefore, furnish a little more explanation to help develop the paragraph.

For example, we might want to know whether the writer merely wakes up, shuts off the alarm clock, and then gets out of bed; or whether he stays in bed a while, debating whether or not he should get up. The topic sentence should supply us with his attitude toward the whole process. After getting up, does he merely take a shower and shave, or does he adjust the water to the right temperature and then soak under the shower? What about the manner in which he gets dressed? Does he do it hurriedly, or does he take time to select the proper clothes?—for example, the right shirt? These questions and others could be answered in detail, thus developing the miniature paragraph into a well developed one that completes the picture of getting up.

Let us now supply the much-needed detail just mentioned, to help develop the paragraph.

MODEL 4

Every weekday morning, just before seven o'clock, the clang of the alarm clock abruptly jars me awake from a sound, deep sleep, to remind me that as much as I would like to stay in my warm bed, I have no alternative but to get up and tackle the dreary process of **getting ready** for work. **Automatically, I turn off** the **alarm clock, then** struggle with my conscience, debating whether or not I have **time** to doze for another five minutes. Invariably, my **conscience** wins, and I stumble out of **bed** toward the bathroom where I enter the stall shower, turn on the water to hot, **and** wait for about two or three **minutes until** the ice-cold **water** actually becomes hot. **Then** I adjust the **water** temperature to warm **and** stand under the **shower,** soaking, just **soaking,** enjoying every **minute** of it. **Showering** is the only enjoyable part of **getting up. After** some four or five **minutes,** I have reached the stage where I am more than half-**awake, and I then turn off** the **shower,** dry my body vigorously with a large, soft bath towel, and emerge feeling somewhat ready to **begin** the day. I leave my face wet, **however, because** a **wet** beard soaks up lather much more readily than does a dry one, thus making it easier to **shave.** I try not to cut myself while **shaving,** but every once in a while the razor nicks a pimple, and I have to apply a styptic pencil to stop the bleeding. **For that reason,** among others, I hate **shaving. In fact,**

129

next to **getting up out of bed, shaving** is the worst part of the day for me. **After I have finished shaving** and have applied shaving lotion, which cools my face and helps to further **wake me up,** I get dressed rather hurriedly, without making much of a production, except for finding my socks. <u>**My bedroom is rather dark, and I can never seem to find two socks that match and don't have holes in them.**</u> **Consequently,** I end up swearing and wasting about **five minutes** before I finally find the right **socks. By now** I glance at the **clock** and realize that I have only **twenty minutes** left in which to cook breakfast and leave the apartment. **Almost frantically, I rush** into the kitchen, turn on the front stove burner, place a half-filled kettle of water on the burner, **and then** pour myself a glass of orange juice and wait for the water to boil. **Suddenly** I realize that I **still have** about **eighteen minutes left, so** I turn on another **burner,** put a small frying pan on, drop a little margarine into the pan, and then crack an egg into the pan. **After that, I drop** a slice of bread into the toaster. In about three **minutes,** the **kettle** starts whistling, the **egg** starts crackling, and the **toast** pops up. **Almost** in one operation, I **turn** off both **burners,** remove the **egg** from the pan into a dish, and butter the **toast. Then** I make a cup of instant coffee and sit down to eat. I can never quite get used to the idea that **despite** my **frantic rushing** around, I always seem to have about **five minutes left** after **eating breakfast. Almost** reluctantly, **then,** I get up from the table, put the dishes in the sink, **and finally** leave for work.

The paragraph above [*Model 4*] is now a fully developed process theme, for it describes in *detail* a systematic procedure: getting up in the morning. It is superior to *Model 3* because of this detail and because it lets the reader know about the writer's *attitude* toward his topic; that is, it explains how the writer *feels* while getting up in the morning. By supplying abundant detail, the writer has vividly explained the entire process. Even though such detail, particularly as it concerns the writer's attitude, is not absolutely essential in writing a process theme, the more detail you can supply, the more vivid will be your writing, and, generally speaking, the more enjoyable it will be for somebody to read it. Therefore, always try to supply as much detail as you can in your explanations. As a beginning writer, you are much better off with "too much" detail rather than with "not enough."

Notice how the writer achieves *coherence* between sentences, as well as *unity* within each sentence, by the use of *transitions, repetition* of key words and phrases, and *explanations*. Each sentence either leads into or is linked with the next one through these devices. (Some of these devices are in bold face for illustration.) One sentence, which is also underlined, explains why the writer must make a production about finding his socks. The overall effect of each sentence dovetailing into the next is one of smoothness, an uninterrupted flow from beginning to end. Thus, even though the paragraph is unusually long, the reader does not have to stop or even pause in order to recall what he has been reading; each sentence relates directly to the previous one, and they all deal with only one topic.

**WRITING ASSIGNMENT No. 2—SEE PAGE 141
AT THE END OF THE CHAPTER.**

H. DEVELOPING OR EXPANDING PARAGRAPHS INTO AN ESSAY.

You will recall that a paragraph has been defined as a miniature essay. In other words, an essay is a series of closely related paragraphs explaining a particular topic. The paragraph you have just read [*Model 4*], beginning on page 129, is rather long to be classified as a paragraph; in fact, if it were any longer, it would read better as a series of two or three paragraphs, each dealing with a particular *aspect* of getting up, such as showering or eating breakfast. Even in its present state, it could well be divided into two paragraphs, the first one describing the process of getting up, and the second one dealing with breakfast. However, it has been written as only one paragraph on purpose, in order to illustrate how a paragraph can be fully *developed* by means of detail.

1. Paragraph Length—Unity

The average paragraph usually runs about one hundred to two hundred words in length. If you are writing on regular (8½ x 11) lined paper, and if you double space (write only on every other line)—so that you can make corrections with ease—you will require just over a page for a hundred-word paragraph. Therefore, you can guide yourself accordingly if you are wondering about how many words you have written, although there is certainly no hard-and-fast rule about how long a paragraph ought to be. Some paragraphs, particularly when used for effect, are only one sentence long; others may be as much as four hundred words long. But the average length of a well developed paragraph, such as this one, is approximately 150 words. That is only an estimate, because I never count the exact number of words. Basically, a paragraph should be long enough to develop *one* particular aspect of a topic, but brief enough for the reader to remember what he has read.

If a paragraph deals with only one aspect of a topic and is brief enough so that the reader can remember what he has read, the next question you might ask is this: How do I know when one paragraph is supposed to end and when another is supposed to begin? (This is one of the confusing problems with beginning writers.)

Again, there is no hard-and-fast rule. A paragraph deals with one aspect of a topic. If the paragraph becomes a burden, that is, if it becomes so long that it gets out of hand, obviously it no longer fits the classification of a paragraph because the writer has included more than one aspect of the topic. In other words, *he has not organized his paragraph.* Instead, he has probably expanded his paragraph into an essay without bothering to divide his essay into paragraphs. Although there is nothing grammatically wrong with what he has done, the error is really one of form. For the convenience of the reader, more than for any other reason, a long theme (essay) should be set off into less cumbersome units, called paragraphs. Otherwise, the form would be extremely hard to follow and understand. Moreover, by dividing an essay into paragraphs, the writer also benefits, for he is better able to organize his theme, to make a point and to stick to it. Consequently, for the sake of convenience, particularly for the reader, but also for the writer, *an essay must be set off by paragraphs, each one dealing with only one aspect of the general topic.*

2. The Essay—A Sequence of Related Paragraphs.

To illustrate the divisions between a paragraph and an essay, let us think of a topic about which we could easily write a process theme. This topic is familiar to practically everyone who has ever experienced a flat tire while driving a car. If I were to ask you now to write a detailed essay explaining how to change a flat tire, you would probably begin something like this: "In order to change a flat tire, the first thing one does is to loosen the lug bolts and jack up the car." Your essay would thus involve about four or five steps. Remember, though, the assignment requires a *detailed* account of the procedure, from beginning to end. Therefore, you must analyze the sequence of steps from the very beginning, when you first hear the blowout or feel the flat, until you have completed the process of changing the tire and have driven away. Since you must explain every step in detail, your theme cannot possibly be developed fully in only one paragraph; it will have to be expanded into a *series* of well developed paragraphs on the same subject. Your theme will be classified then as an *essay.*

The first thing you must do, therefore, is to list the sequence of steps to be used in changing a flat tire. You must begin at the very beginning, when you first realize that something is wrong with the steering. After a second or two, you will probably realize that you have a flat tire. Your detailed sequence of steps for the process theme might be listed thus:

Detailed Sequence of Steps to be used For Changing a Flat Tire:

1. Hold wheel firmly to control car, but do not apply brakes.
2. Reduce speed gradually by taking your foot off gas.
3. Glance in rear-view mirror and side mirror to survey traffic.
4. Determine which shoulder of the road can be reached most safely.
5. Glance quickly behind to confirm your observation in step 3. (This step is necessary because of possible blind spots in the car.)
6. Begin to signal immediately for a turn. (Assume the traffic following allows for a right-hand lane change.)
7. Continue signaling and gradually pull over to the right-hand *shoulder* of the freeway, *gradually* bringing the car to a stop.
8. Park the car *off* the freeway.
9. Set the signal indicator (red flashing lights) to "on" position. (If car does not contain dual flashers, use left-hand signal indicator to warn approaching traffic.)
10. Pull the keys out of ignition, after putting the car in *park.*
11. Set the emergency brake on.
12. Survey rear traffic.

13. Exit from right-hand side of car.
14. Raise hood to indicate car trouble.(This rule varies in different states.)
15. Walk around car to determine which tire is flat.
16. Open the trunk.
17. Remove jack, other tools, and spare tire.
18. Examine spare tire.
19. Assemble jack and other equipment. (List equipment.)
20. Place jack under proper bumper, next to flat tire. (Assume flat is on right-rear tire.)
21. Block opposite wheel with heavy object.
22. Remove hub cap.
23. Loosen lug bolts on flat, with lug wrench.
24. Jack up car about two inches, so tire can be removed.

25. Remove lug bolts and place them in hub cap.
26. Remove flat tire.

27. Raise tire so new tire can be put on wheel.
28. Attach new tire to wheel.
29. Finger screw lug bolts on tire, as tight as possible.
30. Lower car until it is again level.
31. Tighten lug bolts with lug wrench in alternate pattern, as tightly as possible.
32. Replace hub cap.

33. Remove jack and other equipment, and replace them in trunk.
34. Put flat tire in trunk. (Note: Steps 34 and 33 may be reversed, depending on where spare tire is located.)
35. Remove blocks and put them in trunk.
36. Close trunk.
37. Re-inspect newly replaced tire.
38. Lower the hood back to normal position.
39. Re-enter car from right-front side.
40. Replace key in ignition, and after making sure that enough clearance is left to re-enter freeway safely, signal with left indicator and drive away.

I. SELECTING THE MAJOR PARAGRAPH BREAKS BY BROAD CATEGORIES.

Now that we have listed in detail the sequence of steps involved in changing a flat tire, we must determine which *steps* would logically *fall into broad categories* that might serve as paragraphs by themselves. Strictly speaking, "our" decision depends upon both you and me; therefore, it is quite possible that what I feel should be included in a particular paragraph will not necessarily be included in your paragraph. In other words, your decision as to which step belongs in which category is largely arbitrary. You may differ with what I suggest as the *natural breaks* in this particular theme. And you might very well be right. Furthermore, you—as the writer—might even decide that you want to write as many as four or five paragraphs instead of the three which I suggest. Again, the decision is arbitrary. However, as a guideline, we all will probably agree that the procedure of steps could easily be classified in three broad categories, as indicated in the outline by means of a double line; or the steps could fall into four classifications, as indicated by the single line separating steps 26 and 27.

The first category or paragraph should include driving the car off the freeway onto the shoulder of the road, and getting out of the car (steps 1 through 12 or 1 through 13). The second division would probably include the examination of the car and equipment, and possibly the removal of the flat tire (steps 13 through 26). It might even involve the replacement of the flat with the new tire (steps 27 through 32), although these latter steps would probably fall into another category or paragraph in the estimation of many writers. Therefore, a single line indicates the separation of this paragraph. Finally, the last category or paragraph should include the final steps, either 33 through 40, or 27 through 40, depending upon whether the writer uses three or four paragraphs.

Again, let me emphasize that these steps appear to me as the natural breaks for paragraphs in such an essay. You—as mechanic or writer—have every right to disagree with me. It really doesn't matter, so long as you divide your essay into logical divisions, which will become paragraphs, each one dealing with one aspect of the topic. Finally, the outlining mentioned above should enable you to develop your paragraphs adequately. (See pages 128-131.) Therefore, you would be better off attempting to write three or four paragraphs in such an essay rather than five or six paragraphs. Remember, one sentence does not *normally* constitute a paragraph, nor do two or even three sentences. As a *guideline*, I again suggest that you allow at least one page, double spaced, for a paragraph. That way you will soon get the feel of an adequately developed paragraph.

J. LINKING PARAGRAPHS TOGETHER.

As I have already mentioned and illustrated in this chapter, there are three basic methods of achieving coherence, whether between sentences or between paragraphs. These methods include the use of *transitions,* the use of *repetition* of key words and phrases, and the use of detailed *explanation.* Therefore, if you have studied this chapter, you should now be able to develop a theme into a unified essay of well developed and coherent paragraphs.

**WRITING ASSIGNMENT No. 3—SEE PAGE 141
AT THE END OF THE CHAPTER.**

K. STUDENT MODELS.

Study the following process themes, all of which were written by my former students, following an instruction period similar to that explained in this chapter.

THE LIFE AND DEATH OF A STEAK

Although almost everyone enjoys eating a good steak, very few people have ever given a second thought to the creation and development of a steak. Its history could even be considered personal. A calf is born, little suspecting that his future has already been destined. He soon learns to stand on his underdeveloped and shaky legs. During his suckling stage he is kept in the barnyard, where he is given every possible protection. This protection does not last long, however, for he will soon become a full grown steer; and all-too-soon he will be a steak. Now that he has grown, he is led into the pasture and grazed on alfalfa and green grass. And each night he is led back to the cattle pens. Then one day he takes a walk down the road, through the gate, and off into the sunset he goes, for the long, hot and dreary cattle drive. Through sleet and snow, through windstorms and an occasional blizzard, he travels on. Finally, he reaches his destination—the slaughter pens—to be washed, checked for disease, and then slaughtered. Then he is sectioned and sent into the packing house. There he is hung up and bled, then skinned, and cut into halves and quarters, to be sold to the markets. At the meat market he is cut into steaks, ready for the customer to purchase. Soon he is selected over all of the other steaks for a special dinner. He is seasoned with salt and pepper, either fried or broiled, and then eaten. Bite by bite his remains are consumed. Now there is nothing left but bones. But ah! the story doesn't end here; there is man's best friend to consider, good old Shep. Thus, we have the beginning of another journey, for the bones are played with, buried, then dug up, and finally devoured. And so the final curtain falls—the life and death of a steak.

HOW TO BECOME A WILD RICE HARVESTER

Before a person becomes a prolific wild rice harvester, he must have a fundamental knowledge of harvesting wild rice. First, the harvester must have the necessary equipment: a boat, a push pole, two knockers, a seat to sit on, grain sacks, and a lake that is muddy enough to grow wild rice. The rice boat by legal standards must be no more than fifteen feet long, three feet wide, eighteen inches deep, with a flat bottom. The boat can be built of wood, aluminum, or fiberglass. The push pole must not exceed fifteen feet in length and must have a fork at one end. The knockers must be made of wood and must not exceed eighteen inches in length, and they must be no more than one and one-half inches in diameter. The seat is for the pounder to sit on, and the grain sacks are for the harvested wild rice.

Two people are needed in the boat: one to stand and push the boat with the push pole, and the other to sit and pound the wild rice with the two knockers. The pusher guides the boat through the wild rice bed, using the push pole to guide and propel the boat. The forked end of the pole is pushed against the rice stalks to keep the push pole from sinking into the muddy bottom and getting stuck. Don't be ashamed or embarrassed if the pole is lost and you fall into the water and mud; this happens to everyone sooner or later. Meanwhile, the pounder sits in front of the pusher and pounds the wild rice, with a knocker in each hand. The pounder uses one knocker to bring and hold a bundle of rice over the inside of the boat, and with the other knocker he strikes the heads of the rice stalks. In this manner, then, the wild rice is harvested and planted for next year's crop.

When the boat is full of wild rice or when it is time to quit, the wild rice can be put in the grain sacks on shore or on the lake. The wild rice is sold by the pound, at prices ranging from eighty cents to two dollars a pound depending on the ripeness and fullness of the rice. The average yield of one hundred pounds per boat depends very largely upon how well the fundamentals are known by the harvester and how much effort is put into the work.

LURE FISHING

Lure fishing is a suspense filled sport in which man's dexterity is used to its fullest extent. Most of the people who fish with a lure instead of with bait are usually the type of people who like to be active and not sit continuously in one spot. The lure fisherman goes after the fish and knows exactly where to find them; and most of all, he knows how to approach them.

The first thing a fisherman learns is how to set up his line. This is usually done by attaching a swivel, a small safety-pin shaped clip, to the bottom of the line. This swivel serves as a small motor for the lure, to make it rotate in the water when the line is reeled in. To the swivel the lure is attached. The lure is usually a silver or gold color, which will catch the sunlight and attract the fish. At the base of the lure there are three hooks. These hooks must always be kept sharp, for if they are not, they may result in the loss of a fish.

After the equipment is set up, the next question is this: where does one find the right spot in the stream? Most of the fishermen look for a bend in the stream where there may be a small swirling area of water. It is here where the fish feed and where they are most likely to be.

Upon approaching the stream, the fisherman always tries to cast as far from the bank as possible, so that he doesn't alarm the fish by his footsteps or other noises. After casting, the fisherman should allow the current to work the lure across the stream and over the swirling area of water. Finally, after two or three casts, the fisherman feels a sharp tug on his line. He pulls back slightly on the rod in order to set the hook and reel the line in. Behold, he has a beautiful trout on the line, and a surge of excitement runs through him. The excitement of catching a fish, no matter how many times he has done it, is always a unique experience.

THE SIGHTS AND SENSATIONS OF KNEE—BOARD SURFING

Riding the awesome protagonist of pure nature—a wave— gives you a sensation of liberation from reality; it is a journey into the unknown. As an immense swell approaches, a dual feeling of felicity and mistrust runs through you in sudden shocks of animation. Your heart pounds with rapid anticipation of the invincible mass, and you position yourself for the peak, knowing that it can be conquered. But the question of whether you can conquer it or not is racing through your mind constantly.

As you commence down the face of the wave, you feel as though fire is raging through your bloodstream, and excitement mixed with fear grips your mind. The sensations you feel through your board can never be transmitted by anything else. By this time you should be making your bottom turn (turning at the bottom of the wave in a direction enabling you to ride it back up). To do this, you pull on the outside rail and lean back so that the skeg bites hard into the water, bringing about an ultra fast turn. During this time you are always looking up at the face of the wave, which is ready to break, and it looks as if the mouth of Mother Nature is beginning to devour your little body. But to your disbelief, you're back up at the crest, ready to make a re-entry—coming back down the face of the wave. The drop on a re-entry is one of uncontrolled sensibility, so you make another bottom turn quickly and ride the mid-face of the wave, for it is really getting tubed (hollow). Abruptly you get tubed in, enclosed by the hollowness of the wave. For a split second you see nothing. Then suddenly you are in ecstasy—tubed in by an overhanging mountainous wave—and all you see is a gigantic rainbow that enwraps you with fantastic colors. This rainbow, which is caused by the sun shining through the hollow wave, is the most beautiful thing you have ever seen. The crushing sound of the wave breaking is the anger of Mother Nature for being defied.

Finally, you crouch down and hold on for dear life until you reach the shoulder's safety, where you turn and pull out over the backside of the shoulder. By now you are electrified with excitement,for you have conquered the invincible, so you proceed to paddle out for another journey into the unknown—a liberation from reality.

THE OPERATION AND FLIGHT OF THE BOEING 737

The operation and flight of a modern jet airliner is an awesome and magnificent thing to behold, especially if you are fortunate enough to be doing the operating and flying yourself. As a former pilot for one of this nation's major airlines, I would like to render the flight crew's viewpoint of a flight in a particular type of jet airline: the Boeing 737.

Initially, the aircraft is inspected in two phases of what is called the "pre-flight check." The outside of the plane undergoes a close examination of such components as the wing devices, the tail structure, the landing gear assembly—including tires, brakes, brake linings, and wheel well—in addition to other items of vital importance to the operation of the aircraft. This outside inspection, sometimes called the "walk-around," is usually conducted by the third pilot, who is officially known as the "Second Officer."

While this is being done, the First Officer, who will be doing the actual flying of the aircraft, is busy in the cockpit (now known as the "flight deck"), going through a thorough, systematic checklist of the aircraft's systems, making certain that everything is operating within an acceptable tolerance.

The Captain, meanwhile, is in the operations office, checking the weather and possible routings, and filing a flight plan. He will also secure what is known as a "release" for the aircraft. This release consists of two basic parts: the certification from the dispatch office, specifying the plane's airworthiness for the intended trip, as well as its fuel consumption; and a card showing various data computed for this particular aircraft, on this particular day, for this particular flight. This card and its data will become a vital part of the operation of the aircraft, from take-off to landing, for it shows specific values, primarily with regard to power settings and airspeeds for specific stages of the flight. This card is called the "Take-off data card."

Soon all three pilots are seated at their respective positions in the aircraft. While the other two pilots are conducting an instrument and systems cross check, the First Officer is calling Air Route Traffic Control to obtain an airway clearance to his destination. This clearance will be issued on the basis of conflicting or potentially conflicting traffic along the planned route, and will be selected by ground controllers to allow the flight to have the safest and most direct route possible.

After all checks have been completed and all passengers are on board, clearance is given to start the engines and to taxi out to the assigned take-off runway. During this taxi roll, the pilots recheck everything, in particular those items on the "pre-take-off" checklist. Since the First Officer will be flying the plane, the Captain will act as "second pilot," handling the radio communication and responding to various commands. Shortly after this check, the tower will announce take-off clearance, at which time the pilot will position the aircraft on the runway in such a manner as to align it to the center stripe. The critical take-off sequence now begins.

Holding the control wheel firmly with his left hand, the pilot grips the thrust levers (once called throttles) with his right hand, moving them smoothly into the maximum power range. The Captain, backing him up on the power, makes five adjustments to acquire this precise "maximum take-off power" setting indicated on the data card. In addition to power settings, this data card also shows various reference speeds, such as the "decision speed" or "V-1." This is one of the most critical of all reference speeds, for it is at V-1 that the pilot is legally required to continue the take-off, regardless of any problems that might develop. If for any reason he wishes to abort the take-off sequence, he must make the decision **before** he reaches the V-1 value.

Shortly after V-1, the flight will encounter the "nose-up" speed, called "V-R" or "rotation." The Captain will call out each of these reference speeds as they are attained. On the Boeing 737, V-1 and V-R come very close together, so by the time the pilot has heard the V-1 call, he is mentally poised to rotate the aircraft and get into the air. Within a few seconds after rotation, the plane is flying, and at the first indication of a rate of climb on his instruments, the pilot calls the command, "Position rate; gear up." The Captain then activates the landing gear level to the "up" position, and the wheels slowly grind their way up into the wheel well.

Occasionally (as I can testify from personal experience), the pilots may receive a warning light at this point, indicating a wheel well overheat condition. This will frequently occur on exceptionally hot days, when the revenue load (passengers plus baggage) has been high and the wheel brakes have been used to excess during the taxi phase. The brakes simply heat up. The pilots correct this potential hazard by lowering the wheels again and allowing the action of the outside air to cool them.

The plane has now taken off, and one of the most critical phases of the flight is over. By this time the pilot has "locked on" the autopilot, and our 737 is virtually flying itself to its destination.

WRITING ASSIGNMENTS FOR CHAPTER NINE: PROCESS ANALYSIS

NOTE: Before you attempt these assignments, study each section of the chapter dealing with the assignment.

1. GIVING SIMPLE DIRECTIONS:

   a) Using at least four of the transitions listed below, write a well developed paragraph in which you describe in detail how to get from your classroom to your home. (Refer to Model 1 on page 122.)

   ## TRANSITIONS FOR SERIES:

   1) initially, first, first of all, to begin with;
   2) second, secondly;
   3) third, thirdly;
   4) next, after that, afterwards;
   5) to conclude, in conclusion, finally.

   ---

   b) Using at least four of the transitions listed above, write a well developed paragraph in which you describe in detail how to get from your home to a particular destination. Be sure to supply landmarks.

2. Using detailed explanations and transitions, write a well developed paragraph describing the process of getting up in the morning.

3. Making liberal use of transitions, as well as explanations and repetition, write a detailed essay of three or four well developed paragraphs, describing the process of changing a flat tire. For your outline, use the material listed (in sequence) on pages 133-134.

4. Write a process essay in which you describe in detail a particular process or procedure with which you are thoroughly familiar. Your essay should include about three or four *well developed* paragraphs; therefore, it will probably run about four pages in length—double spaced. (For examples, see student model essays beginning on page 136.)

CHAPTER TEN

PERSUASION THROUGH
THESIS-AND-SUPPORTING EVIDENCE

SPECIAL NOTE: Since the purpose of writing is to transfer a particular message from the writer's mind to the reader's mind, all written communication by intent is persuasive; that is, it is designed to convince the reader that the message he receives is the correct one, that the writer knows what he is writing about. Obviously, all explanatory writing falls under this category. Any explanation must have a particular purpose: to convince the reader that the writer's assessment of a particular subject is correct. Therefore, the purpose of writing is persuasion.

Because this chapter explains a particular type of organization used in logical persuasion—thesis-and-support—it may very well be the most important chapter of the entire book. If you master the thesis-and-support type of organization, you will have no trouble mastering essay examinations or critical papers in college, and you will have no trouble in writing business letters or in preparing speeches. You will also become aware of the logic or lack of it in political arguments as well as in commercial advertising. Consequently, you should pay special attention to this chapter.

I. PURPOSE: THE CENTRAL IDEA EXPRESSED
BY A TOPIC SENTENCE.

A. Narrowing the Topic.

Imagine for a moment that this is the first chapter of the book and that you don't know anything about writing an essay, a paragraph, or even a topic sentence. Now suppose that I asked you to write a few hundred words about a person—your friend, husband, wife, or anyone—but gave you no further instructions. What would you do? In all likelihood, you would become so confused that either you would give up, or you would attempt to tell the reader *everything* about the person, his whole life history: his name, where he was born, where he was raised, what he did for a living, what his hobbies were, whether or not he was married, etc. In other words, you would have listed your subject's entire life history without explaining a single point, and in so doing *you would have written almost nothing about everything.*

What could you call such a conglomeration? Certainly not an essay! And most certainly not a paragraph! Why, you may ask, could it not be called a paragraph? If you have studied the previous chapter, the answer should be obvious: lack of organization. Your hypothetical paragraph would contain too many ideas but *no central idea,* and, therefore, it would *lack purpose and unity.*

By contrast, suppose that now I were to ask you to write the same theme. What would you do? Would you not want to ask me this question: "What specifically do you want to know about the person?" If you have thought of this question, you are already aware of one of the most important aspects of writing: *purpose.* Communication must have a purpose. Every piece of writing must have a purpose. If there is no purpose, why bother to write? Even more to the point, if there is no purpose to your writing, why should anyone bother to read it? Obviously, then, *even before you begin to write, you must have a purpose.*

Continuing with our hypothetical theme about *somebody,* you will almost certainly want to pursue your questioning by asking, "What *particular aspect* of the person do you want me to describe?" You are now demonstrating clear and organized thinking, for you are trying to analyze the question in order to answer it as precisely as possible. Simultaneously, you are trying to *narrow your topic.* You are thinking about the *purpose* of your writing: to describe one particular aspect of one particular person. To summarize, you are trying to isolate the *central idea* of your writing.

Once you have decided on a particular aspect of your topic, you are well on your way to organizing a unified paragraph; for as you will recall, a paragraph must be *unified: it must deal with only one aspect of a very narrow topic, in order to express one central idea.* Once you have narrowed your topic so that it expresses one central idea, your paragraph is almost certain to hold together, for its framework has already been laid. Conversely, if you have not narrowed your topic

144

but instead have decided to write about everything, you have failed to isolate the central idea, and therefore, you have failed to lay a solid framework for your paragraph. Consequently, your writing is almost certain to fall apart, the result of which is confusion for the reader trying to figure out what you tried to say. It follows, then, if you have no central idea, you have nothing. But if you have a central idea, and if you elaborate on it and stick to it, you have everything that a well organized paragraph demands: unity, development, clarity, and coherence. In brief, *the central idea is both the purpose behind and the key to good writing.* It is for this reason that you must know not only what a central idea is, but also how to express one.

B. The Topic Sentence.

1. DEFINITION AND SIGNIFICANCE.

The central idea in practically any piece of writing can be summarized normally in one sentence, which is called a *thesis statement,* meaning a statement of one's belief. Often, particularly within the paragraph itself, the thesis statement is called a *topic sentence.* This book will refer to the thesis statement as a topic sentence because it is more commonly known by this term.

Time and again, thousands of English instructors have uttered these very words: "If you learn nothing else from this course but how to write a good topic sentence, you will have learned a great deal." That is why I cannot overemphasize how important it is for you to learn how to write an effective topic sentence. If you know how to write a good topic sentence, and if you can support it with even one good example, you will be able to pass almost any essay exam, provided, of course, that your topic sentence answers the question correctly. On the other hand, if you cannot write a good topic sentence, you are almost certain to fail any essay examination, no matter how well you know your material. It is imperative, therefore, that you learn how to write a good topic sentence.

2. RULES.

Although the topic sentence, along with other terms, was briefly defined in the previous chapter (page 124), the definition must now be developed so that you will know exactly what constitutes a good topic sentence. The following rules apply to the topic sentence; that is, the topic sentence does each of the following things:
a) It introduces the subject of the paragraph and is therefore usually placed at the beginning of the paragraph.

b) It narrows the subject into one aspect of a particular topic.

c) It is never framed as a question or title.

d) It is framed as a generalization or positive assertion that poses the question *who, how,* or *why.*

e) Since it is an assertion, it demands proof by specific, supporting examples.

f) It expresses the *central idea*—that is, the writer's *purpose* or *attitude* toward a particular topic, usually by means of one word.

g) Its attitude (central idea) is usually placed at the *end* of the topic sentence.

h) It is usually most effective when written either as a *simple sentence* or as a complex sentence, in which case the attitude should be placed in the main clause, just before the period.

i) It is least effective as a compound sentence (which expresses two ideas), and therefore should not be written as such.

3. ILLUSTRATION OF PURPOSE IN THE TOPIC SENTENCE: ATTITUDE.

In order to illustrate what an effective topic sentence is, let us imagine that you are a prosecuting attorney in a murder trial involving a defendant, John Smith, who is accused of murder. You, as the prosecuting attorney, are in court for one particular *purpose:* to convince the jury that John Smith is guilty of murder. Everything you say to the jury must pertain to that purpose. You are now required to communicate your purpose to the jury by means of one, single sentence that summarizes your central idea: your belief. This statement of your belief must obviously include your attitude toward your subject, John Smith. Such a sentence is called a *thesis statement,* because it is a statement of your belief about a particular subject. Since your thesis statement must be framed as an assertion—in this case an outright accusation—you must be able to prove it. Can you write such a thesis statement or topic sentence? Try it. It's really very simple. Perhaps your thesis statement is similar to these:

a) Ladies and gentlemen of the jury, I, as prosecuting attorney, believe that John Smith is guilty of murder.

b) Ladies and gentlemen of the jury, I am going to try to convince you that John Smith is guilty of murder.

c) John Smith is guilty of murder.

Upon examining each of the sentences above, we find that although they are very similar, they differ considerably in their *attitude* toward the subject and, consequently, in their *emphasis;* that is, they differ in their degree of certainty about the defendant's guilt. Sentence a, for example, qualifies the assertion with the words "I believe." The writer has not actually accused John Smith of being guilty; he has said merely that he *believes* John Smith is guilty. Hence, the statement is not really an assertion, not in the true sense of the word, and it is certainly *not an accusation.* It does not demand proof. Anyone is entitled to believe anything, so long as it does not infringe upon the rights of others.

By contrast, the writer of sentence b says nothing about his belief, nor does he even accuse John Smith of being guilty. He says merely that he is "going to try to convince" us that John Smith is guilty. For all we know, he may be paid to try to convince us that black is white or white is black, without believing in either. In other words, *we still do not know what he truly believes.* Although one may argue with me and say that the *attitude is implied* in the sentence instead of being explicitly expressed, the point is that a topic sentence must make an assertion; *it must explicitly express an attitude;* it must demand proof. The second sentence does not quite meet these requirements.

Differing considerably from the two previous sentences, the third one makes a very clear assertion about the subject. So positive is the assertion, in fact, that it is actually an outright accusation which demands proof. Such an accusation leaves no doubt whatsoever in the reader's mind as to the writer's intent or belief. In other words, the thesis statement is crystal clear. In as few words as possible, the thesis statement expresses a precise attitude about a particular topic, thereby fulfilling all the rules applicable to an effective topic sentence. Hence, sentence c is the most effective topic sentence of all.

A further point should be made with respect to conciseness. Usually (but not always), the more concise a topic sentence is, the more effective it is. The reader should not have to wallow through "deadwood" in order to get to the heart of the idea. Introductions and casual explanations have their place, but not in a topic sentence. Although a prosecuting attorney in a courtroom is expected to make some introductory remarks, which include addressing the jury in a polite manner, his central idea is in no way made any more clear by these additional words, "Ladies and gentlemen of the jury. I as prosecuting attorney believe that," nor by these,"I am going to try to convince you that . . ." It should be obvious, therefore, that the most effective topic sentence (or thesis statement) is the one that gets right to the point by making a positive assertion or accusation which demands proof. *It lures the reader on.* He wants to know what will happen next. As a rule of thumb, then, the briefer the topic sentence, the better.

To summarize, a topic sentence not only introduces the topic, but also expresses the writer's *attitude* toward his topic, by making an assertion or accusation that *demands proof,* or at the very least poses the question *why* or *how.* The topic sentence should be brief. Unless explanations are a part of the topic, the more concise the topic sentence, the better.

4. SELECTING EFFECTIVE TOPIC SENTENCES: ATTITUDES.

Bearing in mind the concise definition of a topic sentence just summarized above, determine which of the following are effective topic sentences.

a. Teresa is my cousin.

b. Teresa is my favorite cousin.

a. Mr. Sklove is my history teacher.

b. Mr. Sklove's history class is exciting.

a. I am now nineteen years old.

b. As an independent adult of nineteen, I have just begun to live.

a. I attended public school for twelve years.

b. I wish I had not wasted so much time during my twelve years in public school.

a. We have had a cat for eight years, and it eats regularly.

b. At mealtime our eight-year-old cat reminds me of a hungry lion.

a. While I was doing library research, I met my wife.

b. I shall never forget how I met my wife.

a. Our friends from Canada wrote us and told us that they will be visiting us soon.

b. We are thrilled about the forthcoming visit of our Canadian friends.

a. Three months ago we planted a garden in our backyard, and now we have vegetables.

b. Nothing equals the satisfaction of growing our own backyard vegetables.

a. Pollution can be found everywhere in the United States and abroad.

b. Pollution is threatening our survival.

a. Overpopulation will become a problem of some concern in future years.

b. The population explosion is already causing widespread starvation.

It should be obvious that the most effective topic sentence for each subject above is the last one in each group. Each ("b" lettered sentence), you will note, expresses a definite attitude. The other sentences contain no attitudes and are therefore classified as *dead-end;* they lead nowhere. The only reaction one might have after reading such sentences is indifference. "So what else is new?" would probably express the typical reader's reaction. Consequently, the writer should always strive for a topic sentence that not only expresses an attitude, but also lures the reader on.

An attitude is usually best expressed by a *key word* that connotes a particular emotion. It is the emotion provoked in the reader that lures him on. Thus, it is very important that you select the proper word that best describes the particular emotion you want to evoke. You should avoid such words as *good, bad, nice, fine, like, dislike, etc.,* because they are much too nebulous. Instead of depicting a particular emotion, they only generalize, and in so doing, they are virtually meaningless. Instead of being content with generalizations, then, scratch your head, consult the dictionary and thesaurus, and locate the particular word that best describes exactly how you feel about your topic. Remember: *good writing must communicate how you feel about your topic.*

An attitude, which is the crystallization of a central idea, may be expressed by a modifier, such as *favorite, exciting,* etc.; or it may be expressed by a noun or complement, such as *independent, satisfaction, starvation,* etc.; or it may be expressed by a verb or verb phrase, such as *thrilled, had not wasted, is threatening,* etc. Occasionally the imagery used in a comparison also provokes a particular emotion because of the association connected with that image. Consider, for example, how you feel when you think about this image: *a hungry lion.* The two words—hungry lion—paint a vivid picture which leaves little doubt about the writer's attitude toward his topic.

Sometimes it is necessary to write a complex sentence in order to explain your topic. When you find this necessary, make sure that your *main idea* is placed in the *main clause.* For example, note the following sentence:

Unless we do something about the terrible pollution destroying our environment, all life on this planet may someday become extinct.

Although the writer's attitude toward his topic is expressed in the introductory clause, through the use of such emotive words as *terrible* and *destroying* our *environment,* the bleak image depicting the effect of the serious problem is saved for the main clause, where it is placed at the very end of the sentence—right before the period—for greatest emphasis. The message is thereby made crystal clear: all life on this planet someday may become *extinct*.

Note the generalization: *all life* on this planet may someday become extinct. Does the writer mean *all life*—fish, birds, animals, man? Yes, that is exactly what he means. In order to prove his thesis, he would have to show how pollution has already killed a significant amount of plant and animal life, and how it will probably continue to do so until life becomes extinct unless we do something about the problem. Instead of relying on generalizations, though, he would have to use specific examples of life that have already been killed by specific types of pollution. He might show, for example, how oil drilling along the Southern California coastline has resulted in the loss of enormous numbers of fish, millions of them, washed up on shore at Long Beach during the late 1950's; and how the once abundantly plentiful crab and lobster have also continued to disappear from these waters, as the result of being poisoned by pollution dumped into the Pacific.

A *generalization,* therefore, is a *label applied to a whole class* of something; that is, it covers a number of specific examples. It is used in a topic sentence because *it summarizes* the *writer's attitude* about his subject in general as a result of specific examples. Since it is applicable to a number of examples, it obviously demands proof.

II. SUPPORTING EVIDENCE: PROOF.

In order to best *illustrate* the concept of *specific, supporting evidence* for a thesis statement—a concept that is vitally important in organizing a paragraph—let us return to the courtroom, where you are now sitting in the jury box, listening to me, the prosecuting attorney. I have just uttered my thesis statement, "John Smith is guilty of murder," a statement which you obviously recognize as an accusation. Would you now believe me and condemn the defendant to life imprisonment merely on the basis of my generalized thesis statement, merely on the basis of my accusation? Of course not! You would rightfully demand proof. Well, then, would you accept any of these statements as proof?

1) The accused has long hair and needs a bath.
2) The accused looks like a mean person.
3) The accused is a mean person.
4) The accused is a bad man.
5) The accused is a Communist.

6) The accused was once arrested for possession of marijuana.

7) The accused was in love with the victim's wife.

8) The accused was overheard arguing with the murder victim.

9) The news media claims that the accused is guilty.

None of these statements, of course, would be accepted as relevant evidence in any court of law anywhere in the world. You as a juror would likely laugh at the absurdity of such statements if they were introduced as evidence in the first place. Instead, you would want *facts* as evidence to support my accusation against the defendant, and you would not settle for anything less. A fact, you would insist, is something that is true because it has already happened or had been observed or proven, and not because it is somebody's opinion. An opinion may or may not be fact. In the opinion of some people still alive, the earth is flat, but their opinion does not make it so. Likewise, I as prosecuting attorney may believe that the defendant is guilty of murder. I may believe a lot of things, but that does not mean they are necessarily true. More often than not, an opinion is based merely on heresay or on emotion. By contrast, a fact is based on objectivity. Obviously, then, there is a great deal of difference between an opinion and a fact. You—as a member of the jury—realize the difference. You realize that regardless of what opinions you may hold, *you must be objective.* Therefore, you want *facts* which *prove* that the defendant killed the victim. You cannot possibly settle for any other kind of argument. To summarize, you will demand that the prosecuting attorney *support* his accusation (thesis statement) with *specific, relevant evidence* in the form of *facts* that *prove* the defendant killed the victim.

A. Facts.

Let us consider these statements now. *Are they specific facts, and do they pertain to the case?* Do they *prove* that the defendant killed the victim?

1. The bullet that killed the victim was fired from a particular .38 caliber revolver, according to ballistic experts of the homicide division of the Centralia Police Department, who conducted ballistic tests on the bullet which was removed from the victim's body.

2. The particular .38 caliber revolver, known as the "murder weapon" because of the ballistic tests, was found by Officer Henry Jackson of the Centralia Police Force, in the possession of the defendant, at exactly 10:07 PM.

3. The murder weapon contained the defendant's fingerprints, and

his hand contained powder burns.

4. An eye witness, John P. Bigmouth, of 3315 N. Sunburst Drive, Okanogen, California, saw the defendant aim the revolver at the victim and fire it, at exactly 10:01 PM.

5. Another eye witness, Allan Slowmouth, of Glenbourne, Manitoba, Canada, saw the victim fall straight backward, blood gushing from his head, immediately after the shot was fired, at exactly 10:01 PM.

6. The defendant confessed to the crime.

It is quite obvious that each of the statements above is a specific fact that pertains to the case and helps to support the accusation against the defendant. The first two statements point almost conclusively to the defendant's guilt. The third statement lends strong, additional support. The fourth statement, even by itself, is so incriminating that it almost ensures the evidence, as does the fifth statement. Certainly, the five statements combined illustrate beyond any shadow of a doubt that the defendant killed the victim. But just in the event that the evidence is still not adequate, the final statement concludes the case and leaves no doubt in the minds of the jurors that the defendant is indeed guilty of murder as charged. In brief, *the specific facts listed above,* especially those from statement 2 on, *are* excellent *examples which support and prove the thesis statement:* John Smith is guilty of murder.

A thesis-and-support type of essay is organized, theoretically, exactly as we have illustrated above. The writer makes a thesis statement in the form of an assertion. He then supports it with specific facts or examples that pertain to the case. He sticks to the point, discarding all irrelevant material that does not specifically support his thesis. His material is arranged in such a manner that it follows a logical order, each point being explained before proceeding to the next. He concludes by convincing his reader that because of all the evidence presented, his thesis statement has been proven to be correct.

III. EXAMPLE OF THESIS-AND-SUPPORT DEVELOPMENT IN THE ONE-PARAGRAPH THEME.

A. Selecting and Narrowing the Topic.

Now that you know what constitute an effective topic sentence and supporting evidence, let us return to our original assignment: *To write a one-paragraph theme about one particular aspect of somebody you know.* So that we can all work on this assignment together, let us create a fictional character whom we will write about.

Let us call this person Raymond. Now we have selected a *subject* for our essay. The first step is to *narrow* the subject into a *topic;* that is, we must select a particular aspect about Raymond—a trait that is particularly noticeable and one that we either admire or dislike. In other words, we must have an attitude toward this particular aspect of Raymond's character. Can you describe this aspect or trait in the form of a *topic sentence?* Can you write such a topic sentence?

1. Raymond is eighteen years old. (So what? Dead end.)
2. Raymond is my cousin. (Another dead end.)
3. I dislike Raymond. (Much better, but the sentence could be improved by focusing on why you dislike him.)
4. Raymond is a poor driver. (Much improved, but not specific enough. The word *poor* is rather vague.)
5. Raymond is a reckless driver. (Vastly improved. Good.)

The fifth topic sentence, you will notice, meets most of the requirements previously mentioned for an effective thesis statement or topic sentence. Not only does it *introduce* the *subject* of the paragraph or essay—Raymond—but it *narrows* the subject into a particular *topic:* Raymond's *driving.* Furthermore, it expresses the *central idea* by means of an *attitude—reckless—*which thus becomes an accusation. Since it is an accusation, it *demands proof:* how or why.

The *second step,* therefore, is to present *specific, supporting evidence* that clearly *proves* "Raymond is a reckless driver." (It doesn't matter whether or not we exaggerate, because the purpose of this assignment is to illustrate how a paragraph is organized, developed, and finally written. Consequently, we will require some good examples to illustrate how Raymond's driving is so bad that it is actually reckless.) Let us now compile a list of "reckless" things Raymond does when he drives. Perhaps we should start at the beginning.

B. Gathering Preliminary, General Supporting Evidence.

1. He backs up recklessly.
2. He drag races.
3. He is constantly speeding.
4. He sometimes drives through amber and red lights.
5. He is forever cutting in and out of traffic without signaling.
6. He never signals when changing lanes or turning.
7. He never comes to a complete stop at a stop sign or flashing

red light.

8. He never stops for pedestrians in a crosswalk.

9. He does not stop when school buses are flashing their red lights.

10. He does not pull over when police, fire, or ambulance sirens are sounding.

All the statements above are considerably *more specific* than the *original* topic sentence because they give the reader a "slightly" better picture of Raymond's reckless driving. For example, the generalization "reckless" can *include* any and even all of the statements above; however, the term "constantly speeding" does not necessarily include "backing up" or coming to a "complete stop." Nevertheless, these statements are still *accusations* which demand specific proof in the form of examples. In other words, each of the statements could become a *sub* topic sentence of the original, because each explains a little more clearly what we mean by "reckless." Yet each accusation in turn is still a generalization; it demands proof by concrete examples. For these reasons we should call the original topic sentence a *thesis statement* and each of the other ten statements a *topic sentence*.

Now our task becomes much simpler. Since each topic sentence lists a particular aspect of Raymond's "reckless driving," all we need to do is to *narrow* our topic by *selecting one* of the topic sentences so that we can *focus* on it, thereby describing this particular aspect of Raymond's reckless driving. In other words, we want to "paint *one* picture" about Raymond's driving, a picture the reader will not soon forget. Remember: it is better to write a great deal about a little, than a little about everything.

Our third step is to decide which topic sentence we want to use, in order to prove that Raymond is a reckless driver. Since I would like to illustrate, first of all, the development of a paragraph, and since Raymond's "backing up" doesn't have too much to do with "drag racing" or "speeding" or "cutting up" or any of the other accusations, let us concentrate on this first accusation or topic sentence. In other words, let us describe in as much detail as possible *how* Raymond backs up recklessly, and *why* his backing up is actually reckless.

Revised Topic Sentence: *While backing up, Raymond is a reckless driver.*

Now we must gather *specific* evidence to back up our topic sentence.

154

C. Gathering Specific Evidence: Supporting Examples.

1. While backing up he rarely looks behind.
2. He backs up very quickly.
3. He runs over objects in his driveway.
4. He runs over the curb.
5. Sometimes he backs into another vehicle.
6. He narrowly misses hitting pets or children in the driveway.

D. Classifying the Evidence.

You will notice that although the six examples prove Raymond to be a reckless driver while backing up, some of the examples are related. If you examine the statements carefully, you will notice that both 1 and 2 illustrate *how* he backs up (without looking to his rear, and very quickly). In other words, he backs up *recklessly,* or as the dictionary defines the term, "carelessly, heedlessly; without regard to consequences." Statements 3, 4, 5, and 6 all illustrate the *result* of his reckless driving. To summarize, the first two statements are the *cause* of what is about to happen, and the remaining statements are the *result*. This process of examining and then grouping "like" with "like" is called *classification*. It will be explained more fully in the next chapter. If you classify the evidence before you draw up your final outline, your paragraph will be organized logically, so that each sentence will relate to the next, and all sentences will relate to the topic sentence.

E. Writing a Brief Paragraph.

We are now ready to write our brief paragraph, merely by filling in the appropriate sentences and *explaining* them, by supplying *additional detail.*

BRIEF PARAGRAPH: MODEL No.1

While backing up, Raymond is a reckless driver. He rarely looks behind and usually backs up very quickly. As a result, he runs over objects in his driveway. For example, he has run over toys, a lawnmower, and even a bicycle, completely wrecking all of them. He also runs over the curb, and he has even backed into cars recklessly. Once he backed all the way into a car that was parked directly across the street. Another time he backed into a car that was passing by his

155

driveway. That's how reckless he is. He is just lucky that nobody was seriously hurt. He is also lucky that he hasn't killed any pets or children that happen to be on his driveway. Once a neighbor's child was playing nearby and Raymond barely missed hitting the child. How reckless can a person be?

WRITING ASSIGNMENT ONE: TURN TO PAGE 171.

F. Outlining for the Well Developed Paragraph.

Although the paragraph above is a good example of a brief, unified paragraph, it could be improved by further development—by supplying additional details and explanations. Let us therefore revise our simple outline and supply even more detail to explain each of the supporting examples. Then, after we have elaborated on our outline, we can rewrite our paragraph.

REVISED OUTLINE

TOPIC SENTENCE

I. *While backing up, Raymond is a reckless driver.*

PRIMARY (MAJOR) SUPPORTING EVIDENCE

A . He rarely looks behind.

SPECIFIC EXPLANATION

    1. He simply relies on his rear-view mirror.

    2. Sometimes he doesn't even use the mirror.

B . He backs up very quickly.

    1. He releases the brakes quickly.

    2. He steps on the accelerator.

C . He runs over objects.

    1. He ran over a lawnmower.

    2. He demolished a bicycle.

D . He frequently runs over the curb.

    1. He scraped his muffler once.

    2. The car's rear end needs frequent alignment.

E . He backs into other vehicles.

    1. He has backed into another car across the street.

    2. He has backed into another car that was driving by.

F . He narrowly misses hitting pets and children.

    1. He almost hit his neighbor's cat and its kittens.

    2. He barely missed hitting a neighbor's child.

G. Writing the Well Developed Paragraph.

Our outline is now complete and ready for use in writing our paragraph. All we need to do now is to write the topic sentence exactly as it is written and *to fill in the outline with appropriate sentences.* Remember, though, to achieve *coherence* (smoothness), we should supply *transitions, explanations,* and we should *repeat key words* and *phrases.*

WELL DEVELOPED PARAGRAPH: MODEL No.2

While backing up, Raymond is a reckless driver. For example, he rarely looks to his rear. He simply relies on his rear-view mirror, and sometimes he doesn't even use that. Even if he did use the mirror, his car would still have blind spots. His negligence in not looking back, therefore, is an illustration of sheer recklessness. A further example of his complete disregard to consequences is the way he backs up. He doesn't believe in gradually backing up, not Raymond. Instead, he backs up very quickly, releasing his brakes, stepping on the accelerator, and shooting straight back, running over everything in his path. He has run over a lawnmower, badly damaging both the lawnmower and his tires in the process. He has also demolished a bicycle, not to mention less costly objects, including a number of toys left on the driveway. Because he backs up so fast and doesn't look where he's going, he frequently runs over the curb, damaging not only the car's muffler, but also its rear end. The most costly consequences of his recklessness are the two cars that he backed into, on separate occasions. Once he backed into another car parked directly across the street from his home, and another time he backed into a car that just happened to be passing by his driveway. Both cars sustained rather costly damage, but fortunately nobody was seriously injured. It is also fortunate for him that he has not yet injured any of the pets, like his neighbor's cat and its kittens, which frequently crawl under the car. And it is most fortunate that he missed hitting a neighbor's child that happened to be playing nearby. As usual, Raymond wasn't looking where he was going, and in his recklessness he just barely missed hitting the child. How reckless can a person be? That's why we call him "Reckless Ray."

DETAIL AND COHERENCE: Notice how the paragraph above vividly depicts Raymond as a reckless driver, merely on the basis of his "backing up." We haven't even mentioned his "constant speeding" or any of the other reckless traits described earlier, on page 153, while we were gathering our preliminary, general supporting evidence. The reason we have been able to paint such a vivid picture is that we have supplied specific detail to back up our topic sentence. Notice how each statement numbered 1 and 2 is a *specific explanation* for the *preceding primary (major) support* (A, B, C, etc.) Remember, the more specific your explanation is, the more vivid will be your picture. And that's what good writing is: a picture through words.

Notice also how the coherence devices—*transitions, explanations,* and *repetition*—are underlined. Study them carefully, so that you will know how to supply them in your own writing. The more coherence a piece of writing has, the easier it is to read and to understand.

IV. DEVELOPMENT OF THE TWO-PARAGRAPH ESSAY.

Just as the sentence is the basic unit of communication to express one idea or more, the paragraph is the basic unit of organization for the theme or essay. An essay is usually considered to be a piece of writing that contains two or more well developed paragraphs. It should therefore be obvious that before you even attempt to write an essay, you should first master the paragraph form thoroughly. For if you can organize and write one paragraph well, you can easily write two. And if you can write two, you can easily write three, and so on. The only major difference between the organization of a one-paragraph theme and a two-paragraph theme is the *additional topic sentence,* which must then be developed in the second paragraph. The introduction of the second topic sentence is usually achieved by a transition, such as *second* or *secondly, in addition* or *furthermore* or *moreover, another reason* or *another example* or *another illustration of,* etc. Let us now select an additional topic sentence for the second paragraph of our two-paragraph theme. We will therefore return to our original thesis statement—*Raymond is a reckless driver*—and to the preliminary, general supporting evidence.

A. Developing the Two-Paragraph Outline— Preliminary

THESIS STATEMENT

Raymond is a reckless driver.
SUPPORTING STATEMENTS—POTENTIAL TOPIC SENTENCES
  1. He backs up recklessly.
  2. He drag races.
  3. He is constantly speeding.

4. He sometimes drives through amber and red lights.
5. He cuts in and out of traffic without signaling.
6. He never signals when turning or changing lanes.
7. He never completely stops at a stop sign or red light.
8. He never stops for pedestrians in a crosswalk.
9. He does not stop when school buses are flashing red lights.
10. He does not pull over when police, fire, or ambulance sirens are sounding.

CLASSIFYING THE EVIDENCE

Each of the supporting statements above is a potential topic sentence. However, if you examine the statements, you will notice that some are related to each other. For example, you will notice that statements 2, 3, and 4 deal with Raymond's "speeding," although drag racing is a separate form of speeding. Statements 5 and 6 deal with "not signaling." Statements 7 through 10 deal with "not stopping." Therefore, we could quite logically group all of the statements (2 through 10) into three broad classifications: "speeding," "not signaling," and "not stopping." For our second paragraph, we would now have the choice of three generalizations (or accusations), any of which could be developed into a paragraph. Again, these generalizations deal with:

a. *speeding*
b. *not signaling*
c. *not stopping.*

Can we rewrite these three generalizations into three topic sentences?

REVISED TOPIC SENTENCES

2. *Raymond's constant speeding is reckless.*
3. *Raymond's failure to stop is reckless.*
4. *Raymond's failure to signal is reckless.*

(Note that his failure to stop is more closely related to speeding than is his failure to signal; hence it is the third topic sentence.)

Which of these revised topic sentences would you care to use in your second paragraph? Any one of them would be excellent. However, since speeding is usually associated with reckless driving, let us choose that one: Raymond's constant speeding is reckless.

The procedure now for developing our two-paragraph essay is exactly the same as what we have already done in the one-paragraph theme. We merely draw up an outline for each of the two topic sentences and then fill in the outline with appropriate sentences, adding transitions and explanations where necessary. Although each topic sentence can be expressed as it is written above, we would introduce it (as I have mentioned) by an introductory transition. Let us now complete the outline.

B. Revised and Completed Outline for Two-Paragraph Essay.

THESIS STATEMENT FOR TWO-PARAGRAPH ESSAY
Raymond is a reckless driver.

FIRST PARAGRAPH
FIRST TOPIC SENTENCE (Choose One)

I. *While backing up, Raymond is a reckless driver.*
(OR) *To begin with,* Raymond is reckless while backing up.
(OR) *First of all,* Raymond is reckless while backing up.
(Outline and paragraph already completed. See pages 156-157.)

SECOND PARAGRAPH
SECOND TOPIC SENTENCE (Choose One)

II. *Raymond's constant speeding is also reckless.* (OR) *Secondly,* Raymond's constant speeding is reckless. (OR) *In addition to backing up recklessly,* Raymond also speeds recklessly.

PRIMARY (MAJOR) SUPPORTING EVIDENCE
A. He rarely observes posted or unposted speed laws.
SPECIFIC EXAMPLES:
    1. In residential areas, he drives 15-20 miles faster than the legal limit.
    2. In business areas, he also exceeds the limit.
    3. On freeways and interstate highways, he drives 70.
    4. He speeds even on parking lots.

PRIMARY (MAJOR) SUPPORT
B. He drives through amber and sometimes even red lights.
SPECIFIC EXAMPLES:
    1. He speeds up to make a green light, from as far away as three blocks.
    2. He races through amber lights.
    3. He sometimes races through red lights.
    4. He even drags, anticipating the green.

C. Writing the Two-Paragraph Essay.

In order to illustrate how the essay is now written, I shall merely write the first two sentences of each paragraph, following the outline we have just completed. Then you will have an assignment: to complete the second paragraph by filling in the outline with appropriate sentences.

EXAMPLE OF TWO-PARAGRAPH ESSAY

Raymond is a reckless driver. For example, he backs up recklessly. He never looks to his rear. (Paragraph is already written, page 157.)

Raymond's constant speeding is also reckless. To illustrate, he rarely observes posted or unposted speed signs.
[Complete the paragraph by following the outline on page 160 and expanding on it.]

WRITING ASSIGNMENT NO. 2: TURN TO THE END OF THE CHAPTER FOR THE ASSIGNMENT. (Page 171)

V. DEVELOPMENT OF THE THREE-PARAGRAPH ESSAY.

The three-paragraph essay can be developed in exactly the same manner as the two-paragraph essay was developed. The only difference would be the addition of the third topic sentence which would then be developed into the third paragraph. Let us now proceed to develop a three-paragraph theme.

A. Outline for Three-Paragraph Theme.

THESIS STATEMENT
Raymond is a reckless driver.

FIRST PARAGRAPH

I. *First of all, he backs up recklessly.* He never looks to his rear. (Outline is already completed. See page 156.)

SECOND PARAGRAPH

II. *Secondly, Raymond's constant speeding is reckless.* To illustrate, he rarely observes posted or unposted signs. (Outline is already completed. See page 160.)

THIRD PARAGRAPH
THIRD TOPIC SENTENCE (Choose one)

III. *Thirdly, Raymond's failure to stop is reckless. [OR] Still another example* of Raymond's reckless driving is his failure to stop. (OR SEE OTHER EXAMPLES OF INTRODUCTORY TRANSITIONS, PAGE 141)

PRIMARY SUPPORT

A. He never comes to a complete stop at a stop sign or flashing red light.

EXAMPLES 1. He merely slows down and then continues through.
2. He turns right at a stop sign or red light without first stopping.

PRIMARY SUPPORT

B. He never stops for pedestrians.

EXAMPLES 1. He doesn't stop for them in crosswalks.
2. He doesn't stop for them in the middle of the road.

PRIMARY SUPPORT

C. He fails to stop on other important occasions.

EXAMPLES 1. He doesn't stop when school buses are flashing their red lights.
2. He doesn't even pull over when police, fire, or ambulance sirens are sounding.

B. Example of the Three-Paragraph Essay.

Raymond is a reckless driver. First of all, he backs up recklessly. He never looks to his rear.
(First paragraph is already completed. See page 157.)

Secondly, Raymond's constant speeding is reckless. To illustrate, he rarely observes posted or unposted signs.
(Second paragraph should have been completed already by you, in previous assignment.)

Finally, Raymond's failure to stop is reckless. For example, he never comes to a complete stop at a stop sign or a flashing red light. [Complete this paragraph by following the outline on this page and expanding on it.]

WRITING ASSIGNMENT NO. 3: TURN TO THE END OF THE CHAPTER FOR THE ASSIGNMENT. (Page 171)

VI. THE MULTI-PARAGRAPH ESSAY.

It should be obvious now that if you can write one well developed paragraph, you can write two; and if you can write two well developed paragraphs, you can write three; and if you can write three, you can write four, and so on.

Another type of development, however, requires an introduction and a conclusion, with the major supports in the middle. That is to say, the writer includes in his opening paragraph not only his thesis statement, but also the two or three or four topic sentences (or generalizations to be proved)—all within his introduction. He then proceeds to prove each generalization or accusation in a separate paragraph. And finally, he concludes with a brief, separate paragraph that summarizes what he has just proved. For example, we might have "listed" or "summarized" all of Raymond's reckless driving habits in our introduction and then proceeded to focus on each trait in a separate paragraph, concluding with another summary of what we had proved. The basic outline might then have read like this:

Raymond is a reckless driver. Not only does he back up recklessly, but he constantly speeds and fails to stop when he should.

First of all, Raymond is reckless while backing up . . . .

Secondly, his constant speeding is reckless . . . .

Thirdly, Raymond's failure to stop when he should is outright recklessness . . . .

To conclude, Raymond's driving habits clearly indicate that he is too reckless to be allowed to drive.

For an illustration of such a multi-paragraph development, I urge you to study the essay entitled, "Effects of the Working Woman's Absence from Home," on page 165. Notice that the introduction contains a summary or overview of the entire essay. It contains not only the thesis statement, but it also defines the family and indicates how each member is affected by the working woman's absence from home. The second, third, and fourth paragraphs in turn are each devoted to one particular member of the family; and the final paragraph—the conclusion—briefly reinforces the introduction.

VII. MODEL STUDENT ESSAYS.

NOTE: Although I have hundreds of students' essays in my files, I have tried to select for reproduction those which best illustrate the major points I have explained concerning organization. All of these student essays, like those in the previous and following chapters, have been reproduced almost exactly as they were written, without major editorial changes or corrections. The thesis-and-support essays reproduced below were *all* written in class, the first two within a seventy-minute period, after approximately six weeks of instruction; and the remainder within a fifty-minute period, after fourteen weeks of instruction. I must emphasize that these essays are not masterpieces. They were not written by professional writers. They are merely good student essays, written as class assignments, by entering college freshmen, both in regular, transfer courses and in remedial courses. I hope that you, as another student of mine, will soon be able to write as well as these students have. Perhaps in a very short time you will be able to write even better.

CLEAR EXPRESSION

OUTLINE:

The ability to express oneself clearly is the key to success.
I. Clear expression is important in community life and social life.
II. The skill to express oneself clearly will promote a successful educational career:
A. Oral expression is needed before school.
B. Both oral and written expression are needed in school subjects.
III. Clear expression is required in the business and professional world, both for employers and employees.

The ability to express oneself clearly is the key to success. In community life and social life a person may find himself in conversational situations that require clarity and coherence of thought and expression. Since discussion and argumentation may become necessary in community life, the success of presenting an idea or an opinion depends largely upon the ability to express oneself clearly, an ability which may be rewarded with leadership. When explaining a new method, a situation, or exchanging an idea with a neighbor, the ability to explain oneself clearly creates a sense of confidence. The ability of a parent to give clear instructions and explanations to a child enables the child to absorb the information clearly, to think clearly, and to express himself clearly, all of which are essential for success in his school career.

The skill to express oneself clearly will promote a successful educational career. Although a person may develop oral expression skills while attending school, he must have some oral expression ability before he even starts school. Every subject in school requires oral and written expression. A clear oral summary, a clear written report, or the ability to ask a clear question may lead to higher grades and achievements.

The skills to express oneself clearly will affect one's position in the business world and professional world. In many positions a person may be confronted with the responsibility of explaining specialized aspects of a problem and giving professional instruction. A person may have the knowledge and the facts of a particular procedure, but he must also have the ability to present the instructions and facts in a clear and concise language, an ability which may be an indicator for the employer in judging an employee's competence for advancement.

In all aspects of life, therefore, the ability to express oneself clearly is the key to success.

EFFECTS OF THE WORKING WOMAN'S ABSENCE FROM HOME

OUTLINE:

The working woman's family is often adversely affected by her absence from home.

I.   Introduction: Her absence affects the entire family, which includes her children, her husband, and even herself.
II. The children are affected in several ways:
     A. No encouragement.
     B. No stimulus.
     C. Empty house—psychological problems.
III. The husband is affected:
     A. He feels inadequate as a provider.
     B. He feels she is neglecting her responsibilities as a mother.
IV. She, herself, is affected:
     A. No time for her household chores.
     B. No time for her husband and family.
     C. She blames herself.
V.   Result: The entire family is adversely affected by her absence.

The working woman's family is often adversely affected by her absence from home. Since her hours at home are lessened, naturally, she does not have as much time to attend to household affairs as she might otherwise have. Her neglect of the household affairs causes discomfort to the entire family. The man of the house does not want to have friends over. The children are embarrassed to ask playmates to come over with them. Even the lady of the house is irritable, since she would like to have a tidy home but does not have time. The meals, too, are neglected. The lack of time does not allow the working woman to plan meals as she used to do. The meals at times are unbalanced, and the tension at the table could easily cause indigestion.

The working woman's absence from home has an adverse affect on each member of the family in a particular way. First of all, the children are affected. When the mother leaves for work before the children leave for school, she is not there to prompt them to do their best that day. Naturally, she does not have as much time in the evening to help and encourage them in their homework, since she must attend to washing, ironing, and other household duties. Therefore, the children do not receive the stimulus necessary for higher achievement. If Mother is not home when the children return from school, they must come home to an empty house that may seem strange and unfriendly to them. This may even cause psychological problems. At any rate, Mother's presence would make things a little more comforting.

Secondly, the working woman's absence from home causes adverse effects on the husband. Down through history man has had the prime responsibility of providing food and shelter for the entire family. When his wife secures a job, it may lessen his sense of responsibility and make him feel inadequate as the provider. Just as man has had the responsibility of providing, woman has assumed the responsibility of child bearing, child rearing, and teaching. If she begins working, her husband might feel that she is neglecting her responsibilities to the children and, therefore, he may lose confidence in her as a good mother.

Even the working woman herself may be adversely affected by her absence from home. Although she has so little time after working an eight-hour day, not even enough time to take care of household chores, she blames herself for being negligent and may become irritable. She feels that she does not spend enough time with her family and is sad because of this. She cannot be her usual, cheerful self, and she feels that she has failed the ones she loves the most.

Consequently, the entire family might very well be adversely affected by the lady of the house assuming the responsibilities of a working woman who must be absent from home a great deal of the time.

THE LIBERATED WOMAN

The working woman's family is not necessarily affected adversely by her absence from home. Although the liberated woman now spends less time at home than she did before, she has not given

166

up her responsibilities. She still attends to her husband and children, but with even more warmth than she did before. She sees them less and, therefore, she loves them more intently. Moreover, she may very well be a happier woman now that she is working, and her improved morale will be reflected in her attitude toward her husband and children. In brief, it is not the amount of time one spends that is important; rather it is the quality of time that really matters.

Her improved morale is the direct result of no longer feeling "tied down" to a housewife's role that she can describe only as "boring." Instead of being confined to her home, with all its monotonous chores, day after day, the liberated woman now has the challenge of a different job, with all its compensations: added income, new associates and friends, and a new self-image—a feeling of independence. These compensations more than offset the few hours she spends away from her family.

To begin with, she and her family now have an added income, which may very well liberate them from their previous frustrations. The extra income may be used in several ways: to pay outstanding or pressing bills, to buy frills or luxuries, or even to bank or invest. The previous financial worries, which almost certainly plagued the family when it lived on one income alone, have now been eliminated. Instead of the tension which then existed in the family, trying to make ends meet, a new positive attitude now prevails. The family can afford a few frills, possibly even luxuries. There may even be some money left over to bank or to invest. At the least, her added income should enable her to afford part-time household help, thus liberating her from tedious tasks like dusting, cleaning, and the like. With these frustrations eliminated, her morale improves. And her improved morale cannot help but to make her a better wife and mother.

The second compensation of her new job is a different outlook on life, a wider scope. Instead of being isolated in her neighborhood, with her neighborhood friends and their neighborhood gossip, the liberated woman is involved in the mainstream of the working world. She is exposed to new surroundings, new acquaintances, new ideas, and a new outlook on life. She becomes a different person—a more interesting one. Consequently, when she does spend time with her husband, she will have something else to talk about besides her boring household chores and her children. She thus becomes an interesting companion as well as a wife, and their relationship improves. Likewise, when she sees her children, again her improved morale makes her a better person. Instead of being irritated with them over little matters, she enjoys them and overlooks the trivia. In turn, they appreciate Mother more and no longer take her for granted.

Perhaps the most important compensation of all is her new self-image, her feeling of independence. Whereas she had felt limited in her previous role as wife and mother, she now feels that a new dimension has been added to her life. Now, instead of feeling entirely dependent upon somebody else for a livelihood, she feels that she is more than pulling her weight. For she is more than just a wife and mother; she is an individual. She has her own life to live. She, too, is important.

OBSCENITY LAWS

Obscenity laws are not necessary in American society today. Obscenity can only be defined by each individual for what it means to himself. The strictest of obscenity laws would banish great works of art; the most lenient would diminish the freedom of some individuals.

Although "freedom of choice" is not detailed in the United States Constitution, the liberty of "the pursuit of happiness" was the basis of the Declaration of Independence. If one's happiness is fulfilled by pornography, by all means he should have the right to employ any (and all) "instruments" which will complement his needs, so long as he does not interfere with the pursuits of another's happiness. On the other hand, one who is offended by pornography is entitled to his right of happiness. But he is **not forced** to be disturbed by "obscenity"; he has the choice of whether or not he will employ the implements of pornography. A cliche could very well sum up this choice: "One man's medicine may be another man's poison."

Not everyone can agree with each other's tastes in art. One cannot say that Michelangelo's **David** is a work of obscenity. By carving marble, Michelangelo expounds on the beauty of the human body. His works cannot be banned simply because they upset a few people, by showing the erogenous zones of the male. That would not be justice, because the statue also brings joy to many who marvel at the sculpture. Neither can one ban the writings of William Shakespeare, long to be known as "the greatest English writer." Can one censor **Romeo and Juliet,** a play which has lasted for centuries, merely because two lovers have a bed scene? It is not up to the discretion of a few to establish the "forbidden" for all.

Therefore, this writer objects to all laws on obscenity, for obscenity means a different thing to each individual. Laws (such as the recent California Proposition Number Eighteen) could ban the works of the greatest artists in English history, as well as deprive the "pursuit of happiness" for many Americans. And laws are based on the judgment of a few, who govern all. These lawmakers cannot please the interests of all individuals; therefore, they should not make regulations which conflict with the ideals that founded this nation.

CAPITAL PUNISHMENT

Although capital punishment should exist as a deterrent to violent crime, the administration of the death penalty should be sharply revised. In a recent article that appeared in the Los Angeles **Times,** a New York City bank robber was quoted as saying, as he held his hostages at gun-point, "Do you realize I could kill you all and get away with it? There's no more death penalty. You should have a death penalty." (The robber was a psychopathic homosexual, who was later shot and killed by police in his escape attempt.) His statement strikes the reader as being a frightening truth, especially when stated by a member of society who was capable of robbery and probably murder. Where no deterrent to violent crime exists, there is no reason not to commit violent crime. Fear of death is the most absolute deterrent available, and while society may never reach or be able to prevent the actions of the psychopathic killer or the hardened criminal who both feel they have "nothing to lose," the presence of the gas chamber as a reward for violence will deter the petty stick-up artist or juvenile mugger, whose trigger finger is frozen by the fear that the life he takes will cost him his own.

In the administration of executions, changes are needed. A black inmate of Illinois State Penitentiary at Joliet stated, on the night before his electrocution for murder, "The rich and famous don't burn, baby, only guys like me!" This unfortunate act has long been one of the key issues in capital punishment's own lengthy trial. The rich, who can afford the best legal aid and publicity, don't "burn." Stays of execution have dragged on for years, when they could be afforded. When they could not be afforded, death was quick. Truman Capote, in his best selling novel, **In Cold Blood,** showed the contrast when he stated, "A New York City rapist's case has just gone into its twelfth year of appeal, approaching the U. S. Supreme Court for the third time. In Louisiana, an armed robber was electrocuted after only thirty days." (Both figures represent the time elapse after formal sentencing.) Further background by Capote showed the rapist was a man of money, property, and social position. The robber was an indigent share-cropper. Both men stood equal in the eyes of the law during trial. But when the sentence was pronounced, the rich man could afford to prolong his life, but the poor man could not. One revision to the law of capital punishment would be to make free legal services for appeal available to all those convicted of a capital crime and sentenced to death, regardless of their financial position. Another reform would be to increase psychotherapeutic testing and counseling at school level. If the killer were reached in time, he might not become one.

Society needs capital punishment for the sake of its own safety. But society needs to reform capital punishment for the sake of its

169

own social conscience.

CAPITAL PUNISHMENT: A MORALISTIC AND PRACTICAL VIEW

Capital punishment is an outrage. It is a flagrant violation of our natural law and must be outlawed. The cries of indignation from the public over our horrible crime rates are indeed justified, but the advocation of capital punishment as an answer to the problem is only self-deception on society's part. A look at the reasons for punishment will reveal a sensible approach. There are four reasons for punishment: deterrence, restitution, elimination of criminals from the streets, and vengeance. Studies have shown that capital punishment—indeed, any kind of punishment— is not an effective deterrent to crime. The type of criminal who would be affected most by punishment is the hardened or professional criminal. However, it is a fact that this is not the type of criminal who is the prevailing one in our prisons. Very few of these individuals are caught. Instead our prisons are filled with misfits, mentally unbalanced individuals, who are sick rather than evil, and with those who commit crimes of passion against their nature or finally explode against the pressures of their social or economic backgrounds. Executing these individuals will not prevent others like them from following the same course.

As to the question of restitution, what possible benefit will society gain from the murder of these persons? Some argue that first-degree murder is the only justification for capital punishment, but from where do we get the right to take another's life? Capital punishment certainly does remove these criminals from activity in society, but this act is too extreme in its finality. Once done, it cannot be undone. Man is not infallible and should not have the power of life or death. Better methods must be found to solve our problems.

Capital punishment—vengeance—is not the answer to our crime problem, nor is the life sentence. Our penal system is totally wrong, not just inadequate. We need a viable alternative. The way to fight crime is not to practice vengeance—punishment after the fact—but to correct society's ills before the damage is done. We must get to the root of the problem, the cause of the crime, before we can undertake the treatment. We must make it possible and easy for all individuals to lead happy, prosperous, harmonious lives. This is undoubtedly a formidable task.

ASSIGNMENTS FOR CHAPTER TEN.

First, study Section III-F on page 156, "Outlining for the Well Developed Paragraph," and III-G on pages 156-157, "Writing the Well Developed Paragraph."

1. WRITING A BRIEF PARAGRAPH.

Select one of the topic sentences in Group A, page 172. Now develop it into a brief paragraph of approximately one page (double spaced).

2. COMPLETING THE SECOND PARAGRAPH OF A TWO-PARAGRAPH ESSAY.

Complete the second paragraph of the two-paragraph essay on page 161, by following the outline (on page 160) and expanding on it. Follow the outline exactly, but do not merely copy the sentences. Elaborate on them, supplying detail. Also, use a variety of sentence patterns, and be sure to use transitions and plenty of explanation.

3. COMPLETING THE THIRD PARAGRAPH OF A THREE-PARAGRAPH ESSAY.

Complete the third paragraph of the three-paragraph essay on page 162, by following the outline (on page 162) and expanding on it.

4. DEVELOPING TOPIC SENTENCES INTO PARAGRAPHS.

On page 172-173 is a list of topic sentences. Choose *one* of them (from Group A, B, C, *or* D) and then develop an outline for a well developed paragraph. After you have developed your outline, follow it exactly and write a well developed paragraph.

5. WRITING FIVE DIFFERENT PARAGRAPHS.

After you have completed assignment 4, select *five* other topic sentences for five different paragraph assignments. Following the same instructions as you did for assignment 4, write a well developed paragraph for each topic sentence. Remember, though, *work on only one paragraph at a time,* regardless of how long it takes you.

6. WRITING THE ESSAY.

After you have completed assignment 4 or assignment 5 (your teacher will specify which), select the same topic sentence that you used for assignment 4. Now develop it into an essay of at least two or three well developed paragraphs, each one dealing with a particular aspect of the original topic sentence (thesis statement).

7. Your teacher will assign you a certain number of three-paragraph themes based on the topic sentences above. Complete each theme—one at a time.

8. WRITING YOUR OWN TOPIC SENTENCES.

Group E contains a list of broad subjects. Select one at a time, and then write an effective *thesis statement* for each. Remember, you must narrow the subject so that you can handle it in a two-paragraph or three-paragraph essay.

9. WRITING ESSAYS FROM YOUR OWN TOPIC SENTENCES.

After your teacher has approved your topic sentences, select one of them, draw up a detailed outline for a three-paragraph essay, and then write a well developed three-paragraph theme.

10. Following the same procedure as you did for assignment 9, select *four* other sentences that your teacher approved, and then develop each into a three-paragraph or four-paragraph theme.

LIST OF THESIS STATEMENTS (TOPIC SENTENCES)

GROUP A

1. Mr. X (or Ms.X) is the worst teacher I ever had.
2. Mr. X (or Ms.X) is the best teacher I ever had.
3. My biggest gripe is . . .
4. My parents don't understand me.
5. My cousin (or friend) is extremely considerate.
6. Alice (or somebody else) is extremely selfish (or jealous).
7. In class Joe is obnoxious.
8. Theresa is my favorite cousin.
9. Mr. X's class (or Ms. X's class) is exciting (or boring).
10. Right now I wish I were somewhere else (be specific).

GROUP B

1. Nothing equals the satisfaction of gardening (or something else).
2. I shall never forget how I met . . .
3. I shall never forget the day . . .
4. Alice (or someone else) is the most unforgettable person I ever met.
5. Girls' sports should receive as much financial support from the schools as boys' sports do.
6. High school students should be allowed to attend any movies they wish.
7. High school students should have the choice between vocational and academic programs for graduation.
8. Girls are discriminated against in the public high schools (and junior high schools).
9. Smoking should be allowed (or should not be allowed) on the high school campus.
10. The compulsory attendance age for school should be lowered (or

should not be lowered) to fifteen.

GROUP C

1. As an independent adult of 21, I have just begun to live.
2. I wish I had not wasted so much time during my earlier years in school.
3. I am thrilled about my forthcoming vacation (or something else.)
4. At mealtime our eight-year old cat reminds me of a hungry lion.
5. Many television programs are aimed at the lowest common denominator.
6. Pollution is threatening our survival.
7. The only way to learn an art is to practice it.
8. Inflation (or unemployment) is creating a severe hardship on many people.
9. The lack of public transportation in certain areas (specify) is creating a severe hardship on many people.
10. Attendance in class is vitally important for the student.
11. One of the major causes of violence is frustration.
12. The ability to express oneself clearly is the key to success.
13. The Concord should not have been permitted to land in the United States.
14. Nuclear power plants should (or should not) be allowed to operate freely.
15. Learning how to write effectively is (or is not) important.

GROUP D

1. Should smoking in public places be outlawed?
2. Should gambling (or the smoking of marijuana) be legalized?
3. Should students have a decisive voice in the hiring and firing of teachers?
4. Should final examinations be eliminated in high school and college?
5. Should all high school students be required to meet the same standards for graduation?
6. Should the 55 mile-per-hour speed limit in the United States be maintained permanently?
7. Should Canada become the 51st state?
8. Should letter grades be eliminated in school (and college)?
9. Should students be required to read and write at the eighth grade level minimum before being allowed to graduate from high school?
10. Should persons under eighteen be allowed to go into bars?

173

GROUP E: BROAD SUBJECTS

1. College
2. Communication
3. Conformity
4. Conservation
5. Current Events
6. Discrimination
7. Drinking
8. Drugs
9. Energy
10. Grades
11. Medicine or medical care
12. Nutrition
13. Politics or politicians
14. Pollution
15. Postal service
16. Rapid transit
17. School
18. Sports
19. Violence

CHAPTER ELEVEN

CLASSIFICATION

I. DEFINITION.

Classification is the *grouping* of related objects into a broad category. *Analysis* through classification is the reverse process: the *division* and sub-division of a broad subject into its lesser components. The grouping of Gremlins, Hornets, Matadors, and Ambassadors into the category of American Motors Cars would be a form of classification because it classifies all cars manufactured by the American Motors Corporation. Conversely, the analysis of the types of cars manufactured by American Motors would include the Gremlin, the Hornet, the Matador, and the Ambassador. Classification is particularly important in writing because it enables the writer to systematically divide a broad subject into narrow, related topics on which he can focus his thoughts.

From infancy on, classification in some form or another is a vitally important thought process. As soon as an infant can recognize his mother, he begins to classify people into two groups: his mother and others. As his mind develops, so does his system of classification. People are classified according to those he recognizes, and those he does not. His food falls into two categories—pleasant and unpleasant. His toys are classified according to whether they can be licked or chewed, and whether they are hard or soft. Later on he makes differentiations between animals: those he can play with and those he cannot, or those that are big and those that are small. As he grows a little older, he distinguishes between some animals, such as dogs, cats, horses, and others he comes in contact with. Later he learns that people have grouped these animals into further classifications according to breed. Dogs may be terriers, bulldogs, poodles, police dogs, or mongrels. And eventually he learns that such breeds as poodles may be classified even further into teacups, toys, miniatures, and standards. Ultimately he may learn that there are classifications for classifications, and that practically everything has been grouped and labeled according to certain systems.

Classification, however, is not only a system of grouping similar things into broad categories; it is also a system of analyzing a subject by dividing it into its lesser elements. For example, people can be classified according to their sex, size, color, racial origin, religion, nationality, intelligence, education, occupation, or other such category. Each category in turn could be further classified according to some similar characteristic possessed by the group as a whole. Religions, for example, could be classified into very broad categories whose followers believe in one God, two gods, more than two gods, or no gods. Within any one of these categories, further classification exists. To illustrate, Christianity, which is merely one of several major religious movements practicing a belief in one God, could be classified according to its denominations, which include Greek Catholics, Greek Orthodox, Russian Orthodox, Protestants, and others. Of these denominations, some may be further classified. For example, Protestants may include Anglicans, Baptists, Episcopalians, Lutherans, Methodists, Quakers, and so on. Indeed, the list seems endless, so long as there are basic differences within a particular group to warrant a particular classification.

To further illustrate analysis through classification, let us examine two broad subjects by dividing each into a number of categories, each of which in turn could be sub-divided.

1. *Crude Oil:* lubricating oils, paraffins, fuel oils, and petrolatums.

2. *Alcoholic Beverages:* beer, wine, hard liquor, and liqueur.

Each category above, which has already been divided from its parent subject, can be analyzed by examining its components and classifying them according to their basic similarities and differences. For example, if we consider one of the categories of crude oil—lubricating oils—we realize that there are many, many types of lubricating oils, which can first be classified according to their thickness as *grease* or *oil,* and then further classified by the same standard. The lubricating oil used in cars is labeled as 10 weight, 20 weight, 30 weight, or multigrade, depending upon its viscosity or thickness. Another product of crude oil—fuel oil—can also be classified. Among the more common classifications of fuel oil are *gasoline, benzine, naptha,* or *kerosene,* depending on the stage of refinement. One of the most common of these fuel oil products is *gasoline,* which can be classified as "regular" or "ethyl," according to its additives, particularly tetraethyl lead, and then further classified by its octane rating.

If we examine the second broad subject—alcoholic beverages—we need only consider the classification of *hard liquor* to realize how many sub groups fall under this heading: Canadian (rye), bourbon, gin, Scotch, vodka, and tequila. Numerous other (illegal) hard liquors, such as Saskatchewan home brew and Kentucky white lightning, could also be listed under this category. The classification of *wine* merely according to aperitifs, dinner wines, and champagnes, is an enormous study in itself. Wines can also be classified according to their generic variety, vineyard, or vintage quality, or vintage year. Again, any such study could be conducted either superficially or in depth.

To summarize, almost anything can be analyzed by examining its lesser parts, which in turn can be further examined through a systematic process or organization known as *classification.* Obviously, then, classification is an extremely important type of organization, not only in writing, but in any type of thought process, because it selects and groups similar things: food with food, fruit with fruit, apples with apples, and peelings with peelings. Consequently, it enables one to organize his thoughts and to focus them on one particular thing at a time. Without some form of classification, one's thoughts—and obviously one's writing—would be a hodgepodge of unrelated, meaningless ideas.

II. BASIS: LOGICAL, CONSISTENT, ALL-INCLUSIVE.

Any logical system of classification must have a guiding principle, that is, a *basis* for selecting and grouping. The basis that determines the similarities among different things must be *consistent* and *all-inclusive.* For example, if you were the manager of a large men's clothing store that featured thousands of suits in practically every conceivable size, color, style, fabric, and price range, you would have to determine *how* you wanted to group the suits; otherwise, nobody could find what he was looking for. If you grouped them by size, you would have to be consistent, because if a customer needed a 39 short, he (or his salesman) would expect to find his size in the section that contained all the 39 shorts, not in the section that contained the 48 talls. (In fact, many a salesman has been fired because he failed to put merchandise back in its proper place.) Again, if you grouped the suits strictly according to price range, the customer would expect to find a $77.00 suit with the $77.00 suits, not with the $250.00 suits. The basis for your classification would be one of those mentioned above: size, color, style, fabric, or price range. You would determine the basis only after analyzing your *need* to group the suits in the first place: the reason *why* you wanted to put certain suits in a particular group and why you wanted to put others in another group. Once you determined your need or reason for grouping the suits in a certain manner, you would have to be consistent and group *all* of the suits the same way. Otherwise, your classification system would be useless, because it was not a real system.

The same rule of logic, consistency, and all-inclusiveness applies to any type of classification. If you were analyzing the world's great religious movements in terms of those that believe in monotheism—one, all-powerful, personal God—you would probably arrive at three major classifications: Christianity, Islam, and Judaism. You could not then select another category like Catholicism or Protestantism, for example, because each is a subdivision of the original classification, Christianity. Nor could you include outside classifications which believe in more than one God or in no gods at all, classifications such as Hinduism or early Confucianism. In short, the basis for your classification was monotheism; therefore, you would have to stick to it. You could not suddenly change your mind in midstream.

To further illustrate the rule of logical consistency and all inclusiveness when selecting a basis for your classification system, let us examine the different makes of cars listed below:

Cadillac	Mercedes	Pinto
Vega	Toyota	Thunderbird
Continental	Lincoln	Alfa Romeo
Volkswagen Rabbit	Gremlin	Hornet
Dodge Colt	Datsun	Rolls Royce

You will notice that they have not been grouped according to any logical or consistent pattern. Can you now select a basis or bases we might use in order to classify them? At least three bases are evident. What are they?

First of all, we could group the cars according to their *size*—big or small. Second, we could group them according to their *price*—luxury or moderate. (Because of inflation, I will no longer use the term "economy.") Third, we could classify them on the basis of whether or not they were assembled in the United States or in foreign countries— that is, *domestic or foreign.* Fourth, we could classify them according to which *country* manufactured them. Even further classifications exist, such as horsepower, gas consumption, and so on. For this illustration, however, let us stick with the first three groupings: size, price and domestic or foreign maker.

SIZE	PRICE	COUNTRY
Big	*Luxury*	*Domestic*
Continental	Rolls Royce	Cadillac
Cadillac	Continental	Vega
Thunderbird	Cadillac	Continental
Rolls Royce	Thunderbird	Lincoln
Mercedes	Alfa Romeo	Gremlin
	Mercedes	Pinto
Small		Thunderbird
Alfa Romeo	*Moderate*	Hornet
Vega	Vega	
Pinto	Volkswagen	*Foreign*
Toyota	Dodge Colt	Volkswagen
Datsun	Toyota	Dodge Colt
Dodge Colt	Gremlin	Mercedes
Gremlin	Datsun	Toyota
Hornet	Pinto	Datsun
Volkswagen	Hornet	Alfa Romeo
		Rolls Royce

You will notice that we have been consistent in our classification. Once we decided to group the cars according to size, we did not suddenly include a small car (like the Alfa Romeo) with the big ones, simply because it is expensive. To be inconsistent like that would have invalidated our classification. Moreover, we stuck to our three bases for grouping; we did not suddenly decide to include a fourth. We did not suddenly decide that because the Vega, Pinto, Gremlin, and Hornet are fairly economical to run and get good gas milage, they should be placed in the same grouping with the foreign cars, most of which also get good gas mileage. One class or category has nothing to do with the other. We do not mix oranges and lemons with lettuce when we are talking about citrus fruits. We must be consistent.

To *summarize,* the basis for your classification system will depend upon what similarities and differences you detect among various items, so that once you decide to use certain criteria to group the items, you will be able to group *all* the items in their various categories according to the criteria or standards you selected. You will not suddenly make exceptions, because then your classification system will be meaningless.

> **ASSIGNMENTS: Turn to the assignments at the end of the chapter. Study them carefully and then complete them, for each will illustrate the concept and application of classification.**

WRITING A CLASSIFICATION ESSAY.

Since the concept of classification was introduced in Chapter Ten, dealing with the narrowing of a subject into a particular aspect or central idea, the composition of a classification type of essay should now be relatively simple. In fact, you have already written such an essay by describing "Raymond's reckless driving." You illustrated different *types* of recklessness in his driving (backing up, speeding, not stopping, not signaling). The same concept applies in any type of analysis through classification. For example, you could analyze somebody's *jealousy* or *generosity* or *kindness,* or any such characteristic. So long as you select a basis for your analysis, stick to it, be consistent, and include examples that pertain only to the basis for your analysis, your essay will be well organized. Finally, never jump from one basis of analysis to another without completing the first. If you are explaining how Mary displays her jealousy toward her sister, complete that analysis before proceeding to explain how Mary also displays her jealousy toward her brother. Remember, concentrate on and complete one thing at a time.

Before proceeding to write your classification essays, study the MODEL STUDENT ESSAYS which follow. *Then,* turn to the writing assignment at the end of this chapter.

> **WRITING ASSIGNMENT: Turn to Section B of the assignments at the end of this chapter.**

III. MODEL STUDENT ESSAYS.

PROGRESS IN TRANSPORTATION

An attempt to analyze man's progress in transportation leads one to three obvious categories: transportation by land, by sea, and by air. The oldest of these modes is, of course, land transportation, and its most elementary form is man himself. Thousands of years passed before a progression was made from walking to the employment of animals as a mode of transportation. Only minor variations of this method appeared until the nineteenth century, when the introduction of the locomotive revolutionized travel on land. Although trains could go only where rails were laid, the rapid development of extensive networks, both in America and Europe, quickly followed this innovation.

Another century passed before an entirely new, and this time individual, means of conveyance was introduced into society. This invention was the automobile. It has since undergone a population explosion of its own, growing from the relatively few cars of the 1900-1910 period to the millions of vehicles on the road today. However, the automobile has become a hindrance as well as an advantage to man. The massive pollution its numbers have brought to heavily populated areas throughout the world is now prompting many people to realize that man and auto are not completely compatible.

Transportation upon the waters presumably saw its advent during prehistoric times when crude rafts and later variations of the canoe were used on rivers and seas. Eventually the sail was developed and then, as in land transportation, a stalemate followed that was not broken until the 1800's, when the steam engine was successfully adapted to marine engineering. The next two hundred years saw further technological breakthroughs that incorporated new and improved power plants in ships' designs, resulting eventually in the present diesel engines and nuclear reactors.

While these innovations were being developed for shipping, a whole new field of transportation, this time in the air, was beginning to mature. During the past seventy years, air travel has, in fact, eclipsed both the railroads and the ocean liners in passenger appeal and popularity. This phenomenon represents a fantastic advancement from the ventures of the early air pioneers at the turn of the century. Those first planes, like their waterborne contemporaries, were fragile, one-or two-seat, death-defying machines. Now, huge jet airliners, each carrying hundreds of passengers, can span continents and oceans in a matter of hours.

An off-shoot of air travel, even though it is still in its very infancy, requires an additional category of its own. Not even a decade old, space travel is developing so rapidly and is presenting so many possibilities that its only limitations are man's ability to imagine and to endure. The moon has already been visited in this short period, and it is foreseeable that perhaps in our lifetime, even interplanetary travel shall one day cease to be an experience reserved exclusively for the highly trained astronaut.

From the days of our ancestors' initial upright steps to man's first, hesitant walk upon the moon, progress has been the brother of transportation; and as long as mankind uses and develops wisely all aspects of transportation, the relationship will continue.

CLASSIFICATION OF AN ORCHESTRA

An orchestra is a group of musicians playing a musical arrangement together. There are many members in this group; however, they must perform as a whole. An orchestra consists of four main sections, each contributing a particular quality of sound. All of the qualities are equally important, and none can compare with the other. This is the reason, then, an orchestra can create so many different conceptions and moods. The four main sections of an orchestra are divided into the following classifications: strings, woodwinds, brass, and percussion.

The string section is represented by the violin, viola, cello, and bass violin. These instruments are characterized by four strings played with a bow. The highest pitched instrument of this family is the violin. The next member is the viola, which is slightly larger than the violin and tuned a fifth lower. The third largest instrument is the cello. It is pitched half-way between the viola and the bass. All of the preceding instruments are played by their musician in a seated position. Largest of all, the bass, is played standing upright. Its pitch is so low, it would be impossible to duplicate vocally. All members in this section are used mainly for melody or for the main theme in an orchestra.

The next group of instruments are the woodwinds. From highest to lowest pitch, they consist of the piccolo, flute, clarinet, oboe, and bassoon. These instruments are played by blowing. The piccolo and flute are blown through a small hole at one end of the tube. The clarinet, oboe, and bassoon are blown through a reed connected to the rest of the instrument. This group is used for special effects in soft passages of the music. Their tone quality is more resonant than other sections.

The boldest of all are the brass, whose sound is the hardest of all. This section contains the trumpet, coronet, trombone, baritone, and tuba. These instruments are played with a mouthpiece. If this group plays to its fullest extent, it can be heard above the others.

Last of all, yet very important, is the percussion section. This section uses the smallest number of musicians, yet it has the largest number of instruments. This group is used for very special techniques. Excitement is held as its character. A few instruments in this section are various sizes of drums, chimes, cymbals, triangles, tambourines, glockenspiels, castanets, and other gadgets too numerous to mention.

An orchestra has no boundaries. A live stage concert will display the magnificence in itself. Moreover, it is the inspirational background from grand opera to musical comedy. Less costly to the public on television, its performance makes any television show more enjoyable. An orchestra is an emotional experience for all.

POLLUTION

Pollution is threatening our survival. It is a faceless adversary which comes to us in many different forms, such as air pollution, water pollution, and noise pollution. Pollution has grown out of control in our short lifetime, and like a monster, it continues to grow, spreading its destruction to every living organism on earth.

First of all, there is air pollution, which is already showing its destructive effects upon life. For example, air pollution has been directly related to the cause of certain types of respiratory diseases. Likewise, in certain experimental situations, air pollution has been found to affect the chromosomes of rats, with disastrous consequence upon their offspring. Another problem created by air pollution is its effect on plant life. For instance, in the Lake Arrowhead vicinity, trees are rapidly dying because of a disease directly related to air pollution.

Next, there is water pollution. In its wrath it is already claiming lives. For example, last year in North Carolina a man and his son both died after swimming in a river that was later determined to contain contaminated water. Similarly, water pollution is destroying our many different forms of marine life, forms which are so important in the balance of nature. Moreover, contaminants are even finding their way into our drinking water, thus directly affecting us all.

Last, but certainly not least, is noise pollution. It is the sleeping giant of pollution. For as harmless as it appears, noise pollution is not only affecting us physically, but more importantly, it is having a detrimental effect upon our minds. For instance, the many disturbing sounds of each day can be very distressful and can slowly change a person's entire outlook on life. This in turn can have grave consequences upon everyone around him. For this reason, then, noise pollution is the worst of all pollutants.

The air we breathe, the water we drink, and even the sounds we hear, all affect our very existence. That is why pollution is threatening our survival.

MUSIC IN THE ROMANTIC ERA

The Romantic era in music extended from about 1820 to 1900. The music of this period may be classified into four types: the song, the short piano piece, program music, and absolute music.

The Romantic Art Song is the perfect blend of poetry and melody. The Romantic artist longed to express his most personal feelings, and the song satisfied this need. While France and Italy concentrated on opera and the folk song, the German temperament created the art song. Love, the beauty of nature, and the transience of human happiness were the favorite themes expressed by art song composers. Although the master of the art song is, of course, Franz Schubert, both Robert Schumann and Johannes Brahms are also famous for their lovely songs.

The short piano piece is the instrumental equivalent of the art song within a small frame, in its lyric quality and expression of the artist's feelings. The piano really did not come into its own until the Romantic era. Its great range and expressiveness were ideally suited for the intensely emotional type of music favored by the Romantics. These short piano pieces are most frequently titled "Impromptu" (on the spur of the moment), "Intermezzo" (interlude), "Nocturne" (night song), "Rhapsody," or "Romance." The most delightful short piano pieces were written by Schubert, Chopin, Liszt, Mendelssohn, Schumann, and Brahms. These short pieces show that size is no criterion in art. The artists of the Romantic era believed that an exquisite miniature may contain as much beauty as that in a symphony.

Much nineteen century instrumental music was given literary or pictorial associations. This is called program music. One type of program music is the concert overture. It is a single movement piece written for orchestra, based on a literary or patriotic idea, and not associated with any opera. A good example of such music is Tchaikovsky's "Romeo and Juliet Overture." Music originally written for a play is sometimes arranged for concert performance. Grieg's "Peer Gynt Suite" was originally written for Ibsen's drama Peer Gynt. An entire symphony may be associated with a literary theme. The best examples are the program symphonies of Berlioz: Symphonie Fantastique, Harold in Italy, and Romeo and Juliet.

The type of music for which the composer has not indicated any nonmusical ideas is called absolute music. The symphony and concerto are the forms generally associated with absolute music. These forms are large scale works in several movements written for orchestra, or in the case of the concerto, for solo instrument and orchestra. The form of the symphony and concerto in the Romantic era is much more relaxed in contrast to the formal structure of the Classical period. This music is highly melodic and emotional. Above all, the Romantic composers were experts at orchestration. They used the instruments of an ever expanding orchestra in a highly colorful and sometimes exotic way. Much of this music is nationalistic in character, for Romantic composers made use of melodies from the folk songs of their native countries. The meaning of absolute music is in the organization and continuity of the music itself. Brahms, Mendelssohn, Dvorak, Tchaikovsky, Grieg, and

Schumann are the most prominent composers of the symphony and concerto in the Romantic era.

Nineteenth century Romantic music is the backbone of the orchestral repertoire today. The Romantics created few new forms, but the lush, uninhibited, melodic music they did write will always be popular.

List of Subjects for Classification Essay

1. Airplanes	22. Magazines
2. Armed forces	23. Marriages
3. Athletes or athletics	24. Movies
4. Attitudes	25. Newscasters or news programs
5. Ball games	26. Newspapers
6. Boys	27. Novels, stories, or plays
7. Cars	28. Parents
8. Children	29. Pets (or animals)
9. College instructors	30. Reasons for doing something
10. Counselors	31. Roads (or streets)
11. Doctors	32. Salespeople
12. Energy Sources	33. Signs
13. Engines	34. Stores (or markets)
14. Examinations	35. Students
15. Fads	36. Tastes (clothes, books, plays)
16. Foods	37. Teachers
17. Fuels	38. Television programs
18. Girls	39. Traits (generosity, jealousy, kindness)
19. Homes or houses	40. Vessels (sailing)
20. Liquors	41. Wars
21. Love	42. Wines

ASSIGNMENTS ON CLASSIFICATION

A. Analyzing, Listing, and Grouping.

1. First, examine the Table of Contents of this book. Second, examine the book. Third, examine a chapter, any chapter, although Chapters Nine and Ten might best illustrate this assignment. After you have completed this assignment, you should have noted the following:

a) The Table of Contents can be analyzed because the Table contains components, which in turn contain lesser components, which in turn can be further analyzed.

b) The contents contain three major groupings—parts.

c) Each part contains a number of different chapters.

d) Each chapter contains a number of different sections (I, II, III).

e) Each section in turn usually contains a number of smaller sub-divisions (A, B, C).

f) Sometimes each sub-division contains even smaller sub-divisions (1, 2).

g) Occasionally these smaller sub-divisions contain yet smaller sub-divisions (a, b).

h) Finally, these very small sub-divisions (a, b, c) sometimes contain the smallest components of all (i, ii, iii, iv).

i) The reverse process—grouping through classification—is also possible.

2. Examine the table of contents of any other textbook, and then the book itself. Does the classification system follow a consistent pattern similar to the one just explained?

3. Select any newspaper, preferably a large one, and then take out the different sections. Now draw up an outline listing each of the sections, sub-sections, and smaller sub-sections of the newspaper, until your analysis is complete. After you have completed your analysis, reassemble the newspaper by grouping each smaller component under its proper section until your classification is complete.

4. Each of the four automobile makers in the United States—American Motors, Chrysler Corporation, Ford, and General Motors—produces a number of different types of cars, such as the Hornet, the Dodge Dart, the Pinto, and the Cadillac, to name but a few. Think of *two* different classes or *systems* which you might use to classify all the cars manufactured in the United States, and then list *all* the different cars you can think of in their proper category. (Hint: one of the bases for your analysis might be the maker.)

5. The next time you are in a supermarket or food store, examine the different sections of groceries. Note how the store has grouped like items with like: meats with meats, frozen foods with frozen foods, canned soups, vegetables and fruits with similar items, and non-foods with non-foods. Draw up a classification system for the store. How might the present classification system be improved? If you think that your system is more efficient than the present one, show it to the store manager, and ask his opinion of it.

B. Writing the Classification Essay.

1. *After* you have studied this chapter thoroughly, including the Model Study Essays, you will be ready to write a well developed

classification type of essay. Select one of the subjects from the list on page 185. Narrow your topic so that you can focus on *one aspect* of or *basis* for classification. Then write a well developed essay of at least three paragraphs on the topic.

2. Using the same subject as you did for assignment 1 above, focus on a *different* aspect of (or basis for) classification, and then write another well developed essay on that topic.

3. Select another *subject* from the list, and then write a classification type of essay, organized and developed as you did in assignment 1 and 2.

CHAPTER TWELVE

COMPARISON AND CONTRAST

I. DEFINITION.

Comparison and contrast is the notation of relationships—similarities and differences—between objects. *Comparison* reveals *similarities; contrast* reveals *differences.* The noting of similarities in price or size between a Volkswagen Beetle and a Toyota, for example, would be a comparison; the noting of differences between their styles, or between their transmissions, engines, or cooling systems would be a contrast. The points mentioned under a comparison are very much alike; certainly, they are alike in more ways than they are different. On the other hand, the points mentioned under a contrast are more different from each other than they are alike. The Volkswagen Beetle uses an air cooling system; it does not have a radiator. By contrast, the Toyota does not have an air cooling system, but instead uses a radiator. Again, on the basis of price, size, or fuel consumption, the Volkswagen Beetle or the Toyota could be compared with the Datsun, Pinto, Vega, or any such *sub-compact car in that class.* However, on these same bases, the Volkswagen could not be compared with cars in the luxury class, such as the Cadillac, Imperial, or Continental, because the differences would be too great; instead, the relationship would have to be expressed as a contrast. Obviously, then, a basis must first be established before any comparison or contrast can be made. And even more important, the objects or ideas to be compared must be logically comparable; that is, they must be in logically related classes. A man could be compared with other species of animal life on the basis of his anatomy, which is similar; but he could not be compared with a car, even though both are able to travel. They are in two entirely different classes. A horse cannot be compared or contrasted with an apple or a stone, nor can a tree be compared logically with a poem. Any attempted comparison of unrelated classes such as these is not only contrived but ridiculous.

To further illustrate the concept of comparison/contrast, the revealing of similarities between spinach and lettuce in such areas as color, taste, and texture would be classified as a comparison, since the two leafy vegetables are more alike in these areas than they are different. However, on the basis of use, not only can they be compared, but they can also be contrasted. Both are used in salads as well as in sandwiches, but lettuce cannot very well be cooked.

The same concept of comparison and contrast might be applied to other foods. Hamburger can be compared to steak in its origin, nutritional value, and possibly in its taste, depending on one's taste. The two meats could be contrasted with each other on the bases of their price, popularity, prestigious value, and other such criteria. For example, the La Scala Restaurant in Beverly Hills does not feature hamburger, nor does the McDonald's Hamburger chain sell steaks. Red dinner wine can be compared with white dinner wine on the basis of its alcoholic content or the reputation of its winery. However, the two wines could hardly be compared otherwise. They are different, not only in color, but also in taste, body, maturation, and other numerous criteria. In brief, then, comparison is the revelation of how two objects are alike, while a contrast reveals their differences.

Analysis through comparison and contrast is used every day in order to make value judgments and decisions. Before you can make a decision, you must first make a value judgment. Yet even before you can make a value judgment, you must first have a basis for your judgment, a basis which generally you, alone, determine and which will serve as the comparison and contrast of the two or more items you must evaluate. To illustrate, let us say that you have decided to purchase a shirt. You already know what size you need, but you are undecided as to what color, pattern, and style you want. You might even be undecided as to what price you want to pay. You will then compare two or more shirts, both in the same size, but differing slightly, or perhaps contrasting sharply, with each other on the bases you have selected: color, pattern, style, and price. You will eliminate certain shirts through contrast—they are not the right color or price—until you select the one that compares most favorably with the criteria you had in mind. Thus, you will have practiced both comparison and contrast in order to arrive at a value judgment (the best shirt) and your final decision (to buy it).

A similar but perhaps more complicated analytical procedure usually is involved in any serious decision making process. A comparison and contrast of alternatives precedes the value judgment leading to the final decision. Suppose, for example, that you want to enroll in a college course. You must *first* decide what course you would like to take. Your decision will be *based* perhaps on your *need* (if you are working toward a particular goal), *or* it may be based on *other factors,* such as enjoyment. Thus, you first establish a basis, even for your preliminary decision, and then you begin your analysis, through comparison and contrast, of available courses in that area. Let us suppose that you have decided to take English I (freshman composition), and that you have a choice of four sections: two taught by Mr. Brown at different times and different days (Monday mornings and Thursday evenings, for example), and two taught by Mr. White, also at different periods (Tuesdays and Wednesdays). You must now decide what particular section of English I you would like to take. Your decision will be based on one of two criteria: the convenience to you of the particular time slot; or the quality (or ease) of the instruction given by the particular instructor, that is, his reputation. If all other factors were equal (each instructor taught both of his sections identically and had the same requirements), your decision would be narrowed down to which instructor you wanted to take or which time period was most convenient for you. If the time slot was not the deciding factor, then your decision would be based solely on which instructor you preferred. Thus, your evaluation through the elimination of alternatives would have led you to decide on a particular class solely on the basis of its instruction. Before you made your final decision, however, you would have to compare and contrast Mr. Brown's class with Mr. White's class on a particular basis (or bases) which you considered to be most important; for after all, you are the one who must take the class. You would have to decide then the bases or criteria for the comparison and contrast. You would not merely take somebody's word that Mr. Brown's class was good, but Mr. White's class was bad. Such generalizations, as we have already explained in Chapter Ten, are meaningless. What *specifically* is good about Mr. Brown's class, or what specifically is bad about Mr. White's class? How does each class compare with the other on the same basis? Thus, again you would have to first determine the basis for the comparison before you could make any evaluation leading to value judgment.

Through classification you could analyze the term *instruction* into such areas as these: books required, type of writing assignments required, number of writing assignments required in class and out of class, method of instruction (lecture, visual aids, etc.), method of grading, method of returning papers (with comments or with conferences), number and length of individualized conferences, distribution of grades (A, B, C, etc.), and overall reputation of the instructor as to his effectiveness and expertise. Once you established these criteria for evaluating "instruction," you would compare and contrast each item under Mr. Brown's name with the same item under Mr. White's name. In that way you would arrive at an evaluation of each instructor and thereby arrive at a judgment as to which instructor offered the best instruction. (I have usually selected my "best" professors in such a manner, and I have since learned that many of my most perceptive and best students have selected their best instructors in the same way.)

If, however, you were only interested in being processed through the course, and if you learned that Mr. Brown's course was a cinch, then your decision would be based on that factor. (Indeed, many students select their instructor merely on the basis of whether or not he is "easy," or whether or not they can get an A from his course. Unfortunately, the only thing they do get out of such a course is usually the grade.)

The ability to systematically compare and contrast objects or ideas is not only a practical asset, since you are constantly evaluating and judging people, places, things, and ideas, but this ability is also an indication of your intelligence. To begin with, you must be perceptive in order to notice the similarities and differences that exist between two or more objects, which are logically comparable in the first place. The more perceptive you are and the more research you conduct on the subject, the more similarities and differences you are likely to note. Secondly, you must be organized. You must have a logical basis for your comparison or contrast. Once you establish your basis, you must be consistent and not switch from one basis to another without completing the first. For example, if you were comparing a Toyota with a Volkswagen on the basis of economy (a very broad term), and if you listed the price of a Toyota, you would also have to list the price of a Volkswagen; you could not suddenly decide to switch to another basis, such as engine design. You would have to complete the first comparison: you would have to list the price of the Volkswagen, and then you would have to list such items as gas consumption, maintenance, insurance premiums, and resale value, all of which fall under the category of "economy." Then you would have to compare the Toyota with the Volkswagen on the basis of each of these items before you arrived at a final evaluation as to which was the more economical car. After you had completed such a comparison *on one basis*—economy—you could proceed with the next basis for your comparison, which might involve criteria such as performance, design, and so on. Remember, each criterion that you use for a comparison will probably involve several items. Under "economy," for example, the original cost of the car is only the tip of the iceberg. The more thorough you are, the more valid will be your comparison. And remember, too, it is better to be thorough in one area than it is to skim over the surface and try to cover everything. Organization, therefore, is most important in any comparison/contrast. The more organized you are, the more clearly you can reveal the relationships between objects. On the other hand, if you are not organized, and if you do not have a particular and consistent basis for your comparison or contrast, whatever information you do have will be almost useless, because you will be unable to clearly reveal the logical relationships that might exist.

II. TYPES OF ORGANIZATION.

In an essay, usually comparison and contrast go hand-in-hand, although sometimes it is necessary to reveal only one relationship, either a comparison or a contrast. In any event, the process of organizing a comparison/contrast essay begins with first establishing the basis for the comparison. You as the writer determine the basis unless you have been given an assignment requiring a particular basis for comparison. (Many instructors often assign their students a particular question that already contains the basis for the comparison/contrast, for example, the *causes* of two particular wars.) The basis may be a rather broad one, such as the economy factor between two cars, or it may be very narrowly defined, as would be the case if you were comparing the price or weight of two cuts of meat.

After you have established the basis (or perhaps several bases) for the comparison, you should outline the major points of similarity and difference between the two objects, on each basis you have chosen. Such an outline will enable you to determine whether there are more points of similarity between the two objects or more points of difference. You may find that your comparison has turned out, instead, to be a contrast, in which case the focus of your paragraph (or essay) would change; your purpose would then be to reveal a contrast between the two objects rather than a comparison. In short, only after you have examined both sides of the coin will you be able to determine whether your essay lends itself to a comparison or to a contrast—or to both.

Consider, for example, the following point-by-point outline

comparing the 1973 Pinto with the 1973 Toyota Corona on the *basis* of *economy.*

A. Point-by-Point Comparison/Contrast Outline

I. (Basis) Economy

ITEM	73 PINTO	73 TOYOTA CORONA
A. Initial Cost	$3,500 range	$3,650 range
	(approx. $150 less)	(approx. $150 more)
B. Gas Consumption	20 miles/gallon, avg.	28 miles/gallon, avg.
1 yr. (15,000 miles/yr.)	750 gallons ($450.)	538 gallons ($323.)
C. Insurance	almost identical	almost identical
D. Maintenance	$200. yr. approx.	$200 yr. approx.
	(same)	(same)
E. Depreciation	$2,300 approx.	$1,700 approx.
	(approx. $600 more)	($600 less)
F. Total Cost—3 yrs.		
($15,000 miles/year)		
(gas = 60¢ gal.)	$7,750.	$6,919.
	$831.00 more	$831.00 less.

NOTE: The figures above were supplied both by Toyota and Pinto dealers, as well as by two drivers, one who had driven his Pinto for three years, and the other who had driven his Toyota for three years.

After completing the outline above, we notice that although the initial cost of both cars was almost the same, as were the insurance premiums and maintenance costs, the *total* cost over a three-year period was significantly different. Therefore, in writing a comparison/contrast essay, we could have an *option* of four choices.

B. Options.

1. *Comparison (Similarities)—Point-by-Point*

First, we could reveal the initial similarities between both cars, using a point-by-point comparison. We would thus illustrate that during the first year more similarities than differences exist between the two cars. The paragraph or essay would then be classified as a comparison.

2. *Contrast (Differences)—Point-by-Point*

Again, we could use the point-by-point approach, only this time we would focus on the differences. Such a *contrast* would reveal that over a three-year period the Toyota is a more economical car.

3. *Comparison and Contrast—Point-by-Point*

Our third option would allow us to reveal *both* similarities and differences *within* the same paragraph, again by using a point-by-point organization.

4. *Comparison and Contrast—Block Organization*

Finally, we could treat one topic (comparison, for example) in one paragraph, and then in the next paragraph reveal the opposite. In this type of organization, we should use a *transition,* which not only introduces the next object to be compared, but also shows the points of similarities or differences. The second paragraph, therefore, describes the second object and compares it with the first.

C. Model Paragraphs: Comparison and Contrast.

COMPARISON (SIMILARITIES)—Point-by-Point

When comparing the 1973 Pinto with the 1973 Toyota Corona on the basis of economy, one notices more similarities than differences. First, the initial cost of each car is approximately the same. Both are in the $3,500-$3,650 range. Second, the insurance premiums are virtually identical. Third, the maintenance cost for each car is the same—approximately $200.00 a year. The only major points of difference are in gas consumption and depreciation. The Pinto averages about 20 miles per gallon in all types of driving, whereas the Toyota gets about 28. Likewise, the resale value of a Pinto during its first year is slighty less than that of the Toyota, but only about five percent less. Thus, during their first year of operation, both the Pinto and Toyota are very comparable on the basis of economy.

CONTRAST (DIFFERENCES)—Point-by-Point

On the basis of overall cost during a three-year period, the 1973 Toyota Corona is considerably more economical than is the 1973 Pinto. Even though there are virtually no differences on two items—insurance premiums and maintenance—and even though the Toyota actually costs about $150.00 more initially, the savings in gas consumption and depreciation clearly indicate that the Toyota is a better value. First of all, the gas consumption alone makes a significant difference in savings for the Toyota driver. He gets about 28 miles per gallon, in contrast to the Pinto driver, who gets only about 20. If both drivers average about 15,000 miles a year, the savings for the Toyota driver will be considerable, even during the

195

first year. Assuming that the price of gas is 60 cents a gallon, the Pinto driver will have to buy 750 gallons, which will cost him almost $450.00. By contrast, his counterpart in the Toyota will need only 538 gallons, which will cost $323.00, a savings of $127.00. During a three-year period this saving amounts to $381.00, which is more than ten percent of the initial cost of either car. Even greater than the savings on gas consumption, though, are the savings on depreciation at the end of a three-year period. The Pinto driver loses approximately $2,300 on his car at the end of that period if he decides to sell his car. Again, by contrast, the Toyota driver will lose only $1,700—that is, some $600 less than the Pinto driver. Thus, at the end of a three-year period, the Toyota driver saves $831.00 more than the Pinto driver, a significant savings for anyone.

NOTE: The second sentence illustrates a comparison within a contrast essay.

COMPARISON AND CONTRAST—Point-by-Point and Block

If one compares the 1973 Pinto with the Toyota Corona manufactured in the same year, he will notice that on the basis of overall economy during a three-year period, there are both similarities and differences. For example, the initial cost of each car is approximately the same. Both are in the $3,500-$3,650 range. Second, the insurance premiums are virtually identical, as is the cost for maintenance, even over a three-year period. Thus, each car is comparable on these three items.

On the other hand, the savings in gas consumption and depreciation, especially over a three-year period, clearly indicate that the Toyota is a better value. First of all, the gas consumption alone makes a significant difference in savings for the Toyota driver . . . (See Contrast Paragraph)

MOST EFFECTIVE TYPE OF ORGANIZATION

There is no particular method that is best suited for a comparison/contrast essay. You may choose to show *both* a comparison and a contrast within the same paragraph and then proceed to the next paragraph for a similar treatment of another aspect of the topic. Or you may want to use the block type of organization, to show both a comparison and contrast. Or, upon completing your outline, you may find that the number of differences outweigh the number of similarities, and you may therefore decide to reveal more of a contrast than a comparison (or vice versa). Your conclusion will depend upon the thoroughness and objectivity of your analysis. If you compare and contrast only one or two items, your analysis will be superficial and your conclusion, therefore, will reflect this superficiality and may very well be misleading, as is often the case in poorly organized opinion polls. Even worse, if you are not objective and stack the cards, so to say, you can prove anything you want to prove, and your conclusion, obviously, would be biased. Therefore, you should be objective and thorough in your analysis. Focus on one topic, but treat it in depth and with some insight. Where necessary, reveal your relationships clearly by the use of transitions. Do not assume that the reader understands the comparison or contrast. Be specific and show how the items are alike or different. That is one of the major uses of transitions—for comparison or contrast. And finally, review your facts before you draw your conclusion.

SPECIAL NOTE ON TRANSITIONS

Perhaps more than in any other type of organizational pattern, the comparison/contrast essay requires transitions to reveal clear relationships. Therefore, you should make sure that your reader is always aware of the comparison or the contrast, by using transitional words and phrases in your writing. Such words as *likewise, similarly, also, too, however, on the other hand, nevertheless, by contrast,* etc., have already been supplied in Chapter Nine (See page 125.) Refer to the list freely, and use the transitions.

III. STUDENT MODEL ESSAYS.

MY NEW JOB AND THE OLD ONE

My new job, which I started last year, is far superior to any job I have held in the past. Besides the pay being greater than my former pay, the benefits are substantially better, too. For example, I currently receive six hours of annual leave per pay period, the accumulation of which amounts to a calendar month per year of vacation time. My former job could offer only five days of vacation time a year. In my present job, sick leave is accrued at a rate of four hours a pay period, or a total of 104 hours a year; I used to receive only forty hours a year. Another tangible benefit I receive now but did not receive before is my health coverage. A good health plan is hard to find.

In addition to the various monetary related benefits, the working conditions in my present job are a lot better than they were in my previous job. I now have my own desk, office, telephone, and my own secretary. In my former job I had none of these. My present employer, by giving me new responsibilities, has deemed these "extras" necessary. By contrast, my former employer demanded only physical labor, and I therefore had no need for such extras. My responsibilities now require that I work with various high level people, who treat me as an equal, not as an employee. Furthermore, I do not receive constant supervision now as I did in my former job. I am allowed to make certain decisions that were normally reserved for my supervisors before.

My present job also offers me travel opportunities. For example, last July I traveled to Denver, Colorado, to study government contracting procedures. In December of 1973, I attended a class on statistical quality control at Rock Island, Illinois. In the future I am planning to attend a class in San Francisco. Again by contrast, no training or travel was offered to me in my former job.

Opportunity for advancement has greatly improved over that in my former job. Currently, my training program provides for substantial upgrading at one year intervals. Many potential management positions are available. My former job had no training and no method of advancement except for transferring into another unrelated position. The advancement was restricted to only a few individuals.

Obviously, my present job is a great improvement over any job I have had in the past. What is even more important, though, it offers almost unlimited opportunities for the future.

A LARGE OFFICE AND A SMALL ONE

Having a job can be a wonderful, worthwhile experience or a very unpleasant one. There are many different advantages as well as disadvantages to working in a large business office compared to working in a small, privately owned one. For instance, in a large office there are a lot more people to do the work than there are in a small office. In a large office, one has a specific job to do, with little variation. Such is not the case in a small law office, for example, where one uses not only her secretarial skills to the best of her ability, but where one also gains an enormous amount of knowledge in the field of law.

In a large office there is a need for many employees; therefore it is necessary to have a time clock with time cards, to keep track of everyone's hours. The time cards also make it easier on the bookkeeper when making out the payroll checks. However, one of the disadvantages of the time clock is that one cannot sneak in a few minutes late without being docked, as one can in a small office, where there is no time clock.

In many large offices, one works the regular eight-hour day, five days a week, from 8:00 A.M. to 5:00 P.M., or whatever the designated time period might be. Usually in the morning there is a coffee break, then around noon hour there is a lunch break, then possibly in the afternoon there is another coffee break, thus creating a relaxation from the hustle and bustle of the work day. However in the small office, at least where I work, there is no designated lunch hour where one can just leave at noon. There is no morning break or afternoon break. And if one would like to leave at approximately six in the evening, but some attorney needs a letter or something else to go out that night, one must stay and get it out before leaving. In this respect, therefore, a small office has its disadvantages.

The benefits in a large office are many. One may obtain group insurance, medical insurance, retirement plans, or other types of benefits. In a small office, however, where there are individual attorneys, there is no group insurance plan, for each attorney is his sole practitioner. Consequently, any insurance benefits one may receive are obtained solely at the discretion and generosity of the employer.

When one considers the social aspects of offices, large and small, the small office has an advantage, by far, over the large office. For instance, in a large office there are usually so many people that one really cannot get to know a person well. Most of the time no one ever sees the "big boss"; also, everyone is just a number. Moreover, large offices usually have very formal atmospheres, depending, of course, on the particular corporation. But in a small office people take an interest in the individual, not only for the skills one has to offer, but for who and what one is as a person.

Whether one chooses a large office or a small office, there will always be advantages and disadvantages in any job that one undertakes. It is all a matter of personal choice and personal taste. Therefore, I will choose the small law office with my irregular hours and everything else that comes with the job.

MARRIED AND SINGLE LIFE FOR THE MAN

Married life compared to single life has less to offer men. Married life has too many responsibilities, whereas single life has few. The single man is responsible only for himself. Married life means the sharing of everything among the family members. However, a single man does not have to share because he supports only himself. A married man must support the entire family, distributing his income over two or more members. The single man has his income entirely to himself; therefore, he can afford many more luxuries than the married man can afford. The married man must budget very carefully in order to accumulate luxuries for himself and his family, whereas the single man can acquire many luxuries without much budgeting. Without the burden of additional responsibilities, the single man can live a freer and easier life than that of the married man, who has a family to support. The single man does more or less what he pleases—when he pleases. If he would like to take a trip or to go on an adventure, he can usually leave at a moment's notice. By contrast, the married man is tied down by his family and must first think of them before he makes any plans for himself or the future.

If he so wishes, the single man can ignore most of his responsibilities without too many hardships falling on him later. The married man, however, is bound by his family, and he cannot neglect his responsibilities without causing hardships to fall upon his family. The single man does not have to worry about other individuals while living out his life and, therefore, lives a much more carefree life than that of a married man who is always thinking, planning, and worrying about his family.

LIFE IN LOS ANGELES AND TOPEKA

There are many differences between the living conditions of people in the Los Angeles area and those of Topeka, Kansas. For example, the Los Angeles area offers many places to go and see, whereas in Topeka the places are limited. Places such as Disneyland and Knott's Berry Farm or even the mountains and ocean, which are common to Los Angeles, cannot be found in Topeka. Even what little Topeka does have to offer is not close at hand, as is the case in the Los Angeles area, with entertainment, for example.

Another major contrast between these two geographic areas is in the field of job opportunities. Los Angeles has many industries, which in turn create job opportunities, but in the Topeka area there are only a few industries and thus few job opportunities. Also, the people working at their jobs in Topeka stay with the same job for many years because of the limited opportunity for advancement. By contrast, the job advancement opportunity in the Los Angeles area is much better because there are more jobs to begin with and, therefore, people will change jobs more freely.

An equally important contrast is the variation of shopping facilities. In Los Angeles anyone can shop around for the best deal before making a major purchase, such as a new car; in Topeka there are few shopping facilities, especially shopping centers and car dealers. (There is only one car dealer for each manufacturer.) Thus, people in Topeka do not have the choice in the first place, nor can they make the deals that the people in Los Angeles can.

On the whole, the Los Angeles area has many advantages over the entire Topeka, Kansas area.

ADVANTAGES OF COUNTRY LIFE

Life in the country seems to be more pleasant and fulfilling than it is in the city. I have never lived in the country; nevertheless, the many times I have visited it, I have felt a closeness among the people there which I have missed in the city.

One advantage to living in the country is that the schools are smaller, thus allowing the teachers to work closer with their students. Unlike city schools, where sometimes hundreds of students are placed in one large room, and where the instructor must use a microphone in order for the students to hear his lectures, country teachers are able to know their students personally and learn their needs and interests. Thus, students in country schools do not feel as if they are just part of a large mass of animals, moving from one barn to another. Instead, they feel as if someone really cares whether they are learning useful information or just acquiring a grade.

Not only are students and teachers closer in the country, but society as a whole is closer. When walking down a country road, the people are always friendly and never frightened or embarrassed to say "hi" or make small conversation. On the other hand, in the city, people walking down the street will purposely look in another direction, hoping to avoid any contact at all with a stranger. In the country, especially in smaller towns, people know and love each other. Sure, there is the usual gossip that goes around, but I have found that underneath all the talk, there is a love for each other that leads one to do almost anything to help a neighbor or friend. However, in the city one may not know or even care to know his neighbor, let alone help him in time of trouble or need. One example of such indifference is the well known event which took place in New York, in which a woman was brutally stabbed outside an apartment building while the tenants of the building would not so much as call the police for help.

The most important part of country life is the closeness one gains to God and His nature. By just stepping out of a house and looking about, one can see trees, grass, animals, and everything nature has to offer us. Just to look up in the sky at night and to see the many thousands of stars glimmering in the dark, or to see the lightning bugs swarming around tall, majestic trees gives one such a feeling of humility and closeness to God that one may never want to leave but stay there forever, watching and wondering in awe at the beauty of nature. By contrast, in the city when one steps out of a home, there is fake grass in the parkways and along the streets; there aren't many tall trees because their roots clog up drains and the trees must be removed; or they are sitting in a lot, where a new department store is to be constructed. Finally, there is so much smog that at night it looks as though the stars forgot to come out.

I know that I will always love the country, and someday I hope I have the opportunity to live there and enjoy everything that it has to offer, everything which the city could never hope to offer.

ASSIGNMENTS FOR CHAPTER TWELVE.

---

1. ESSAY ASSIGNMENTS.

1. Select one of the topics listed below, organize a comparison and contrast outline on the basis of *one* aspect of the topic, and then write *either* a comparison *or* a contrast paragraph based on the particular aspect you have selected. Your paragraph will probably run about 150-200 words. NOTE: Use transitions freely.

2. After you have done assignment 1, select *another basis* for comparison/contrast dealing with the *same topic*. Develop a detailed outline, and then write a comparison/contrast essay on the topic. If you feel that your topic lends itself better to either a comparison or a contrast instead of both, then write such an essay. Make sure that you use specific, supporting examples freely.

3. Write a comparison and contrast essay on *another topic* in the list.

TOPICS

1. The advantages and/or disadvantages of two occupations or jobs.
2. The working conditions of two jobs.
3. Two ways of life: city-country; military-civilian; policeman-civilian; prewar-postwar; foreign-domestic.
4. Two ways of quitting smoking.
5. Two ways of saying goodbye.
6. Two schools, colleges, universities, or divisions within these institutions.
7. Two cities, states, countries, or geographic areas.
8. Two types of TV commercials (best and worst) or programs.
9. Two different tastes in music, clothes, entertainment, or friends.
10. Two modes of study, travel, work, or relaxation.
11. Two different philosophies on life or two different types of people.

CHAPTER THIRTEEN

DEFINITION

I. SIMPLE DEFINITION.

To define something means to explain its meaning. The meaning of something may be explained in terms of cause, effect, function, appearance, or any number of such criteria. Certain *specific* objects or ideas have a particular, unmistakable meaning when they are pointed out or defined, regardless of who defines these objects or ideas. Such a particular meaning, which is universal and usually good for all time, is called *denotation.* The word *typewriter,* for example, needs very little definition, because anyone who is even vaguely familiar with such a machine knows what a typewriter is. In short, the word *typewriter* has a particular denotation or meaning with almost everyone. However, should such a specific thing as a typewriter or car require a definition, the writer would probably classify the object in a particular category and then compare and contrast it with others in the same class. The meaning would then be clear to a person who previously had been unfamiliar with those objects, provided of course that he was familiar with those objects in a similar class. To this day, for example, I do not know what a "differential" is although I have heard my mechanic use the term several times. I simply never bothered to ask him what it meant. If I did ask him, I suppose that he could illustrate what it was by comparing its appearance or function with that of a gear shift or steering wheel or some other part of a car with which I was familiar. The more specific was his comparison, the more vivid would be his explanation, and the more clearly would I understand what is meant by the term *differential.* The same rule applies to all types of definition.

To a great extent, dictionary definitions are accomplished in such a manner: through classification, comparison and contrast, and example. First of all, the item that is being defined is usually grouped with other items in a broader class, and then it is compared and contrasted with the other items in its general class. Finally—and perhaps most importantly—an illustration of how it functions is generally provided. Explaining how an object can be used is probably one of the most common methods of defining specific items with which we may be unfamiliar.

Suppose, for example, that you wanted to define the word *car*. The most simple definition would be a dictionary definition, such as this one from Webster's New World Dictionary of the American Language, "any vehicle on wheels." To elaborate, you might include several dictionary definitions or several definitions from the same dictionary, such as these: "A chariot or a vehicle that moves on rails as a streetcar. An automobile, an elevator cage, or the part of a balloon or airship for carrying people and equipment." However, unless you illustrated more clearly how a car was used, unless you compared it with other modes of transportation, your simple "dictionary" definition would leave much to be desired. In short, even a simple definition should include a specific example of how the object is used or where it is found. And a comparison or contrast with other items in its class will make the definitions more meaningful to the reader.

II. CONNOTATION: MEANING WITHIN A CONTEXT.

The connotation of a word is the meaning it implies through its use in a sentence or through its use in a larger context, such as a paragraph or essay. Unlike the term *denotation,* which denotes or points out a particular meaning, usually of a specific thing, the term *connotation* may carry a different meaning for a different person, even when the same word is used in the same context. For example, the word *love* has a different connotation for different people, regardless of how it is used, because its meaning is in the mind or heart of the beholder. However, unless it is used in a particular context, the term may be meaningless altogether, because it is an *abstract* term to begin with and depends, therefore, on its use for any meaning it might have. Dictionary definitions of such abstract terms do little to clarify their meaning. Consider, for example, Webster's definition of *love:* To be fond of, desire . . . a deep and tender feeling of affection for or attachment or devotion to a person or persons." What does the term *affection* mean? (If I said to my wife, "I have a deep affection for you," she would start crying and in between sobs she would reply, "You don't love me anymore.") What does *devotion* mean? In short, what do any of these abstract terms mean? The dictionary has merely *substituted* one generalization for another; it has supplied synonyms—words that have similar meanings but are spelled differently. In order to attempt to define abstract terms, dictionaries substitute words with which the reader may be familiar. If, however, he is not familiar with the synonyms, or if the synonyms vary slightly from the orginal term—as they almost invariably do—then the reader may be no more informed than he was in the first place. A dictionary definition of an abstract term, therefore, has serious limitations, and such definitions should be used sparingly by writers to define their terms.

Since the meaning of an abstract term is derived mainly from its context, the most common method of defining such terms (as you must be well aware by now) is by providing examples. An abstract term is in essence a catchall generalization that can mean anything to anybody, depending on one's background, experiences, association, and familiarity with that particular term. What the writer may mean by using an abstract term and what the reader may understand from the same term may be different altogether. The term *religion,* for example, may mean one thing to a Roman Catholic but an entirely different thing to an atheist, an agnostic, a Buddhist, or a Jew. Or it may mean one thing to a rabbi but another to each member of his congregation. It may mean one thing to a college freshman at the beginning of his course, yet something far deeper at the end of his course if he has taken a class of philosophy. To further illustrate, what we Americans in general mean by the term *communism* or the term *democracy* and what the Russians or Red Chinese mean by these terms are quite different. To many of us in America, the term *communism* for a long time has been synonymous with *repression,* while the term *democracy* has been associated with *liberty*. In Russia and Red China these terms have carried opposite connotations. It is because of such differences in meaning associated with different terms by different people that communication gaps exist.

As a writer, therefore, you should be very careful to explain what you mean, by supplying examples whenever you suspect that your explanation has not been complete. All you need to do is to use the expression "for example" or "to illustrate" and then proceed to supply a *specific* example that clarifies your previous sentence. The entire process is really that simple. The problem with most beginning writers, though, is they assume that the reader is their twin brother, that he is in the same room with them, and that he instinctively understands what they mean by a particular term or sentence.

Unfortunately, not all communication is quite that simple, especially when you are using abstract terms. Consequently, you should use examples freely so that your reader understands what you mean by the use of a particular word. Remember, an abstraction means nothing until it is used in a particular context. And the more specific is the context, the more meaning will the word have for the reader.

III. EXTENDED DEFINITION

An extended definition is a type of writing that provides a detailed explanation of a topic, usually an abstract term. There is no particular form or organizational pattern involved in an extended definition; rather, several methods may be involved, such as those already explained in previous chapters: illustration by examples, process analysis, classification, and comparison/contrast. The writer's objective is to explain his topic, usually in terms of one or more of the following criteria: its origin or cause, its function (how or why it is used or how it works), its structure (components), its classification (relationship to others in its class), its effect on something, or its comparison to or contrast with others in a similar class. The criterion or basis for the extended definition is usually up to the writer. Thus, he alone decides how he will define his term or topic.

An example of an extended definition is this particular chapter, as well as every chapter in this book. I as the writer have attempted to explain in detail exactly what a particular term (such as *classification,* for example) means to me and, therefore, what it means to people like me (teachers), as well as to people in general. In order to explain the term, I began by defining the term, first in a sentence, then in a paragraph or series of paragraphs, and finally in an entire chapter. In addition, to make sure that you knew exactly what I meant by the term, I provided not only my own specific examples of paragraphs or essays on the topic, but also those of my students. The model essays, therefore, further illustrated the *function* of the particular term—how it was used—and how it should be used by the reader. Ultimately, I even provided assignments which would make use of the reader's knowledge of my extended definition. In fact, this entire book is an extended definition of the term *explanatory writing.* To summarize, an extended definition is a thorough explanation.

Although an extended definition is one of the most difficult types of writing, you can write extended definitions if you remember and apply what you have already learned in this chapter, particularly as it deals with supplying *specific examples.* Do not try to explain what one generalization means by supplying another. Instead, explain what the particular term means to you—personally—and then give concrete illustrations of what you mean. Remember, the meaning of a word is derived from the context in which it is written. Therefore, be specific. You, the writer, are trying to communicate your particular meaning for a term, not somebody else's definition. And remember also that meanings for abstract terms vary not only from individual to individual, but also from one period of time to another. There is no absolute meaning for all time.

In your extended definition, use comparisons and contrasts freely. They are among the most effective methods of explanation. What is more vivid than a picture of something or somebody you know? Nothing, unless it is a picture of somebody who is the exact opposite of a person you know.

Finally, in order to illustrate what an extended definition is, I strongly urge you to read the section *Definition* under each chapter in Part IV of the book (How to Write Themes: Paragraphs and Essays), and to conclude, read the student model essays that follow.

IV. STUDENT MODEL ESSAYS.

SUPERSTITION

Practically every living person is superstitious. Education, science, and logic have no meaning where superstition is concerned. Although superstition plays an important role in the lives of the less educated and more primitive people, it also affects the lives of even the most sophisticated and intelligent as well. For example, the superstition of number "13" is widely spread all over the world. In France no house will use the number 13. After number 12 follows number 12 1/2 and then immediately number 14. Italian lotteries will never use the number 13. Even in business-like America, many skyscrapers will omit the thirteenth floor. In my apartment building, there is no number 13.

Another superstition commonly held throughout Europe and the United States is the belief that walking under a ladder may lead to bad luck. Instead of admitting that this belief is superstitious, people will tend to use rationalizations to hide their feelings and to explain their actions. Some of the rationalizations are that a workman may splash paint on the person walking under the ladder or even worse, drop the entire bucket of paint. Another may be that the workman could drop a tool or piece of equipment, like a tile. The superstition originally goes back to the crucifixion of Christ, since a ladder was used in connection with the actual crucifixion. Ever since that time, a ladder has been associated with evil and death.

Possibly an even more superstitious belief is the association of a black cat with bad luck or with good luck, depending upon the geographic location and period in history. In Egypt, black cats were considered extremely holy and sometimes hailed as gods. Centuries later, during the Middle Ages in Europe, witches were thought to assume the form of a black cat; therefore, cats were thought of as being evil. Today, in many areas of the world, black cats are still associated with bad luck, and many people are afraid of a black cat crossing their path.

Even though the above mentioned examples are as much a part of our lives now as they were a part of those who lived centuries ago, many experts feel that superstitions belong to the uneducated. One such expert, Dr. R. Barsch, feels that imagination combined with ignorance is superstition full-born. Dr. Barsch also feels that every natural thing our forefathers could not understand was attributed, as it is today by less educated and almost savage-like races, to some good or evil spirits. Diseases were thought to have been caused by malicious demons, evil fairies, or vengeful witches. Shipwrecks were the direct acts of water demons. Dr. Barsch also strongly feels that the more advanced a nation is, the less superstitious that nation is. It would be very interesting to conduct a poll throughout the United States to find out just how superstitious Americans are. The results would probably destroy his theory.

HONOR

Honor is a generic term used to describe anything held in high esteem. Honor is intangible; you cannot see it, taste it, or touch it, but you know it is present. Legal holidays are set aside for honoring the dead, because this country holds their memory in such high esteem. People show honor for the American flag by saluting it. Other people show honor for a church by bowing their heads when they pass one. In other words, honor goes hand-in-hand with respect.

The term "honor" is often used in reference to self-respect and family pride. People often use the expression, "You have dishonored the family name." By this expression they mean that the individual has done something that will cause other people to think with less respect of the whole family, or even with hatred. "He is an honorable man" or "He is a man of honor"—these are expressions people use to describe a man they have come to respect for one reason or another. Whether it is because of the way he handles his business affairs or just because he has never gone back on his word after he has given it, people respect such a man and want to show that they think of him as being special. Therefore, they describe him in a special manner—with honor.

American institutions use the term honor in connection with the way they acknowledge outstanding achievements or deeds accomplished by the people connected with the institutions. Schools and colleges acknowledge students who have done exceptionally well by having their names included on the Dean's Honor Roll, or by graduating the students "with honor."

The Armed Services of the United States acknowledge their people in honor ceremonies in which those honored are presented with medals. This is the service's way of showing respect and admiration for what these people have accomplished. Even American business and industry are starting to acknowledge their employees. Each week certain companies run a two-column writeup, entitled "Executive of the Week," in which an executive is honored for achievements made during the previous week.

Throughout the United States and other countries, the term honor is used every day in connection with people, job titles, holidays, landmarks, deeds, and so on. It is an expression that is easily used to sum up all the deep feelings that are held for someone or about something.

SOCIAL DARWINISM

During the nineteenth century, one scientific theory that had a tremendous effect on other phases of life was Charles Darwin's Theory of Evolution. Darwin explained life as a struggle for existence, in which physically weak organisms die and the "fittest" survive. His theory, moreover, affected ideas outside the field of biology. The term **Social Darwinism** covers the transfer of Darwin's ideas from biology to society and human relations. However, the theories of the Social Darwinists are quite different from Darwin's original theory.

The main idea which the Social Darwinists extracted from Darwin's theory was "competition." Competition in biological evolution means that the organism best suited for its environment is the one that will survive. Other organisms which are unsuited for their environment will gradually become extinct. Therefore "survival of the fittest" by natural selection is a passive process rather than a vicious fight for life. By contrast, the Social Darwinists saw competition as an active force in society. They thought of social evolution as a process in which individuals or groups must engage in intense competition to assure their survival. They applied this idea of active struggle for survival to economic and moral matters.

For example, many Social Darwinists began to think of the human struggle as a struggle for wealth. They believe that the poor were poor because they were unfit for life, and that if a man could not earn enough money to support himself, he should not survive. Herbert Spencer, a nineteenth century British evolutionist, summed up their ideas in his **Principles of Ethics:** "Of man, the law by conformity to which the species is preserved is that among adults the individuals best adapted to the conditions of their existence shall prosper most, and the individuals least adapted shall prosper least." In this case, therefore, Darwin's phrase "survival of the fittest" seems to have been interpreted to mean that the wealthy should be the ones to survive.

Another idea of Social Darwinism is that some races are biologically superior to other races. Racists applied Social Darwinism to groups of humans as a struggle for existence among races. The racists tried to provide a biological basis for racial superiority and justification for racial descrimination. Their idea was carried to an extreme by Hitler during World War II. He tried to instill in the German people the idea that they were a biologically superior race, an idea which was used to justify the mass execution of Jews, whom many Germans felt were an inferior race. Although Darwin saw life as a struggle for existence, he did not seem to be an advocate of racial discrimination, as were the Social Darwinists. In fact, in **The Descent of Man,** Darwin stated, "There is only an artificial barrier to prevent sympathies extending to the men of all nations and races."

It is evident, therefore, that concepts which were derived from Darwin's Theory of Evolution are included among the ideas of Social Darwinism. Nevertheless, it seems that the Social Darwinists have misinterpreted Darwin's original theory. Darwin's ideas were conceived from and applicable to the field of biology; his ideas enabled man to gain a better understanding of nature's evolutionary process. Unfortunately, however, his name was used to support ideas that the evolution of social life could also be understood in terms of heredity and selection. In particular, Social Darwinists believed that "survival of the fittest" could be applied to economics and races. It seems regrettable that some irrational ideas, which Darwin never intended, have been attributed to him by the Social Darwinists.

ESSAY ASSIGNMENTS.

Write an extended definition of ONE of the topics listed below.

1. Anger.
2. Art.
3. Communication.
4. Education.
5. Equality.
6. Ethics.
7. Honor.
8. Humor.
9. Integrity.
10. Justice.

11. Literature.
12. Love.
13. Morals.
14. Persuasion.
15. Propaganda.

16. Politics.
17. Rationalization.
18. Sophistication.
19. Trust.
20. Wisdom.

APPENDIX

CORRECTION KEY

Ab	Improper abbreviation	**QM (or)** "" ""	Quote marks required
Ad	Adjective or adverb misused	**Red**	Redundant
Agr	Agreement (subject-verb; pronoun-antecedent)	**Ref**	Pronoun reference unclear
		Rep	Repetitious
Ca	Case (Pronoun)	**Sp or ○**	Spelling error
Cap	Capital letter required	**SS**	Sentence sense (logic)
←**Coh**→	Coherence and unity	**Sub**	Subordination
Coll	Colloquialism or slang	**T**	Verb tense or mood or voice
Comp	Comparisons incomplete or incorrect	**TS**	Topic sentence
		V	Verb
C/S	Comma splice	**Var**	Variety of sentence patterns
D	Diction or word choice inappropriate	**Voice**	Use active voice OR don't shift from active-passive; passive to active
Dev	Develop paragraph (too brief)	**W**	Wordiness
Dgl	Dangling modifier	**∧**	Omission
Frag	Fragment	**/'**	Possessive or apostrophe
FS	Fused sentence	**∿**	Transpose
Glos	Glossary	**○**	Unnecessary punctuation—delete
Gr	Grammar	**( )**	Close
Ital ___	Italics	**⁋**	Paragraph required for new topic
K	Awkward sentence (rewrite)	**NO ⁋**	No paragraph
L/C	Lower case letter required	**X or /**	Delete OR error
Mis -Part	Misplaced parts: modifiers or split infinitives	**/**	Separate words
		?	What do you mean?
Mix **//**	Mixed constructions — Parallelism required	**✓**	Good (sentence or idea)
M	Mood		
NC	Not clear (not communicating)		
Nos	Numbers: write them out		
P	Punctuation: error, required, or omission		
PTS	Poor topic sentence		
P/V	Point of view shift: pronoun, tense, voice, or mood		

INDEX

216

222

try and, 113
type, 113

U

uninterested, 113
Unity
  coherence, 56
  in paragraphs, 126
unique, 113
Usage
  colloquialism, 55, 89-90
  formal—definition, 89
  glossary, 89-115
  informal—definition, 89
  slang, 55, 89-90
  substandard—definition, 89-90
used to, 114

V

Variety, 82
Verbal noun
  gerund, 55
Verbs, 8, 82-87
  active voice, 86
  assertions, 82
  auxiliary, 85
  changes in, 84
  compound tenses, 84
  definition, 8, 82, 83
  errors committed, 85
  forms of, 83
  function, 82
  helping verbs, 85-86
  imperative mood, 86
  indicative mood, 86
  linking, 85-86
  mood, 86
  passive voice, 86
  placement, 83
  present tense, 83, 85
  progressive tense, 84
  regular, 85

simple tense, 83-84
subjunctive mood, 86
tense, 83-85
voice, 86
Voice, 64, 86
  active, 64, 86
  passive, 64, 86

W

wait on, 114
want in, out, down, up, off,
  through, 114
want that, 114
ways, 114
weather, whether, 114
Wedding rings, 16
  as conjunctions, 16-17
where, 114
where . . . at, 114
whether, 102
which, 114
while, 114
who, 114
wonderful, 115 (*See* also *grand,*
  great, wonderful,)
Word choice (*See* Diction)
Wordiness, 87
worst way, 115
would, 110
would of, 115
would rather, 101
Writing, 118

Y

Yet
  coordinating conjunction,
    17-18
  definition, 17-18
you, 115
you was, 115
yourself, 106
your, you're, 115